'Soeters' book is a landmark study of military institutions and war. Steeped in the ideas of the founders of sociology and informed by the experience of contemporary war, Soeters demonstrates the relevance of classical and current social theory for understanding the social organization of violence. He shows by example how to plow new paths for studying the military and war. Written in a lively and accessible style, the book is an enthralling read for beginning and advanced scholars alike.'

– James Burk, Texas A&M University, USA

'This expansive vision of military sociology is an essential resource for the field. Soeters captures key connections between the founders of sociology and contemporary notions of war, peace and the everyday problems facing military organizations. These remarkable men and women of ideas come alive in this clear and compelling book.'

– Patricia Shields, Texas State University, USA

'This book is a comprehensive attempt to connect sociological insights with practical challenges the military faces. It is a book that military officers would need to read and study before engaging in operations.'

– Major-General Tony Bardalai, ret., Indian Armed Forces

Sociology and Military Studies

This book examines the connection between sociology and the challenges faced by the modern military.

Military sociology has received little attention in the broader academic world, and is mostly focused on civil–military relations. This book seeks to address this gap and combines ideas, theories and insights from sociology's founding authors, with each chapter focusing on a specific thinker. There are chapters on Max Weber, Emile Durkheim, Karl Marx, Georg Simmel, Jane Addams, W. E. B. Du Bois, Erving Goffman, Michel Foucault, Morris Janowitz, Norbert Elias, Cornelis Lammers, Arlie Russell Hochschild, Cynthia Enloe and Bruno Latour, and each essay discusses their ideas and theories in relation to topics that are of concern in and around the military today. Military studies are taken in a broad sense here, so the volume encompasses a wide range of issues, including civil–military relations, military–political affairs, performance and outcomes of military operations, and organizational arrangements including technology and the composition, performance and well-being of personnel. The book intends to provide views and insights that will help the military to innovate their organizations and practices, not necessarily in the usual functional way of innovating (i.e. faster, more precise, etc.) but in a broader way.

This book will be of great interest to students of sociology, military studies, civil–military relations, war and conflict studies, and IR in general.

Joseph Soeters is Professor of Organizational Sociology at Tilburg University, the Netherlands. He is the author/editor of numerous works, including co-editor of *Routledge Handbook of Research Methods in Military Studies* (Routledge, 2014) and of *Military Cooperation in Multinational Peace Operations* (Routledge, 2008); and author of *Ethnic Conflict and Terrorism* (Routledge, 2005).

Cass Military Studies

Researching the Military
Edited by Helena Carreiras, Celso Castro and Sabina Fréderic

Drones and the Future of Air Warfare
The evolution of Remotely Piloted Aircraft
Michael P. Kreuzer

Transforming Warriors
The ritual organization of military force
Edited by Peter Haldén and Peter Jackson

Space Warfare in the 21st Century
Arming the heavens
Joan Johnson-Freese

Strategy Before Clausewitz
Linking Warfare and Statecraft, 1400–1830
Beatrice Heuser

Special Operations Forces in the 21st Century
Perspectives from the Social Sciences
Edited by Jessica Glicken Turnley, Kobi Michael and Eyal Ben-Ari

Civilians and Warfare in World History
Edited by Nicola Foote and Nadya Williams

The Military and Liberal Society
Societal-Military Relations in Western Europe
Tomas Kucera

Israel, Strategic Culture and the Conflict with Hamas
Adaptation and Military Effectiveness
Niccolò Petrelli

War and Strategy in the Modern World
From Blitzkrieg to Unconventional Terrorism
Azar Gat

Sociology and Military Studies

Classical and Current Foundations

Joseph Soeters

Routledge
Taylor & Francis Group

LONDON AND NEW YORK

First published 2018
by Routledge
2 Park Square, Milton Park, Abingdon, Oxon OX14 4RN

and by Routledge
711 Third Avenue, New York, NY 10017

Routledge is an imprint of the Taylor & Francis Group, an informa business

British Library Cataloguing in Publication Data
A catalogue record for this book is available from the British Library

Library of Congress Cataloging in Publication Data
Names: Soeters, J. author.
Title: Sociology and military studies : classical and current foundations /
Joseph Soeters.
Description: New York : Routledge, [2018] | Includes bibliographical
references and index.
Identifiers: LCCN 2017048907 | ISBN 9781138739529 (hardback) |
ISBN 9781138739536 (pbk.) | ISBN 9781315182131 (ebook)
Subjects: LCSH: Sociology, Military.
Classification: LCC U21.5 .S637 2018 | DDC 306.2/7–dc23
LC record available at https://lccn.loc.gov/2017048907

ISBN: 978-1-138-73952-9 (hbk)
ISBN: 978-1-138-73953-6 (pbk)
ISBN: 978-1-315-18213-1 (ebk)

Typeset in Bembo
by Taylor & Francis Books

This book is dedicated to my uncle Matthew ('Ome Jeu'). He was a drafted, twenty-year-old sergeant who was deployed to the Dutch 'policing actions' in today's Indonesia. Fairly soon after he accessed the area of operations, he must have experienced something violent, something really bad, which he did not survive in a stable manner. He passed away at the age of 46, in a mental health institution. Numerous others, Indonesians and Dutch, have suffered a similar fate or worse. Through 'Ome Jeu' I dedicate this book to all of them as well.

Contents

List of figures		xi
List of tables		xii
List of boxes		xiii
Acknowledgements		xv
Prologue		xvii

Introduction		1
1	Max Weber: Bureaucracy, leadership and military music	8
2	Emile Durkheim: The military group, culture and its consequences	22
3	Karl Marx: Critical analyses of society and the military	37
4	Georg Simmel: Networks, conflict, secrecy and the stranger	51
5	Jane Addams: From peace activism to pragmatic peacekeeping	65
6	W. E. B. Du Bois: Race, diversity and inclusion, in society and the military	78
7	Erving Goffman: Total institutions, interaction rituals, street-level bureaucrats	91
8	Michel Foucault: Discipline and surveillance in and by the military	105
9	Morris Janowitz: The professional soldier, civil–military relations and the AVF	118
10	Norbert Elias: Decline of violence, habitus in combat, international relations	130
11	Cornelis Lammers: Strikes and mutinies, occupational styles, and cooperation	143

12 Arlie Russell Hochschild: Emotions in organizations and in the
    military   157

13 Cynthia Enloe: Feminist views of the military and its surroundings   169

14 Bruno Latour: Science and technology in society and the military   181

15 From the classics to the future in military studies: Conclusions,
    themes and prospects   196

    Index   205

Figures

1.1 Continuum of bureaucratic organizing and violence   12
4.1 Military organization seeking partnerships in one closed, dense
     network or in more disconnected networks   53
5.1 Surge in uniformed personnel in UN missions since 1993   69
7.1 Simmelian ties, indicating that A and B belong to one group or
     clique and C and D to another   96
10.1 Fluctuating diachronic decline of violence in two different
     countries   135

Table

15.1 Contributions of founding sociologists at the macro-, meso- and micro-level.　　　197

Boxes

Ambidexterity in the military   13
Limits of military leadership   16
The dark side of the tune   18
Sociology on a bike   26
Enhancing American military effectiveness   28
Comparing military actions   33
The generals' roles?   40
Armies of the poor during the Parisian insurrection of 1848   44
Loss of control, social inequality and former child soldiers   47
Strong ties among special operations forces   54
Theory of supercooperators   56
Why secret intelligence fails   59
NVA officers in the Bundeswehr   61
Unintended consequences of peacekeeping   70
Empowering women in Afghanistan   75
Graduation at West Point   83
Dutch Muslim soldiers on deployment in Muslim societies   86
Military 'duties' in the Russian barracks   94
The 'polymetis' soldier   98
Military violence in non-combat situations   101
The origin of business practices and the West Point connection   108
Airports   114
'Khaki capitalism' and civil–military relations   124
The return of the draft system?   126
Savage restraint   136
The Established and the Outsiders: human interconnectness in the
refugee crisis   139
Rebellion in DR Congo   145
Different occupational and administrative styles   148
Cooperation in UN missions   153
The military and the family as 'greedy institutions'   160
Snipers at work   161
Dutch soldiers' emotions in Indonesia, 1945–1950   164

Military memoirs   165
Disaster as war   170
Feminist reflections about Abu Ghraib   176
Sociological controversies   183
Validating the virtual   186
The *Challenger* launch decision   188
Archeologies of the Spanish Civil War   192

Acknowledgements

This book is a result of being involved in sociology for more than 40 years and having worked in a military context for over 20 years. Those are long, even though overlapping, periods in a lifetime. During such long periods one is likely to collect thoughts, insights and experiences that together create a broad view of what is and what has been happening around one. Clearly, the art of doing sociology profits from experiencing, seeing, talking, listening, reading, travelling and studying a lot. Pursuing sociology in the military is even more the result of long-term experiences, as the military constitutes a fairly closed community that is not easy to access and understand at first glance. It takes time to really comprehend what is going on in the armed forces.

This is my second monograph on military-related issues. The first one concerned the origin and dynamics of civil wars and terrorism; it starts in a problem-oriented manner, in which theories follow the problems related to civil wars and terrorism: *problems first, theories next*. I believe in the value of this way of working and teaching rather than the other way around. Yet, the current book starts with theories that were launched by sociology's founders. This seems to be at odds with what I believe to be the most natural way of presenting academic work. But the theories in this book are immediately applied to current problems. In fact, it does not matter much which comes first, as long as the distance between the two, theories and problems, is not large. Sociology should be valuable in everyday practice; it should not be a kind of *l'art pour l'art*.

A number of people contributed to this book, mostly because they, sometimes inadvertently, came up with ideas and suggestions that turned out to be useful while compiling the various chapters; two of them, Charles Moskos and Cornelis Lammers, had already passed away when the book came into being. During their lifetimes they encouraged and influenced the development of my thinking about sociological aspects of the military in many ways. I am grateful for their influence.

Others are colleagues, near and far, who helped me develop the ideas in this book, in one way or another. They came up with references, sometimes via Facebook, and some provided practical tips revealing secrets of the word processing system that were still hidden to me. They are in alphabetical order: Eyal Ben-Ari, Daniel Blocq, Hans Born, Morten Braender, Lindsay Cohn, Said

Haddad, Jacqueline Heeren-Bogers, Urbian van den Heuvel, Dirk Kruijt, Nina Leonhard, Yagil Levy, Marius Meeuws, Delphine Resteigne, Wilbur Scott, Ad van Iterson, Jan Van der Meulen and Claude Weber. In a way, this book is the product of *crowdsourcing* and *crowdinspiring*.

The librarians Ernst Bertelink and Mirjam Kruize at the Netherlands Defence Academy helped me a lot in retrieving the literature that was outside my range while exploring the internet. Jacqueline Vlek-Schut designed the cover illustration, for which I am really thankful. Marjet Berendsen helped polish my English.

I would like to extend a special word of appreciation to James Burk and Patricia Shields, both scholars in the circles around the journal *Armed Forces and Society* and the Inter-University Seminar on armed forces and society (IUS). They have helped and encouraged me to start and continue working on the book. Patricia Shields made me aware of the importance of Jane Addams' work in the domain of peace and conflict. James Burk not only supported and mentored me, but also helped discover Max Weber's sociology of music, with its possible applications to military music. My colleague Paul van Fenema suggested not to forget technology as a main topic of social and military studies. This advice, together with Maarten van Veen's enthusiasm about this author, convinced me to write the chapter on Bruno Latour. The anonymous reviewers of the book proposal were quite positive, which encouraged me to actually get the work going. My close colleague Rene Moelker in the Netherlands and my colleague Philippe Manigart from the Belgian École Militaire in Brussels read the various draft chapters carefully and helped me avoid many mistakes. They also provided various additional ideas. Of course, any remaining errors, flaws in interpretation and debatable choices are my own responsibility.

Prologue

Bruno Latour, a sociologist of science and technology whom we will meet in the penultimate chapter of this book, once made perfectly clear why sociology is important for engineers, technicians and technological decision-makers. He sought to demonstrate to technicians 'that they cannot even conceive of a technological object without taking into account the mass of human beings with all their passions and politics and pitiful calculations, and that by becoming good sociologists and good humanists they can become better engineers and better-informed decisionmakers' (Latour, 1996: viii).

The same reasoning, I would say, applies to military men and women and to those who decide about their resources as well as the beginning, content and ending of their actions.

Reference

Latour, B. (1996) *ARAMIS or the Love of Technology*. Cambridge MA and London: Harvard University Press.

Introduction

Since the time sociology was founded as an academic discipline, the concepts of war, peace, conflict, violence and the military have been – explicitly or implicitly – elements in its theorizing and research. This is not surprising because those phenomena were part and parcel of everyday life in the days when sociological thinking as an academic discipline emerged. In those early times – in the nineteenth and twentieth centuries – war and violent upheaval, revolutions, military action and conscription, and the corresponding longing for peace were part of every man's and every woman's daily conversation and concern. And they continued to be so during and immediately after the Second World War. In those two centuries Napoleon's invasions of almost all European and Middle Eastern nations, the colonial and civil wars in the United States, the world wars in Europe and Asia, and the many protracted wars of colonization and deco-lonization waged by European states coloured and obscured everyday life. War-related events and experiences simply had to be the subject of sociological analysis, i.e. the analysis of the interaction between groups of men, women, institutions and societies.

Over centuries, military power – *the social organization of concentrated lethal violence* (Mann, 2012: xiii), has undergone considerable transformations. The military developed from unorganized peasant troops and merchant armies in the (late) Middle Ages to sizable forces that relied on a conscription system in the nineteenth and twentieth centuries, and then to the smaller but more professional all-volunteer forces that can be seen in many Western nations today. Throughout history military organizations have gained and lost relevance and urgency, for reasons that have been analysed by sociologists themselves. But military-related phenomena were never far from view. Today's newspapers still report on wars, in Syria, Libya, Yemen and Sudan to name but a few, and there is almost daily news of terrorist attacks and military actions all over the globe. Accordingly, military sociology has developed into a small but healthy branch of the mother discipline.

Military sociology today predominantly deals with civil–military relations, in the broad sense of the word. This includes (political) decision-making about military action, the relation between the state and the military, the impact of public opinion and the media, the representation of a country's population in the military's workforce including gender and minority representation, and organizational, human resources and work-related challenges that the armed forces face nowadays. In a number of publications one can find overviews of this sub-discipline. Bernard Boëne's colossal Ph.D. thesis (1995) on the development of military sociology in the USA since the beginning of the last century is an important source, albeit in the French language. David Segal and James Burk's four-volume anthology (2012) provides a valuable overview of the state of affairs in this sub-discipline, from the 1940s until now. An overview of the state of the art in this sub-discipline in Europe can be found in a volume edited by Gerhard Kümmel and Andreas Prüfert (2000). *The Routledge Handbook on War and Society* edited by Steven Carlton-Ford and Morten Ender (2013) examines the societal impact of the recent wars in Iraq and Afghanistan, especially in the American context. Guiseppe Caforio's new *Handbook of the Sociology of the Military* (2018) provides the most recent and comprehensive impression of the advances in this field.

However, the connection between the origins of sociology – at a time when war and peace dominated elements of everyday life – and today's militaries and their operations has seldom been studied. One could say that the relevance of the theories from those earlier times seems almost forgotten, although Guiseppe Caforio (2003) provided some historical notes in his *Handbook of the Sociology of the Military*. The work by Siniša Malešević (2010a; 2010b) aiming at developing a sociological theory of war and violence is an important exception that needs to be pursued. Malešević (2010b) showed that quite a number of 'founding fathers' saw war and violence as key mechanisms of social change, even though pacifist interpretations of the classics may have rendered a different impression. He even speaks about a *bellicose* sociology, a sociology that is rife with thoughts of war. In a more or less similar vein Joas and Knöbl (2013: viii) have referred to the 'suppression of war' in social theory. They claim that wars have often been constitutive in the construction of social theories – 'as the informative background to ideas' – however, without or hardly ever appearing as such in theories themselves. Dandeker (1990: 29–30) also noted the sociological neglect of military organization and surveillance in the mainstream branches of the profession.

Following these observations, this book aims to explore the connection of elements of the work of the founding fathers and mothers with today's challenges for the military as an institution and organization. More than providing a general overview of sociological thinking about war and violence the way Malešević (2010a) and Joas and Knöbl (2013) did, this book intends to study the military organization and institution in all its facets. Hence, the book is more directed at the meso-level of organizations and institutions and the micro-level of individual soldiers' conduct than at the macro-level of societies and (international) politics. Studying these levels and making use of the insights from classical and more current sociology may serve at least three purposes. These insights are first touchstones of excellence; furthermore they are ways to introduce complexity to students and readers; and they are also simply sources of great ideas, as Stinchcombe once put it (1982).

The aim of this book is twofold: it provides theoretical insights stemming from previous times while at the same time showing their direct or indirect relevance for today's militaries' decision-making, training and operations. In this, the sociologists' input concerns both the *cold* and the *hot* side of military organizing. This is the military *preparing for* and the military actually *doing* the job of preventing, containing and solving large-scale violent conflicts. The latter is important. In general, until today sociology has not given the study of actual military operations much prominence, leaving the major part of the field to historians and military experts (Giddens and Sutton, 2013: 1028). That situation is in need of change, which is what this book intends to achieve.

Focusing on everyday concerns in the military implies that the book strives to be theoretically and practically important. The idea is that both military students and practitioners may profit from it, and so, hopefully, may civilians with an interest in military affairs, such as students of international relations, security studies, political science and sociology in general.

The book intends to provide views and insights that will help the military to innovate their organizations and practices, not necessarily in the usual functional way of innovating (i.e. acting faster, being more precise, less polluting, less labour-intensive, less detectable, etc.), but in a broader manner. As sociologists would say, this book does not specifically intend to help improve the military in a functionally rational manner. Instead it is also, and perhaps even more, focused on substantive rationality, to use the concept as described by Karl Mannheim (e.g. Ritzer, 1998: 20–29). Functional rationality refers to action-oriented knowledge when the means-to-ends-relation is clear. It intends to respond to questions such as: has the bridge that has been targeted been destroyed properly, without causing (too much) collateral damage and casualties, without using too much ammunition? Substantive rationality, however, puts broader values and questions into the equation; often these values and questions are of a social and ethical nature, implying that means-to-ends-relations are much less clear. Does the destruction of the bridge that was targeted indeed contribute to the cessation of hostilities; does a destroyed bridge help to solve the violent conflict in the area? Are the combat skills of a platoon conducive to ending combat or – on the contrary – do they aggravate the violence in the area of operations? What will happen once the combat has ended? Who bears the consequences? This book is not only about functional issues related to the military, but also – and perhaps more in particular – about those more general questions, the questions that sociology was meant to raise and ponder.

The book's set-up

The book is limited in scale and scope: it does not claim to be an introduction to the icons of sociology; there are other textbooks that do this perfectly well (e.g. Aron, 1989 [1967]; Giddens, 1971; Nisbet, 1976; Coser, 1977; Turner, 1991; Levine, 1995; De Jong, 2007). The book is also selective, in two ways. First, it presents a selection of the formative and contemporary sociologists to be discussed and, second, it is selective as to which parts of their work is presented.

The selection criterion was whether the authors produced work with a coherent message that has impacted on the development of theories, insights and methods in the field of today's military studies. Given its orientation to the military institution and organization, sociologists focusing on macro-level phenomena such as the connection between war, revolution and upheaval and the formation of states and international relations are beyond the scope of this book. This literature is elsewhere abundantly available. Sociologists with a penchant for general, abstract theorizing do not act as leading figures in this book either.

Hence, this book can be considered to be a presentation and discussion of sociological *capita selecta* that are relevant to the military. Even though these *capita selecta* from sociology may seem quite varied and different, it will soon become clear that there are common and recurring themes. As the book progresses, the chapters will gradually start 'speaking to one another'. At the end of the book, the variety of topics will have provided a broad and comprehensive picture of the military.

This book is very much inspired by two previous publications; the first one is an edited volume that examines the contributions and importance of classical sociologists in the field of organization studies (Adler, 2009). In that volume founding sociological theorists such as Alexis de Tocqueville, Max Weber, Emile Durkheim, Karl Marx, Gabriel Tarde, Georg Simmel, Joseph Schumpeter, Norbert Elias, Thorstein Veblen, W. E. B. Du Bois, John Dewey, Mary Parker Follett and Talcott Parsons have been discussed in search of their relevance to today's organization studies. In addition, Paul Adler and associates (2014) compiled a follow-up book on contemporary sociologists and their works' influence on organization studies. The sociologists discussed in this volume were European scholars such as Michel Foucault, Pierre Bourdieu, Bruno Latour and Niklas Luhman, and Anglo-American authors such as Charles Wright Mills, Erving Goffman, Arlie Russell Hochschild and Anthony Giddens. Both volumes led to surprising and important results, and, as said, these volumes have been a major source of inspiration for the present book.

This book on sociology and military studies differs from the volumes that were initiated by Paul Adler, as it deals with military studies as a specific branch of organization studies. Military organizations are specific because they tend to be a type of organization *sui generis*, an organization of its own kind that is not often included and discussed in general organization studies. The task of using violence sets them apart from the rest of the organizational world. More than organization studies, military studies as a discipline has clear connections with other scholarly branches, in particular political science and administrative studies, the study of international relations and theories of civil–military relations.

This book is also different because it brings together names that appear in one or other of the two previous publications on sociology and organization studies; it brings together older and newer scholars. Next to the famous classical sociologists Max Weber, Emile Durkheim, Karl Marx, Georg Simmel, Jane Addams and W. E. B. Du Bois, we will meet here with more recent scholars, in particular Erving Goffman, Michel Foucault, Morris Janowitz, Norbert Elias, Cornelis Lammers, Arlie Russell Hochschild, Cynthia Enloe and Bruno Latour. Only the latter three are alive at the moment of writing. Only Morris Janowitz can be considered to be a true military (and political) sociologist; the others are generalists, but with theories and findings that have implications for the study of the military, as we will see.

Through this selection of sociological scholars one can also observe two main developments in sociology. First, it starts in Europe but over time it gets bigger across the Atlantic Ocean and, second, in the beginning sociology is over-whelmingly a man's business, but later women catch up rapidly; current advancements in the field of social sciences and the military are unthinkable without the contribution of female scholars.

All authors brought forward theories and insights that have been leading the study of the military to where it now stands. They did so by writing about the military intentionally and explicitly, or inadvertently and implicitly, and sometimes by paying hardly any attention to the military at all. However, even though none of these authors exclusively worked on and for the military, all of them produced work that is important to better understand the structure, functioning, performance and effectiveness of today's armed forces, right across the globe. This does not necessarily imply that these authors are the only ones to meet this criterion, but they are among the most prominent ones, at least in my eyes.

The impact of these authors on military studies was direct, or indirect, through the help, mediation and input of others. Karl Marx's views on social inequality and elites, for instance, have become specifically relevant to the study of the military through the work of Charles Wright Mills. Later sociologists such as Yagil Levy also focused on social inequality and its connection to military action and its consequences. Max Weber's theories on the bureaucracy have been translated and applied to the military by many scholars, most recently by Morten Ender following up on George Ritzer's update of Weber's work. Jane Addams' insights concerning conflict mediation through public administration were very much inspired by pragmatist ideas conceived by John Dewey and recently applied to the military by Patricia Shields. Theories on diversity in society developed by W. E. B. Du Bois have been advanced and applied to the military by Charles Moskos and fellow sociologists. Contributions by Randall Collins and Michael Lipsky have been helpful in furthering the use of Goffman's theories in military studies. Christopher Dandeker's work has been important for seeing the influence of Foucault in connection with Weber on some of today's challenges for security forces. Eyal Ben-Ari put the issue of emotions in the military on the agenda, following up on Arlie Hochschild's work on this terrain. Many American sociologists, including James Burk and David Segal, have furthered Morris Janowitz's impact on the field. These are only a few names in this connection; this book will present more, and more recent, theoretical insights in addition to those from the selected authors.

In what follows the various authors and their work will be introduced and discussed one by one: each author has one chapter. The order of presentation is historical, but in a slightly loose manner; for instance, I preferred to start with Max Weber and not Karl Marx, even though the latter predates the former.

The collection of chapters provides a whole gamut of ideas, theories and empirical studies that perhaps may seem overwhelming and possibly even disorienting at first. The topics range from military bureaucracy and military music to cohesion in primary groups, via peacekeeping, race and gender issues and occupational styles, to emotions in the military and science and technology; and there is so much more. The chapter subtitles indicate the wide range of topics that will get attention. Yet, as said, gradually the various authors will start 'speaking to one another'. Despite their differences, the founding scholars also have many ideas and insights in common. Younger authors are likely to pursue and elaborate the ideas of the older ones, creating cumulative and consistent patterns that are less apparent at the very beginning.

Throughout the book many examples, stories and illustrations will be given in the main text or in text boxes adjacent to the main argument. Sociological theories tend to be abstract. In my view, they can only be properly understood through constant leaps from theory to everyday realities and practices, and back. The illustrations will be from all over the world and they will be from historical as much as from current times. Additionally, sociology should not be interpreted too narrowly. Hence, authors who are known as anthropologists or political scientists are also included in this book. Sociology, anthropology and political science belong to one extended family, I believe.

Having said all this, I need to acknowledge that the sociological insights that will be presented here are mainly European and American. On those continents, in Europe earlier than in the USA, sociology started to develop. Those are the regions that still dominate sociological thinking and research, including the sociology of the military, today. This comes at a cost. It is argued that North-centric and Western-centric thinking is based on problematic cultural premises. Therefore, a number of scholars advocate the need to embark on the development of so-called 'connected sociologies'. In these 'connected sociologies' theoretical categories will be reconstructed 'to create new understandings that incorporate and transform previous ones' (Bhambra and de Sousa Santos, 2017: 6). One claims that such a broadening approach, paying much more attention to developments in the southern and eastern parts of the globe, will not only add to our knowledge but will actually transform it. Adding or transforming is a matter of words, but for sure the current book has a North and Western bias. Even though a number of studies and findings herein pay attention to other parts of the world, one of our ambitions for the future should be to enlarge our understanding of the military beyond the Western hemisphere, which consists mainly of Europe, the USA, Israel, Canada, Australia and the like.

Where the texts that constitute the foundation of this book were originally written in another language (French, German, Dutch, Spanish), English translations have been used with an indication of the date of the original publication. It was not always possible, however, to find English translations.

Bibliography

Adler, P.S. (ed.) (2009) *The Oxford Handbook of Sociology and Organization Studies: Classical Foundations.* Oxford: Oxford University Press.

Adler, P.S., P. Du Gay, G. Morgan and M. Reed (eds) (2014) *The Oxford Handbook of Sociology, Social Theory and Organization Studies: Contemporary Currents.* Oxford: Oxford University Press.

Aron, R. (1989 [1967]) *Main Currents in Sociological Thought, Vols I and II.* New York: Anchor Books Doubleday.

Bhambra, G.K. and B. de Sousa Santos (2017) 'Introduction: global challenges for sociology'. *Sociology* 51(1): 3–10.

Boëne, B. (1995) 'Conditions d'emergence et de développement d'une sociologie specialisée: le cas de la sociologie militaire aux Etats-Unis'. Ph.D. thesis, University of Paris V René Descartes.

Caforio, G. (2003) 'Some historical notes'. In G. Caforio (ed.) *Handbook of the Sociology of the Military.* New York: Kluwer Academic/Plenum Publishers, pp. 7–26.

Caforio, G. (ed.) (2018) *Handbook of the Sociology of the Military.* Cham, Switzerland: Springer.

Carlton-Ford, S. and M. Ender (2013) *The Routledge Handbook of War and Society: Iraq and Afghanistan.* London and New York: Routledge.

Coser, L. (1977) *Masters of Sociological Thought. Ideas in Historical and Social Context, Second Edition.* Long Grove, IL: Waveland Press.

Dandeker, Chr. (1990) *Surveillance, Power and Modernity: Bureaucracy and Discipline from 1700 to the Present Day.* Cambridge: Polity Press.

De Jong, M. (2007) *Icons of Sociology.* Amsterdam: Boom.

Giddens, A. (1971) *Capitalism and Modern Social Theory: An Analysis of the Writings of Marx, Durkheim and Max Weber.* Cambridge: Cambridge University Press.

Giddens, A. and Ph.W. Sutton (2013) *Sociology.* 7th edn. Cambridge: Polity Press.

Joas, H. and W. Knöbl (2013 [2008]) *War in Social Thought: Hobbes to the Present.* Princeton NJ and Oxford: Princeton University Press.

Kümmel, G. and A. Prüfert (eds) (2000) *Military Sociology: The Richness of a Discipline.* Baden-baden, Germany: Nomos Verlaggesellschaft.

Levine, D.N. (1995) *Visions of the Sociological Tradition.* Chicago and London: University of Chicago Press.

Malešević, S. (2010a) *The Sociology of War and Violence.* Cambridge: Cambridge University Press.

Malešević, S. (2010b) 'How pacifist were the founding fathers? War and violence in classical sociology'. *European Journal of Social Theory* 13(2): 193–212.

Mann, M. (2012 [1986]) *The Sources of Social Power, Volume 1.* Cambridge: Cambridge University Press.

Nisbet, R.A. (1976) *The Sociological Tradition.* London: Heinemann.

Ritzer, G. (1998) *The McDonaldization Thesis: Explorations and Extensions.* London: Sage.

Segal, D. and J. Burk (eds) (2012) *Military Sociology.* 4 vols. Thousand Oaks, CA: Sage.

Stinchcombe, A.L. (1982) 'Should sociologists forget their mothers and fathers?' *The American Sociologist* 17(February): 2–11.

Turner, J.H. (1991) *The Structure of Sociological Theory.* Belmont, CA: Wadsworth.

1 Max Weber

Bureaucracy, leadership and military music

Max Weber (1864–1920) from Germany is one of the most famous names among sociology's founding scholars, and his contributions to the discipline have been enormous. One only has to recall his work on the sociology of religion, culminating in his theory on the impact of the protestant ethic on the development of Western capitalism. But there were other studies on religions as well, on Judaism and on Islam in particular, which broadened his scope of comparison and theorizing. His approach of broad historical-sociological systemizing also stressed the relevance of the state for the monopolization of legitimate force upon a territory. Hence it stressed the importance of the military in the formation of states, an idea that has been elaborated in many later sociological studies (e.g. Tilly, 1992; Joas and Knöbl, 2013).

In general, Weber's texts are rife with observations that pertain to the military. Weberian thinking on state formation led sociologist Randall Collins to predict the coming demise of the Soviet Union in the early 1980s, a number of years before it actually happened. This prediction, based on the idea of overstretched borders leading to unmanageable logistical problems for the military, was met with severe disbelief and criticism by the international and military experts of the time (Collins, 1995). We will see throughout the present book that sociological insights and predictions often provoke irritation, disbelief and rejection. Sociology frequently provides a critical analysis of common sense, as it often points to the unexpected and the unintended (Portes, 2000), which can be quite irritating indeed.

Next to this macro-sociological work, Weber contributed fundamentally to methodological issues, such as the importance of *sinnhaft Verstehen*, trying to understand people's actions instead of merely observing or counting them, as well as the development of the so-called *Ideal Type,* one of which is the *Bureaucracy* (e.g. Coser, 1977). It is here where our discussion about the relevance of Weber's work to the study of the military institution starts. But it ends with a surprising topic: military music.

Bureaucracy

For organization studies, and for military studies in particular, Weber's work on bureaucracy theory has been tremendously influential, and despite signals to the contrary (Lounsbury and Carberry, 2005), its impact can hardly be overestimated (e.g. Du Gay, 2000; Shields, 2003). Bureaucracy as an organized form of human action has developed over centuries, as far back as the Egyptian and Roman empires and before. It is a manifestation of the continuous *rationalization* of organized social life throughout history. It is also a vehicle to encapsulate 'naked power' – the potential to fully dominate others and make them do whatever you want, even against their own needs, wishes or well-being. The bureaucracy does so by well-described legal arrangements and organizational practices. Max Weber, in the early twentieth century, was the first to systematically analyse the bureaucracy's elements and characteristics based on instrumental rationality and standardization.

Weber needed just a couple of pages to define the bureaucracy as an ideal type, i.e. as a theoretical construct in a pure form extracting the essentials of a phenomenon that perhaps are never present as such in reality (Gerth and Wright Mills, 2009: 196–204; Weber, 1976 [1914]: 124–130). This ideal type applies to both public and business bureaucracies. It stresses

- a firm, stable and elaborated division of labour and duties,
- hierarchically arranged positions,
- formal rules, regulations and work practices,
- fixed salaries and career patterns, and
- the appointing and promoting of civil servants on the basis of their educational qualifications and previous performance (merit).

Other particular characteristics, such as employees' race, religion, family or geographical origin, are, or should be, irrelevant in hiring and promoting personnel. Additionally, workers are protected by law and regulations against external impact but also against the leaders they serve. There is equal treatment for all employees, and career paths are based on seniority, achievement or both. There is compulsory retirement, implying that all employees occupy organizational positions only for a limited period of time. Furthermore, there are no extra-organizational prerogatives related to the position that employees or their leaders ('die Herren') occupy. Employees are personally free and only need to be obedient to their leadership in relation to their bureaucratic obligations (e.g. Perrow, 1972: 4; Dandeker, 1990: 9). Finally, the employees do not own any of the resources that belong to the bureaucracy, implying that they cannot use the organization's resources for their own purposes.

This stands in contrast to patrimonial or pre-bureaucratic organizations, where the servants are 'at the disposal' of the leader, and tasks, positions and remuneration, sometimes in kind, can change all the time depending on the insights and moods of the leader. Most importantly, the servants have acquired their positions based on their affiliations with the power elite, and not, or not so much, because of their professional qualifications and merits. Those affiliations may be regional, religious, political, tribal, family- or language-related, or combinations of those.

All this very much applies to military organizations. Western military organizations, in their various stages of development, may be characterized as bureaucracies par excellence: procedures, skills and drills are maximally elaborated, rationalized, standardized and hence impersonalized. In turn these are collectively transferred to the newly enlisted men and women whose salaries are related to objective criteria connected to qualification and merits. Similarly, promotion to higher ranks follows well-described patterns, implying that career paths are clear to everyone and are also based on qualification and merit.

Weber was among the first to point out the enormous impact of discipline as a source of military superiority, even exceeding the influence of technological innovation in the times before Weber's era (Gerth and Wright Mills, 2009: 255–261). The disciplined behaviour of troops conducting their moves and actions precisely in accordance with the prescripts they had learned during exercises turned out to be a decisive factor on the battlefield. Greek and Roman forces in ancient history and later examples such as the Dutch army under Maurice of Orange or Chaka Zulu's troops in Africa clearly evinced the weight of military discipline as a key element in military bureaucratic organizing. King's (2013) interpretation of the 'collective virtuosity' of today's combat infantry groups echoes this view.

In addition to discipline, skills and drills, legal considerations play an increasingly large role in operational decisions and conduct in military bureaucracies. In today's military operations, the legal advisor is seen as the most important officer, next to the commander. Every operational decision can and will be evaluated and judged beforehand from a legal perspective, and also much later after the mission or operation has ended. The emphasis on law at the state level and regulations at the level of the organization itself is part and parcel of Weber's concept of bureaucracy, which is not so surprising since he, like his father, enrolled as a student of law.

The bureaucratic organizational system has been refined over centuries. It aims to ensure predictability, rationality, calculability and protection against arbitrariness of those in power, particularly for the inmates of the organization but also for those affected by state conduct or, in the case of the military, state violence. The system has clear advantages. For instance, possible derailments of military people leading to violence getting out of control will be legally dealt with. Seen from this perspective, the 'bureaucratic ethos' cannot be praised enough (Du Gay, 2000). It also constitutes the foundation of what Ritzer (1993) has termed the 'McDonaldization' thesis, which relates to the ubiquitous presence of bureaucratic organizing in today's societies. American sociologist Morten Ender used this idea when pondering whether American soldiers deployed to Iraq were 'McSoldiers' or innovative professionals. He concluded that American soldiers vacillated between being dependent McSoldiers ceaselessly repeating their learned skills and drills, and innovative actors making their own decisions more or less independently in a given situation (Ender, 2009: 153).

This conclusion already indicates that obedience has its disadvantages. Following the bureaucracy's prescriptions is not always good as there may be far reaching negative consequences. Bauman (1989) contended that the Holocaust – with its elaborated chains of intelligence, administrative, transport and other logistic organizations and finally the militarily-organized death camps – could never have occurred without the 'logic' of rational, bureaucratic organizing (see also Soeters, 2005). Every person, every unit, every organization, within the machinery or supplying the machinery, knew what to do and did so. While acting in this manner they usually were not fully aware of, or did not feel responsible for, their contribution to the final result: the genocide of millions of people.

The transporting of about 100,000 Dutch Jewish citizens from various cities to the Nazi death camps in World War II was possible through the assistance of many. First, there was the help given by Dutch city clerks who provided the names and addresses, then there were the Dutch city police (next to Nazi police and activists) who summoned these citizens to leave their houses. Next, there was the Dutch railway organization that provided the transport to the country's two transition camps that were built by ordinary construction companies and supplied by local bakeries, grocery stores and farmers. Everyone did their bit, but no one was, or felt responsible for what would happen later on, further away in Germany and Poland. This interpretation is not uncontested but it undoubtedly points at the possible 'irrationality of bureaucratic rationality'.

This interpretation, however, does not only seem relevant to an understanding of the Holocaust. In today's world, it may help to come to grips with questions pertaining to the responsibility for the use of high-technology devices in violent conflicts, devices such as drones or robots. Many top-level individuals are involved in the use of such devices: suppliers, meteorologists, maintenance engineers, target planners, intelligence officers, commanders and operators. Given the elaborated division of labour, each person is responsible for only one (small) aspect of the whole operational machinery. Yet, who will be accountable if a drone misses its goal and causes tens or hundreds of innocent people to lose their lives?

This question fits into a more general development occurring inside the military, which is the increasing elaboration, regulation and standardization of war-fighting and combat (King, 2013). We will encounter this phenomenon more often throughout this book. For now, it suffices to point at this development that Malešević (2010: 221) has described as the 'cumulative bureaucratization of coercion'. As said, this development implies one giant question: if everyone simply follows the rules and instructions, and if everyone practises the skills and drills that they were ceaselessly trained in, who is responsible for possible mishaps? Who is responsible for the actions of over-bureaucratized military organizations?

On the other side of the continuum (see Figure 1.1), current non-Western armed forces such as in many African nations or Afghanistan are often seen as patrimonial or pre-bureaucratic organizations. Such military organizations are under-bureaucratized so to speak, because they are based on particularistic and nepotistic staffing of various kinds. Tribal, ethnic, religious or political affinities are more important in decisions regarding hiring men than mere skills and competences. One can argue that in such armed forces politics trumps rational

Biased, irrational	Rational	Over-disciplined
violence by patrimonial, <------------	bureaucratic ---------->	violence by irrational
pre-bureaucratic forces	forces	bureaucracies
(under-bureaucratization)		(over-bureaucratization)

Figure 1.1 Continuum of bureaucratic organizing and violence

organizing. To be hired because you belong to the leader's group is more important than merely knowing your job. The workforce composition in such armed forces creates (extreme) loyalty to the ruling power elite. In Perrow's words (1972: 15): 'In most cases, the exchange of loyalty for competence is in the executive's interest.'

In such forces the lack of formal and legal recruitment and appraisal procedures, as well as the absence of clear career prospects and fixed payments, are likely to be detrimental to military performance, at least in Western eyes (e.g. Davids and Soeters, 2009; Erikson Baaz and Verweijen, 2013). Talmadge (2015) has provided an enormous contribution in this connection.

She convincingly showed that armed forces whose workforce is primarily directed at preventing coups from inside and protecting the regime in power are much less effective on the battlefield than those whose composition and staffing is based on military professional criteria, i.e. qualification and merit, only. She made two comparisons: the North Vietnamese with the South Vietnamese army and the armed forces of Saddam Hussein's regime in Iraq with those of Iran. Basing her analysis on these comparisons, she concluded that the defeat of the South Vietnamese army, despite massive US support, was the consequence of failing conventional war practices because inner-directed coup protection practices had been dominant in the organization. The Vietcong on the contrary did not have to face the risks of coups and had adopted conventional war practices far more successfully. As to the Iraq–Iran comparison it turned out that both armed forces performed poorly when their militaries were uniformly subject to coup protection practices; in times when those practices were not in place, however, military performance had been noticeably better (Talmadge, 2015: 8–11). Haddad and colleagues' work (2015) on the militaries in Arab countries similarly points to the divergent outcomes of military interventions, in this case with respect to the protest movements during the so-called 'Arab Spring'. The armed forces in Arab nations pledged allegiance either to the state or to the ruling regime, which denotes the difference between the bureaucratic and the patrimonial or pre-bureaucratic military.

A major additional problem with pre-bureaucratic militaries whose personnel is hired because of affiliations with the power elite is that they tend to take sides in internal conflicts against the groups that oppose the power elite. This so-called 'civil service issue' is almost always a factor in the origin and perpetuation of civil wars. In such cases the military becomes part of the problem instead of part of the solution. Examples abound: the pro-British composition of security forces in Northern Ireland aggravated the troubles between the adversary population groups; police forces in India, with its large majority of non-Muslims, have often been criticized for harassing and victimizing Muslim citizens; the security forces in former Yugoslavia were dominated by Serbs; and officers of European descent ordered indigenous conscript soldiers in Bolivia to shoot at protesters on the streets who were also predominantly indigenous. More recently, in Iraq, the religiously biased staffing of the Iraqi armed forces after the Americans had left the country spawned the flaring up of hostilities there. In the various African conflicts, this problem emerges and re-emerges ceaselessly. Again and again, it is the civil service issue that highlights grievances (Horowitz, 1985; Soeters, 2005: 24–26).

These distinctions are not a matter of black and white, of course, and they are also in constant flux. Besides, there has been quite some criticism of the Western bureaucracy (e.g. Crozier, 1964; Perrow, 1972; Masuch, 1985). Too strict regulations ('red tape'), coercive leadership, ritualism, 'trained incapacity', over-conformity, goal displacement and too little information-sharing within the organization, vertically and horizontally, may be consequences of elaborated bureaucratic organizing. These hamper the bureaucracy's performance in many situations, as has been argued by Merton (1968). Vicious circles of all these phenomena, e.g. implementing new rules to enforce compliance with older rules, are likely to make things worse. These bureaucratic processes also apply to Western armed forces (Davis, 1948; Feld, 1959), as has been described so famously in a number of novels, of which *The Good Soldier Švejk* (Hašek, 1973 [1923]) and *Catch-22* (Heller, 2004 [1955]) are probably the best known.

These often-criticized characteristics have led more recently to the development of new variants of bureaucracy, such as the 'enabling' or 'post'-bureaucracy that is intended to replace the older 'coercive' bureaucracy (e.g. Adler and Borys, 1996). Less authoritarian leadership, less 'bad rules', and more self-steering in the form of mission-oriented command are elements of these newer forms of (military) bureaucracy. Already in 1959 Morris Janowitz pointed to the need for the military to introduce changing patterns of organizational authority in its bureaucracies. He aimed at the organizational development of patterns of authority that were less based on the domination of superior ranks and corresponding hierarchical considerations.

Ambidexterity in the military

One of the new elements in military organizing pertains to the growing number of tasks that the military is requested to do. No longer is traditional combat the main, let alone the only, task the military are set to do. The military also needs to act in crises and disasters, in reconstruction and peace building, in special operations hunting down terrorists, in new domains such as cyber- and space security, and the conduct of drone operations. This expansion of tasks connects to what organizations in general experience these days, which is the need to cope with new and growing demands, pressures and innovations from the outside world. The way to do so is to combine exploitation – doing the usual 'stuff' – and exploration, discovering how to get along with the new 'stuff'. Hence, organizations need to be ambidextrous: equally skilful, as it were, with the left and right hand (Shields and Travis, 2017).

There are two ways to deal with new demands. Either one creates new units and professions in the organization, which is increasing the degree of structural differentiation. Or one prepares and trains conventional units and professions for multi-role performance. In the lingo of organization studies this refers to respectively structural and contextual ambidexterity. Even though structural ambidexterity is the usual bureaucratic reflex and contextual ambidexterity is often seen as unnatural, creating new units and professions comes with disadvantages: it decreases the flexibility in the organization and it incites turf battles and fights over budgets and manpower. It has been shown that the enlargement of special operations forces in today's militaries was not only induced by external developments but also by military entrepreneurs and the dynamics of internal competition; animosity, or institutional hostility, between special operations forces and conventional units is one of the consequences (Shamir and Ben-Ari, 2016).

For sure, one can argue that these new developments do not render the military much better than it was before, and that Weber's *stahlhartes Gehäuse* of rationalization remains the 'iron cage' it always was (Barker, 1993). But these newer forms can also be seen as true improvements, certainly because the general population from which new recruits are hired is increasingly better educated, and better educated new recruits no longer tolerate being stifled by old-time bureaucracy.

Still there are problems with today's military bureaucracies, one of which is that Western forces may be susceptible to forms of nepotism, too. Today's military bureaucracies in the Western hemisphere still seem to cherish some aspects of patrimonial organizations. Getting hired or promoted may be the result of being best friends with, or being family of, the people at the top. One cannot claim that such tendencies do not occur at all in today's Western security forces. A study of the French military academy at St Cyr indicated the importance of being from a military officer family (Weber, 2012: 194). Having attended the same 'elite' school or academy may still help to obtain the highest positions in the military, as has also been demonstrated by a British study (MacDonald, 2004).

Patrimonial military organizations in a number of developing countries, on the other hand, often feel the pressure of international influences or democratic tendencies in their own societies to transform into more rationally, bureaucratically organized forces. Convergence, 'isomorphism' in the argot of organizational sociologists, will emerge one way or another. This is what Western armies specifically aim at when they are assigned to restructure and train the armed forces of developing nations, such as in Africa, the Middle East and Latin America. Sometimes these efforts end up with satisfying results, sometimes the results are much less so.

Authority and leadership

Connected to bureaucracy is the issue of legitimate, i.e. accepted and endorsed, leadership and authority. This stands in contrast to coercion, 'naked power', which is the ability to dominate others even at the expense of their own well-being or the continuation thereof. In Weber's thinking, three types of such legitimate authority exist (Weber, 1976: 130ff). First, there is *traditional* authority that dominates in patrimonial organizations, implying that the leader belongs to the established and ruling affiliation, i.e. a tribe, region or religious group. Patriarchalism and patrimonialism are two characteristic forms. Next to traditional authority Weber distinguishes between *legal* and *charismatic* authorities (Giddens, 1971: 154–163). Rational-legal authority belongs to bureaucratic organizations as it is based on impersonal, standardized rules, norms and regulations that have been established within a context of purposive or value rationality. Rational-legal authority is bestowed on people who merit the job because they have displayed excellent previous performance and obtained proper results in rationalized training and education. Legitimate leaders have to obey to the impersonal rules themselves; after all, these rules are standardized and hence apply to all. With rational-legal authority, the laws, rules and regulations are more important than the leaders themselves.

Charismatic authority (or leadership to use a more modern word), in contrast, is a creative, driving force that is very much based on extraordinary, supernatural qualities that others attribute to the person in charge (Gerth and Wright Mills, 2009: 245–252). Charismatic authority hence emerges in the interaction between leader and followers, such as in revolutionary and religious movements. It occurs all over the world and in all kinds of atmospheres: from Mohammed to Marx as the saying goes. Unlike rational-legal authority, charismatic authority is not based on rational principles; it is essentially non-rational in Weber's view and because of the increasing rationalization of society it belongs more to the past than to the present: 'the further back we look in history, the more we find this [leadership based on charisma] to be the case' (Gerth and Wright Mills, 2009: 245).

Charismatic authority is mysterious, seductive and enchanting, but it is erratic and sometimes problematic, too. Weber himself sceptically suggests 'that charismatic imputation involves the *misattribution* of supernatural or extraordinary powers to individuals who were prone to "epileptoid seizures" […], to those who simply worked themselves into a "bloodthirsty frenzy", or to those who could cunningly pull of a "rank swindle"' (cited in Joosse, 2014: 274). Followers worship and fantasize about their leaders but because of their frightening and intimidating appearance they fear them too; think of Adolf Hitler for instance. Charm and fear are more connected than may appear at first sight. More than traditional and rational-legal authority, charismatic authority may turn into 'naked power', as again the examples of the Führer or Stalin have demonstrated much too clearly.

In the domain of today's violence and conflict this type of leadership can still be seen particularly in ferocious political movements, such as today's Islamic State, or in Mafia-type criminal gangs involved for example in human or drugs trafficking. Osama Bin Laden for sure was a charismatic leader whose attraction was expanded through his performances in mass media and the Internet. And today's charismatic jihadist hate preachers who are also influential through their presence on social media, have followed his example.

Remarkably enough, commanders of Western bureaucratized armed forces are sometimes also seen as charismatic leaders because of their communicative skills and convincing performance in action. This goes back to Weber's *charismatische Kriegshelde* – 'charismatic war heroes' – of ancient times when military states of emergency were part of everyday life (e.g. Moelker 2003). However, the charisma of some of today's military commanders is necessarily blended with rational-legal authority, as modern bureaucracies cannot tolerate anything but administrative reasoning based on laws and procedures. In today's military bureaucracies, charisma inevitably gets *routinized* and embedded in rationalized and legal practices. Military decisions, like those of of medical doctors, professors and accountants, increasingly need to be based on rational reasoning and proven knowledge and evidence. Leadership needs to develop from 'eminence'-based to evidence-based practices.

Nonetheless, some of today's commanders are indeed seen as charismatic, which usually refers to the talent to use a large gamut of communicative means. They express messages that are based on creative intuition and *Fingerspitzengefühl*, and that energize and satisfy the needs and confidence of their followers, the rank-and-file. Through these behavioural attributes charismatic commanders have acquired reputation and eminence. Examples abound. Yet, there is always debate about what constitutes true military quality and what really makes a great leader. General Stanley McChristal was held in high esteem until the moment he had to step down. Obviously, there are limits to charismatic leadership in the military, as has also been demonstrated by empirical sociological studies (Shamir et al., 1998). As charismatic impact may also be intimidating, studies have reported elements of destructive leadership among senior military leaders (Reed and Bullis, 2009). And usually the enchantment eventually ends. For sure, charismatic leadership is unstable leadership, as Weber never ceased to say (Gerth and Wright Mills, 2009: 248–250).

Limits of military leadership

An example of the power and limits of charismatic leadership was offered in a talk by the commander of a national air force to a selected group of mid-career officers. He told them that the Minister of Defence had approached him with a request to prolong the air force's participation in a UN mission. Continuing, he jokingly and sarcastically referred to the minor importance of the UN as an international institution and the Minister of Foreign Affairs who valued UN missions. The mid-career officers were clinging to every word. The commander continued, saying that he had given some thought to the request and after some thinking to himself he had come to the conclusion that his service could no longer prolong its contribution. His intuition and experience had told him that the air force had already done too much. 'The elasticity of my organization had already been overstretched', he expained, a statement he illustrated with wide gestures. This he had conveyed to the government. Much to the commander's irritation, the Minister had not accepted this message and she had tasked other military to elaborate all options quantitatively, using computer software. Eventually she had decided to prolong the mission, including the air force's input, the commander told his audience, still visibly annoyed. For a short while he had considered resigning in anger, he said, but in the end he had decided not to. But, clearly, the commander's charisma had lost out to pressure from politicians to make decisions based on more than a commander's intuition, experience and authority.

It has been argued that next to these three well-known types of authority a fourth type is needed, which may be called *substantive-rational* authority (Guzmán, 2015). This fourth type is based on value-rationality instead of formal, bureaucratic rationality ('these are the rules and procedures here'). Value-rationality is based on the use of broader, general, and scientific information and views, Plato's philosopher-king being a prime example. Military commanders who rely on a broader approach to violence and conflict may be another example. US Army General David Petraeus developed a remarkable and novel approach in the Iraq mission through the introduction of so-called Red Teams. These teams consisted of outspoken intellectuals and non-conformists questioning the military staff's assumptions, ideas and plans. These teams, however, were not entirely successful as they met with resistance and obstacles. The Army was not used to such probing of orders, plans and ideas, especially if they came from higher ranking members (Hajjar, 2014: 131). As in all types of legitimate leadership, there are limits to this fourth type's success and effectiveness.

Music

A final token of Weber's relevance to the military, although at face value perhaps less essential, is music (Weber, 2010 [1911/1912]). In his life Weber combined his love of music with one of the main themes in his sociological work, which is the rationalization of organized social life. He sees bureaucratization and rationalization as main drives behind the evolution of church music and classical music such as operas. In particular, the development of notational systems, structured harmony, organized choirs, ensembles, orchestras and the standardized production of modern instruments was made possible through these societal processes. Of all forms of musical expression, the conductor-led orchestra is the most bureaucratized form of performance. Even the 'irrational' and mystical sphere of the production and experience of culture and music cannot escape from rationalization and bureaucratization, as Weber showed.

Hence, society influenced music and continues to do so, but the reverse holds good as well. Music has an impact on social life, too, as it plays a role in political movements – cultural nationalism for instance – and in the emergence of new youth cultures such as the rise of hip-hop or dance music (Turley, 2001). Music has the capacity to transcend social divisions, but that is something Weber did not pay a lot of attention to. Yet it is something another sociologist observed and that we will encounter later in the chapter on W. E. B. Du Bois (Kemple, 2009).

Music is important in military life too: it accompanies and facilitates the ceremonial events that are so important in military culture as they give expression to the collective character, the collective mind and memory, of the military. Military music is particularly important in all sorts of ceremonial events, such as graduation and promotion ceremonies or annual celebrations of a unit's establishment. It is particularly important in ceremonies where those killed in action are remembered (Burk, 2008). Marching together makes one feel good and makes cooperative efforts of every kind, physical and psychological, easier to carry out (e.g. Soeters, 2018). In historical times when other means of communication were not available, drums and trumpets were important to indicate the timing and rhythm of operational manoeuvres on the battlefield. A trumpet gave the signal to attack, manoeuvre or retreat. The rhythm of drums made the soldiers march as one collective entity, which made them feel good and less fearful. In classical history, the sound of the Roman legion's loud, unison war-cry was often decisive on the battlefield (Johnson and Cloonan, 2009: 33–34). As Weber showed, all this was very much a process of bureaucratized discipline and standardization. Standardized musical expressions were used in the attempt to bring some clarity to the fog of battle.

As said, music itself has an impact on other social phenomena. One aspect of such influence may be particularly relevant to the military and its actions.

The dark side of the tune

Every musical transaction is potentially an act of aggression, invasion or symbolic or actual violence (Johnson and Cloonan, 2009; 2011). In military operations, such as during the Vietnam War, music has been used in a loud and high-profile way to accompany military action. Used like this it is a means to encourage one's own soldiers and to warn and intimidate the enemy, including the host population. Until the present day, music has also been used as an instrument of torture in military sites all over the world; if played loud enough, music can drive people crazy. Music and violence can very well go together, as demonstrated in Serbia during the Balkan war in the 1990s when a champion of violence married a star performer of nationalist ethno-folk muisic (Johnson and Cloonan, 2009: 148–150). Music can also be performed in complete opposition to violence, as happened in that same conflict when a single musician protested against the violence by playing his cello in a market square in Sarajevo, for days in a row and totally unprotected from snipers' bullets (Galloway, 2008: 225).

Conclusion

Max Weber was a sociological thinker whose influence can hardly be overestimated. His work includes an analytical approach to societal developments, public administration and the military that is still very useful today. His analyses pertain to phenomena as they occur all across the globe. Remarkably, as a citizen he was quite carried away by nationalist sentiments, at least in the period before the outbreak of the First World War (Joas and Knöbl, 2013: 118–121). Apparently, there is a difference between the rational sociologist at work and the private individual with a penchant for all-too-human feelings, even if this is only temporary. This difference seems less applicable to the next founding father of sociology, Emile Durkheim.

Bibliography

Adler, P.S. and B. Borys (1996) 'Two types of bureaucracy: enabling and coercive'. *Administrative Science Quarterly* 41(1): 61–89.

Barker, J. (1993) 'Tightening the iron cage: control in self-managing teams'. *Administrative Science Quarterly* 38(3): 408–437.

Bauman, Z. (1989) *Modernity and the Holocaust*. Cambridge: Polity Press.

Burk, J. (2008) 'Military culture'. In L. Kurtz (ed.), *Encyclopedia of Violence, Peace and Conflict*. Oxford: Elsevier, 1242–1256.

Collins, R. (1995) 'Prediction in macro-sociology: the case of the Soviet collapse'. *American Journal of Sociology* 100(6): 1552–1593.

Coser, L. (1977) *Masters of Sociological Thought: Ideas in Historical and Social Context*. 2nd edn. Long Grove, IL: Waveland Press.

Crozier, M. (1964) *The Bureaucratic Phenomenon*. Chicago: University of Chicago Press.

Dandeker, Chr. (1990) *Surveillance, Power and Modernity: Bureaucracy and Discipline from 1700 to the Present Day*. Cambridge: Polity.

Davids, C. and J. Soeters (2009) 'Payday in the Afghan national army: from Western administrative liabilities to local realities'. In G. Caforio (ed.), *Advances in Military Sociology: Essays in Honor of Charles C. Moskos, Part A*. Bingley, Yorkshire: Emerald, pp. 285–303.

Davis, A.K. (1948) 'Bureaucratic patterns in the Navy officer corps'. *Social Forces* 27(2): 143–153.

Du Gay, P. (2000) *In Praise of Bureaucracy: Weber, Organization, Ethics*. London and Thousand Oaks, CA: Sage.

EnderM.G. (2009) *American Soldiers in Iraq: McSoldiers or Innovative Professionals?* London and New York: Routledge.

Erikson Baaz, M. and J. Verweijen (2013) 'The volatility of a half-cooked bouillabaise: rebel–military integration and conflict dynamics in Eastern DRC'. *African Affairs* 112(449): 563–582.

Feld, M.D. (1959) 'Information and authority: the structure of military organization'. *American Sociological Review* 24(1): 15–22.

Galloway, St. (2008) *The Cellist of Sarajevo*. London: Atlantic Books.

Gerth, H. and C. Wright Mills (eds) (2009 [1946)]) *From Max Weber: Essays in Sociology*. Abingdon and New York: Routledge.

Giddens, A. (1971) *Capitalism and Modern Social Theory: An Analysis of the Writings of Marx, Durkheim and Max Weber*. Cambridge: Cambridge University Press.

Guzmán, S.G. (2015) 'Substantive-rational authority: the missing fourth pure type in Weber's typology of legitimate domination'. *Journal of Classical Sociology* 15(1): 73–95.

Haddad, S. (ed.) (2015) *Les armées dans les révolutions arabes: Positions et rôles. Perspectives théoriques et études de cas*. Rennes: Presses Universitaires de Rennes.

Hajjar, R.M. (2014) 'Emergent postmodern US military culture'. *Armed Forces and Society* 40(1): 118–145.

Hašek, J. (1973 [1923]) *The Good Soldier Švejk and His Fortunes in the World War*. London: Penguin.

Heller, J. (2004 [1955]) *Catch-22*. New York: Simon & Schuster.

Horowitz, D.L. (1985) *Ethnic Groups in Conflict*. Berkeley: University of California Press.

Janowitz, M. (1959) 'Changing patterns of organizational authority: the military establishment'. *Administrative Science Quarterly* 3(4): 473–493.

Joas, H. and W. Knöbl (2013 [2008]) *War in Social Thought: Hobbes to the Present*. Princeton NJ and Oxford: Princeton University Press.

Johnson, B. and M. Cloonan (2009) *Dark Side of the Tune: Popular Music and Violence*. Farnham: Ashgate.

Johnson, B. and M. Cloonan (2011) 'Introduction'. *Popular Music and Society* 34(1): 1–6.

Joosse, P. (2014) 'Becoming a god: Max Weber and the social construction of charisma'. *Journal of Classical Sociology* 14(3): 266–283.

Kemple, Th. (2009) 'Weber/Simmel/DuBois: musical thirds of classical sociology'. *Journal of Classical Sociology* 9(2): 187–207.

King, A. (2013) *The Combat Soldier: Infantry Tactics and Cohesion in the Twentieth and Twenthieth-First Centuries*. Oxford: Oxford University Press.

Lounsbury, M. and E.J. Carberry (2005) 'From king to court jester? Weber's fall from grace in organization theory'. *Organization Studies* 26(4): 501–525.

MacDonald, K. (2004) 'Black Mafia, loggies and going for the stars: the military elite revisited'. *Sociological Review* 52(1): 106–135.

Malešević, S. (2010) *The Sociology of War and Violence*. Cambridge: Cambridge University Press.

Masuch, M. (1985) 'Vicious circles in organizations'. *Administrative Science Quarterly* 30: 14–33.

Merton, R.K. (1968) *Social Theory and Social Structure*. Enlarged edition. New York: The Free Press.

Moelker, R. (2003) 'Technology, organization, and power'. In G. Caforio (ed.), *Handbook of the Sociology of the Military*. New York: Kluwer, pp. 385–402.

Perrow, Ch. (1972) *Complex Organizations: A Critical Essay.* Glenview IL and Brighton: Scott, Foresman and Company.

Portes, A. (2000) 'The hidden abode: sociology as analysis of the unexpected'. *American Sociological Review* 65(February): 1–18.

Reed, G.E. and R.G. Bullis (2009) 'The impact of destructive leadership on senior military officers and civilian employees'. *Armed Forces and Society* 36(1): 5–18.

Ritzer, G. (1993) *The McDonaldization of Society.* London: Sage.

Shamir, B., E. Zakay, E. Breinin and M. Popper (1998) 'Correlates of charismatic leader behavior in military units: subordinates' attitudes, unit characteristics, and superiors' appraisals of leader performance'. *Academy of Management Journal* 41(4): 387–409.

Shamir, E. and E. Ben-Ari (2016) 'The rise of special operations forces: generalized specialization, boundary spanning and military autonomy'. *Journal of Strategic Studies* (online).

Shields, P. (2003) 'The bureaucracy in military sociology'. In J. Callaghan and F. Kernic (eds), *Armed Forces and International Security: Global Trends and Issues.* New Brunswick, NJ: Transaction Publishers/LIT Verlag.

Shields, P. and D.S. Travis (2017) 'Achieving organizational flexibility through ambidexterity'. *Parameters* 47(2): 65–76.

Soeters, J. (2005) *Ethnic Conflict and Terrorism: The Origins and Dynamics of Civil Wars.* London and New York: Routledge.

Soeters, J. (2018) 'Organizational cultures in the military'. In Caforio, G. (ed.) (2018) *Handbook of the Sociology of the Military.* Cham, Switzerland: Springer.

Talmadge, C. (2015) *The Dictator's Army: Battlefield Effectiveness in Authoritarian Regimes.* Ithaca NY and London: Cornell University Press.

Tilly, C. (1992) *Coercion, Capital and European States, AD 990–1990.* Cambridge: Blackwell.

Turley, A.C. (2001) 'Max Weber and the sociology of music'. *Sociological Forum* 16(4): 633–653.

Weber, C. (2012) *A genou les hommes, debout les officiers: la socialisation des Saint-Cyriens.* Rennes: Presses Universitaires de Rennes.

Weber, M. (1976 [1914]) *Wirtschaft und Gesellschaft. Studienausgabe.* Tübingen, Germany: J.C.B. Mohr.

Weber, M. (2010 [1911/1912]) *The Rational and Social Foundations of Music.* Eastford, CT: Martino Press.

2 Emile Durkheim

The military group, culture and its consequences

Emile Durkheim's (1858–1917) contribution to the development of French sociology and sociology in general is undisputable (e.g. Heilbron, 2015: 73–91). He and his collaborators contributed substantially to the understanding of the relations between the individual and society and of social facts in general. Durkheim stressed that social facts need to be distinguished from psychological phenomena and individual-level explanations, no matter how self-evident these may be at first glance. Sociological analysis requires more abstract and comparative thinking, focusing on the collective level only. He also advocated a rigorous empirical and statistical approach, quite different from the philosophical standpoint that dominated intellectual life in France at the time. His interests were wide-ranging: from the transformation in the division of labour and its consequences for society, to elementary forms of religious life, questions of crime and punishment, methodological issues in sociological research, and more. All his studies actually converge because they all address one single question: how do individuals get integrated into society?

Durkheim also got involved in political activities, in an early stage of the Dreyfus Affair that divided France at the turn of the century. This concerned an army captain of Jewish background who was convicted of allegedly selling military secrets to Germany, and it created considerable social and political upheaval. It shows that military issues were in the midst of the social and political turmoil of those times. The events led Durkheim to publish a brief analysis of anti-Semitism that, in his view, was caused by 'a state of social malaise' in the country (Goldberg, 2008: 302). Towards the end of his life he specifically reflected on the causes of the First World War that had just begun, including the role of the Germans in this process (Durkheim, 1915; Durkheim and Denis, 1915). He differs from Max Weber in that he as a private person took the view that there is something more universal and more valuable than one's 'fatherland' (Joas and Knöbl, 2013: 121).

Like Max Weber's academic work, many fruits of Durkheim's thinking and research were and are relevant for the military. Corresponding with the multi-dimensional nature of his work, this relevance is manifold, although the leading Durkheimian question applied to the military remains the same: how do individuals get integrated into the military institution? Answering this question may start with a discussion of human interaction at the level of the small group.

Primary group

The core of military action, at least infantry action, belongs to the small group: the squad or the platoon, currently referred to as the smallest units of action. The success of these primary groups is based on continuous interaction between the members of the group and the development of group cohesion. The concept of the primary group was coined by a later, American sociologist, Charles Cooley, who used the family as a prime example. In this, he paralleled some of Durkheim's insights, at the same time with his own emphases (Coser, 1977: 307–310).

Focusing on the primary group in the military, British sociologist Anthony King (2006; 2013) explicitly refers to Durkheim's work on group formation, which occurs when people – aboriginal tribal societies in one of Durkheim's most famous studies (1976 [1912]) – come together and engage in celebrations in front of a totem. The totem can be seen as a symbol of the god whom they worship, in fact as a symbol of the group itself. These celebrations are elements of religious life that are common to all humankind, so Durkheim claims (Durkheim, 1976 [1912]; Giddens, 1971: 107–112). Durkheim compares these rituals in front of a totem with a soldier dying to recover a lost flag (King, 2006: 500). Like the aboriginal totem, the flag is a symbol of the military unit and the country to which the soldier belongs. The soldier's sacrifice, therefore, is an expression of the pursuit of group goals. The soldier dies for the group, which is represented by the flag (King, 2006: 500). These dynamics of group formation can be recognized in the training of military groups or platoons that aims to create group cohesion; they foster the idea of 'all for one and one for all'. The effect of training on cohesion is dramatic, says King (2013: 273–280). Here one can see the same dynamics Durkheim described in his work. Military life is social life par excellence (King, 2006). This conclusion is related to a number of earlier studies on cohesion at the primary group level in the military.

Perhaps the most famous early example of the significance of cohesion at the level of primary groups is Shils and Janowitz's analysis (1948) of the persistent performance of German Wehrmacht platoons at the end of the Second World War. Based on various documents and interviews with German prisoners of war, they found that solidarity among the soldiers in the platoons, i.e. small-group cohesion or micro-level camaraderie, was far more important in making the men resist until the very end of the war than were ideological reasons (also: Malešević, 2010: 219–233). This conclusion has been challenged by others in more recent studies, but its main implication still stands. More recent is Weick and Roberts' reconstruction (1993) of heedful interrelating among sailors on US Navy flight decks. Heedful interrelating, or carefully paying attention and reacting to another's behaviour, turns out to be a decisive factor in preventing accidents, which are so likely to happen in these complex sea-based air operations. Heedful interrelating, bonding, solidarity, mutual loyalty and group cohesion time and again prove to be decisive in military performance, particularly when the stakes are high.

Interestingly, this occurs in collectivities of people who work in either type of division of labour, as discerned by Durkheim (1933 [1893]). The platoon or the work group as the smallest unit of action shows a simple form of work division, based on resemblance or likeness of tasks, creating *mechanical solidarity* among a unit's members. The flight deck operations rely on a differentiated division of work, based on a system of different interdependent tasks, creating *organic solidarity* among the workers. In the first case one simply feels one belongs together, as in a family. In the second case one simply knows one belongs together because everyone has to do their bit to make the whole system work, like the proper functioning of all organs is needed to keep the whole body healthy.

Somewhat differently, Israeli scholars have pointed to the phenomenon of temporary military groups; these are small units that rely on temporary frameworks of ad hoc and diverse components and aim to achieve high-intensive, complex goals (Ben-Shalom et al., 2005). As an example, such 'instant units' may be composed of infantry soldiers, engineers and bomb-disposal experts, medical personnel and intelligence officers. Hence these groups are based on Durkheim's concept of organic solidarity we have just mentioned. Even though these military men and women are from different units, they can work together to conduct a particular mission because of the 'swift trust' that develops in the process of instant group formation and temporary action. In line with organizational scholars before them, these military scholars put forward that 'such temporary groups constitute an organizational equivalent of a "one-night stand": they have a finite life span, form around a shared and relatively clear goal or purpose and their success depends on a tight and coordinated coupling of activity' (Ben-Shalom et al., 2005: 77).

It does not always work like this, though. The dynamics at group level can go wrong in two ways: because of too little or too much cohesion. Too little or failing cohesion at unit level occurred in the Vietnam War. There have been numerous accounts of fragmentation inside US army platoons and companies during the Vietnam War (e.g. Moskos, 1974). Fault lines within the units were predominantly race-related and hierarchy-related, and they had grave consequences, even leading to the occasional killing of officers by enlisted men (so-called 'fragging'). The bonding within the primary groups, both horizontally and vertically, had failed conspicuously. Tensions within society at large had been imported to the military, also because units did not train and deploy collectively but on a more or less individual basis.

On the other hand, too much cohesion occurs when group dynamics at the unit level reinforce strong affective ties. These may lead to misplaced loyalties, preventing members of the unit from speaking out against the misconduct and inappropriate behaviour of team mates. These dynamics have been uncovered by the late Canadian anthropologist Donna Winslow. She analysed what happened when soldiers of the Canadian Airborne regiment, deployed to operations in Somalia, committed serious offences. She concluded that exaggerated loyalty to the group leads members to work at counter-purpose to the mission's overall goals (Winslow, 1998).

In both cases, too much and too little cohesion, Durkheim's lessons have been insufficiently taken into account in the preparation and actual conduct of military operations. Durkheim's theorizing on primary groups, based on anthropological ideas, was not explicitly directed at the military, but over time it proved to be important to a better comprehension of the socio-dynamics of military units at the primary group level.

Military culture

At a more general level, one can say that the Durkheimian concept of the *conscience collective* has been fundamental to the study of cultures, including organizational and military cultures (Dobbin, 2009). Durkheim's conscience collective, i.e. the beliefs and sentiments common to the average men and women of a society or community, may be seen as the social creation of people's mindset, their *psyche*. It refers to the many social conventions, norms and values and even cognitive dispositions that impact on the individual mind (Zerubavel 1997). Like a language, as an element of the conscience collective, does, not because it is created but because it is used by every one of us.

In the famous words of Mary Douglas, it makes sense 'to think of the individual mind furnished as society writ small' (Dobbin, 2009: 206). Individual and society coincide, not totally of course and not for all people in a similar way, but most certainly to a large degree. It particularly applies to the many people who echo the views, opinions and emotions of others who belong to the same groups or the identities they themselves adhere to. Social conformity within social groups is a driving force in this regard. Summarized in other words, the conscience collective is 'a composite, the elements of which are individual minds' (Giddens, 1971: 67). With a somewhat different emphasis, one can say the conscience collective is something bigger than the sum of individual parts.

This insight constitutes the foundation of culture studies that focus on various levels of collectivity: nations, regions, language groups, religions, occupations, organizations and henceforth also the military (Burk, 2008). The military in particular may profit from a cultural approach, because work often takes place in a 24/7 environment, implying that work and life overlap and take place in a rather closed community, such as a camp, barracks, garrison, international HQ or training institution (Diken and Bagge Laustsen, 2005). As noted, the military is a social group par excellence. Working in the military often also implies studying in the military, doing sports and games in the military, having drinks and meals together, often having intimate relations with other military and finally marrying and possibly divorcing other military people. There is a 'pre-scribed sociability' in the military, as Morris Janowitz (1960) described it. Although military people are tending to become more like ordinary civilians, as we will see in Chapter 9, *the military mind may still be furnished as the military society writ small*. This particularly pertains to the military on deployment. This even applies after people have left the military. Veterans behave, think, enjoy, suffer from and reflect on military life, long after they have quit the force.

Veteran bikers, for instance, tend to organize themselves in a military manner, in military communities so to speak (e.g. Samet, 2014).

> **Sociology on a bike**
>
> Dutch sociologist Rene Moelker (2014) did ethnographic field studies among veteran bikers on tour, both in the USA and the Netherlands. He described how veterans seek comfort by touring together on their bikes: they feel they are different due to past experiences in war zones and because of the lack of understanding, even the feeling of rejection, by civilians in wider society. The groups make pilgrimages to Washington D.C. – the 'Run for the Wall' – or to Lourdes in France, where injured and disabled veterans get together to seek healing for their wounds. Most of all they relive their experiences as military men and women.

From the onset of military organizing, culture in the armed forces has been a masculine affair par excellence. We will turn to this aspect in Chapter 13 that deals with the work of Cynthia Enloe.

In addition, cultural characteristics of the military organization (Soeters, 2018) have been described as:

- *Hierarchy- and discipline oriented*, which manifests itself in all kinds of visible elements such as rank indications on uniforms, the display of standardized drills and skills (for instance saluting), and obedience to the orders of the higher-ranking military;
- *Being inner-directed*, i.e. being an island in society, as can be seen from the bases, forts and garrisons that are fairly inaccessible to outsiders, or from the training and education programmes or other facilities (e.g. hospitals, hotels) that are specifically designed for the military;
- Having a *Janus face*, with one side directed at operations in crisis- and wartime conditions and the other at the placid preparation thereof during peacetime conditions, including the capability to quickly switch from one condition to another; and
- Displaying the tendency of being *averse to outside assessments*, as military people are loyal to one another and tend to defend each other. The military prefer to do things by themselves, including judging whether or not they are doing a proper job or whether or not soldiers have demonstrated misbehaviour (Winslow, 1999). Only the military have their own formal courts of justice and law enforcement agencies.

Of course, not all of these aspects are unique to the military and there may be small differences between nations and situations. Yet, the combination of these aspects makes the military culture a unique phenomenon. However, it is not a monolith one (e.g. Hajjar, 2014), even though it may sometimes look like it is, particularly in comparison with many civilian organizations. In reality the military consists of many organizational subcultures that can be observed at the level of services such as special forces units, the air force, the army and the navy, or in combat units as compared to for instance logistic units. There are also subcultures following the boundaries between regular, full-time military personnel vis-à-vis reservists and civilian employees who work for the defence organization. Sometimes there are culture-related political fault lines within the military, as revealed by the military coup in Turkey in the summer of 2016.

Of course, cultural differences can also be seen in international variations in operational practices, styles and strategic world views; the American way of military organizing and performance clearly deviates from the Italian, Russian, South African or Japanese way (e.g. Vreÿ et al., 2013; Soeters, 2018). In Chapter 11 on Cornelis Lammers we will elaborate on these international differences and how they impact on military operations.

However, there are many similarities among these national armed forces, too, since they are all military. In the military sector, like in other sectors such as health care, there are strong isomorphic, converging tendencies. These are the result of supranational rules and regulations, e.g. NATO's doctrines with respect to training, certification and conduct in operations. Or they result from uniform weapon systems or technologies, F-35's for instance, that require common policies in terms of training, maintenance and actual use that transcend cultural differences. Or they follow from simple mimetic behaviour among people and organizations (Winslow, 2007; Soeters, 2018). These very facts make it possible for armed forces of different nations to work together in military operations, such as in missions under the aegis of the UN, NATO or the African Union.

Nonetheless, cultural differences between national militaries continue to exist. They may hamper the effectiveness of multinational military cooperation in missions because of a lack of understanding of others' values, practices and interests. There are three organizational and operational solutions to accommodate for these differences (Soeters and Szvircsev Tresch, 2010; Soeters, 2018). All of them are used in multinational military cooperation in missions:

- *Assimilation* occurs when smaller partners adapt to and often become similar to a majority or a larger partner on whom they are dependent or whom they deem superior; examples are smaller air forces (e.g. Belgium, Norway) that use the same aircraft as a senior partner, in particular the US Air Force; another example refers to the Estonian and Danish infantry contingents that were attached to the much larger and more highly reputed British contingent in Afghanistan, which intentionally or unintentionally led them to mimic the British approach in the arena that has been described as truly war-like (King, 2010);
- *Separation* as a way of organizing is often applied in operations, by dividing

a   the area of operations in smaller areas that are assigned to different lead nations, such as during the ISAF mission the Afghan province of Helmand to the British, Kandahar to the Canadians and Uruzgan to the Dutch; or

b   by means of time-related separation: in one particular period the task of air patrolling in an area – for instance above the Baltic States – is tasked to one nation, in the subsequent period it is assigned to another; or

c   by task-related separation: for instance Operation Enduring Freedom taken up by the Americans and the British, and ISAF assigned to the Germans and other European forces;

- *Integration* is the most difficult way of obtaining cooperation among armed forces of different nationalities, as it relies on the idea that all partners are equal and can have comparable input to achieving the mission goals. This is most likely to occur in multinational HQs where the contribution of nations is more based on deploying individual personnel than on whole large-sized units.

Enhancing American military effectiveness

The late American military sociologist Charles Moskos (2001) authored a memo about his experiences during visits to one British and various American war and staff colleges and NATO's operational HQs in Belgium (SHAPE). He interviewed large numbers of international officers, non-American officers who received military education and training in the USA or who worked at SHAPE. A number of recommendations to enhance American military effectiveness in multinational military operations followed from these interviews. Language in particular was an issue. Almost none of the international officers are as fluent in the English language as the Americans and British. This produces all kinds of side-effects, such as a lack of understanding of what is being communicated and the rise of informal groups along language lines (Spanish-speaking officers from Spain with Spanish-speaking officers from Portugal, etc.). This, in combination with different access to classified material in the curriculum and the dominance of American lecturers and topics ('the big war mode'), 'aggravates an incipient feeling of being second-class citizens'. All these culture-related observations are from the beginning of the current century, and may have changed over the years. Or not ...

Identifying the importance of cohesion at the level of the primary group (squad, platoon, company) and culture at the level of the organization are among Durkheim's most valuable contributions to sociology and military studies. There is more, though.

Suicide

The relevance of Durkheim's work to the military explicitly comes to the fore in perhaps his most famous study: *Suicide* (2006 [1897]). This study based on extensive statistical documentation and intelligent analysis has lost nothing of its importance and freshness (Heilbron, 2015: 79–81). It demonstrated that an act of suicide is not only a decision of an individual person, but that such a dramatic event is also very much connected to the social group one belongs to and to society at large. The military relevance of this classic study is twofold: it contributes to understanding the relatively high suicide rates among soldiers that persist until today (Mastroianni and Scott, 2011), and it helps to come to grips with suicide attacks by hostile individuals that continue to terrify ordinary people in everyday life.

In his study Durkheim (2006 [1897]: 186–199) spends a full section on analysing suicide rates among soldiers in a large number of countries. As in other studies, he showed the importance of comparative analysis, which methodological issue we will turn to later. First, he observed that 'in all European countries [...] the suicidal aptitude of soldiers is much higher than that of the civilian population of the same age' (Durkheim 2006 [1897]: 186). His interpretation points at military suicide being an expression of *altruistic suicide*, which is suicide *because of the other*; this means that the suicide is related to the strong pressure of the social group, i.e. the military itself.

In Durkheim's own words:

> Influenced by this predisposition, the soldier kills himself at the least disappointment, for the most futile reasons, for a refusal of leave, a reprimand, an unjust punishment, a delay in promotion, a question of honor, a flush of momentary jealousy or even simply because other suicides have occurred before his eyes or to his knowledge. [...] Everything is readily explained when it is recognized that the profession of the soldier develops a moral constitution powerfully predisposing man to make away with himself.
>
> (Durkheim, 2006 [1897]: 198–199)

Military life is so pervasive and intense that even the smallest deviation from everyday convention may spawn formal and informal reactions in work and life that may cause mental problems among its inmates, leading to the suicide of some of them, following Durkheim. Not surprisingly perhaps, troops with the least pronounced military character, such as engineers, administrators or ambulance personnel, are least severely affected by the tendency to commit suicide (Durkheim, 2006 [1897]: 197). Next to these general socio-dynamics leading to higher suicide rates among military personnel, Durkheim points at the phenomenon of the 'heroic suicide', i.e. soldiers sacrificing their lives on the battlefield to prevent the death of others (Riemer, 1998).

In this Durkheimian line of thinking, American social scientists Mastroianni and Scott (2011) have expanded the explanation, pointing out that one should be aware that, unlike the situation in Durkheim's days, not all armed forces today show higher suicide rates than the civilian population. Nonetheless in some countries it is a persistent phenomenon. Mastroianni and Scott (2011) relate the high and even rising suicide rates among American soldiers to all types of suicide that Durkheim discerned. Particularly in the aftermath of the operations in Iraq and Afghanistan, suicide rates among American veterans have been exceptionally high compared to non-veterans; the suicide rate among female veterans has even been considerably higher in comparison with female non-veterans (Hoffmire et al., 2015).

> If you're a veteran and you feel like you can't handle it any more or the world could be better off without you, please call this number.
> Veterans Suicide Hotline
> 800-273-8255
> [...]
> Your loved one will NOT be happier when you are gone.
>
> (Facebook posting in the USA, 16 January 2017)

In trying to analyse this dramatic phenomenon, Mastroianni and Scott (2011) first point to the opposite of the altruistic suicide, which is the *egoistic suicide*: the type of suicide that occurs not because of too much but because of too little social integration into garrison environments. Frequent deployments and individual rotations can be experienced as disruptions to the high degree of social integration the military is known for. It may render individual soldiers intensely lonely, bringing a number of them to the point of killing themselves. A problematic reintegration into the family after deployment(s) may mean that marriage and family life, usually a factor preventing suicides as Durkheim showed, contributes to the tendency among military people to feel isolated, with unhappy events such as divorces and suicides as a result. But the impact may stem from earlier periods in life as well. Recently, Griffith and Bryan (2016) have argued and shown that today's militaries have fewer applicants to select from and hence necessarily accept proportionally more applicants for military service. This includes recruiting more new members from nontraditional, in particular single-parent, households and households of adverse childhood experiences; this characteristic renders them more vulnerable to suicide; this again can be seen as a form of egoistic suicide in the Durkheimian sense of the term.

Additionally, Mastroianni and Scott (2011) relate the high degree of suicides among American soldiers to what Durkheim coined as *anomic suicide*, which refers to suicides as a consequence of sudden negative changes in ordinary life and work. Leaving the socially safe environment of the military and being unable to find a new job in the civilian labour market may be experienced as such a sudden, dramatic change in life. Anomie during operations may occur, according to Mastroianni and Scott, if enlisted men and women experience frustration and despair when their expectations, developed during education and training and nurtured by political or military leaders, are violated by what is happening to them. This may occur when they are made to believe they will be fighting conventional warfare in a mission involving a known enemy, whereas they are confronted with fierce, but irregular hostilities they are unfamiliar and uncomfortable with. Psychological strain and physical threat, particularly when it is unfamiliar and untrained for, go hand in hand. For some soldiers this will simply be too much. Let's not forget in all of this that according to accepted insights, not that many people are actually good at experiencing and using violence.

There are a few, though – the 'violent few' as Collins framed them (2008). They appear on all points of the spectrum, which leads to the phenomenon of suicidal attacks, combining internally with externally oriented violence. Notorious examples are the kamikaze suicide attacks by Japanese warplanes during the sea battles in the Pacific in the Second World War, and more recently the attacks on the USA of 11 September 2001, and thereafter in Bali, Madrid, London, Casablanca, Ankara, San Bernardino CA, Paris, Brussels, Orlando FL, Istanbul, Nice, Barcelona and almost continuously in Baghdad, Kabul and Damascus. These attacks are launched by people who feel frustrated over unsatisfied wants (e.g. Schinkel 2004). The frustration is usually expressed as collective grievance and anger, and transferred to an outspoken and clearly advocated ideology and goal. Terrorist attacks up to the 1970s were often launched in the name of independence and liberation. Most of today's suicide attacks relate to the ideology of the Islamic State group, which uses this 'tactic' also as a defence practice when they are beleaguered themselves.

This phenomenon refers to what Durkheim would indicate as *altruistic and fatalistic suicides* (Soeters, 2005: 94), the latter occurring if the impact of the group and its ideology becomes intensely dominating and even suffocating, leaving no other way out, also because other options in life are perceived as closed. Chronic poverty and deprivation, divorce from family life or earlier criminal convictions may make people believe they will no longer succeed in life anyway. The particular characteristic of suicidal violence is that it is at the same time inwards- and outwards-directed; it also is the convergence of individual psychological trauma and frustration on one hand and ideologies and collective beliefs at the sociological level on the other. Another sociological aspect of this is that the chances in life for some people, in particular some young men, are clearly less than for others, which is often, though not necessarily always, an antecedent of the psychological trauma and anger that precedes the violence.

The comparative method

One of the strong points in Durkheim's work is his development of methods of sociological inquiry. He always stressed the importance of studying *social facts*, i.e. characteristics at the collective, supra-individual level. His study of suicides is a prime example.

In particular, Durkheim's emphasis on systematic comparisons was a breakthrough at the time when studies of single cases, for instance single tribes or single nations, were predominant in the social sciences (Durkheim, 2013 [1895]: 101–110). By systematically comparing ethnographic material collected from tribes in Australia, China and North America he aimed to understand the most fundamental patterns of social life (Dobbin, 2009: 204). The method Durkheim advocated was what he called the study of *concomitant variations* among different cases.

In military research, conducting case studies of singular national armed forces or unique events, such as battles, is still a common approach. In military history, ceaselessly stressing the unique character of events is even more the case than in other disciplines of military studies. This is not really different from a collection of individual 'one-nation, one-case' studies in an edited volume where one tries to find similarities and differences among them. The 'one-nation, one-case' research approach has advantages because it enables reaching for in-depth insights. At the same time, however, it offers a myopic view because the researcher cannot judge the findings in a broader perspective. He or she simply lacks the criteria, the yardsticks, for comparison, which may easily lead to subjective evaluations and judgements. Durkheim would not have approved of that.

There are exceptions, though. Most famous is the study by John Nagl that compares fairly systematically the American operating style in the Vietnam War of the 1960s and 1970s with the British approach to combating communist movements in Malaya in the 1950s (Nagl, 2002). The conclusion was that the American forces could have learned a lot from the way British troops had operated in Malaya, and Nagl's message was that this would have helped them to perform much better in Vietnam. This message struck like a bombshell because it showed the advantages of comparisons in the most practical and operational way. If Durkheim's approach had been pursued much more often and much earlier, commanders would have profited from it.

One way of doing so would be to conduct many more case-comparisons, because a comparison of two cases only is not enough to provide the whole picture. It may even make matters worse: a single comparison may create impressions that are incorrect. Compared with the American operational style in Vietnam the British approach in Malaya was clever, modest and population-centred as John Nagl demonstrated, but later studies have shown that the British struggle in Malaya was also fairly aggressive, suppressive and destructive. Neither were the problems easily solved (e.g. Greene, 1951). This latter aspect has been overshadowed, however, by comparison with the enormous and arguably obscene violence that was used in the Vietnam War. After all, evaluations and comparisons are never absolute.

To avoid myopia by focusing on two cases only, similar or other cases should be systematically compared with other national armed forces' operations, such as those of the French in Algeria, and elsewhere the Dutch in the former Dutch East Indies, the British in Kenya, the Belgians in the Congo, and so forth. Conducting multiple-case comparisons or conducting a series of two-case comparisons, based on one methodological frame of reference, will help to understand the dynamics and effects of military operations much better (Soeters, 2013). In this respect, Durkheim's methodological lessons have so far not been learned and applied enough in the field of military studies. There is progress, though. Young scholars are showing us how to improve this situation: Christoph Harig (2015), who compared the Brazilian participation in the UN mission in Haiti with internal security operations in Rio de Janeiro; Tony Ingesson (2016), who systematically compared military operations through various time periods in history; and Chiara Ruffa (2014/2017), who studied the conduct of four national contingents in the UN's Lebanon mission.

Comparing military actions

Chiara Ruffa is an Italian political and social scientist who provided a prime example of the advantages of using a comparative approach in studying the military. She conducted extensive fieldwork, using mixed methods, to see how the UNIFIL mission in Lebanon was executed by four different national contingents. The mission was conducted in a relatively small area north of the Israel–Lebanon border, by various national militaries who all pursued the same goals defined by the same mandate and who were commanded by one general commander and his staff. Ruffa studied the way of conducting operations by the French, Ghanaian, Italian and South Korean forces in the mission. She was able to demonstrate systematic differences in how the national contingents performed their daily military activities. Among other things she discovered a 'deterrence-oriented' approach among the French and the Korean troops and a 'humanitarian' operational style that was applied by the Italian and the Ghanaian contingents. There could be military operational consequences of such differences in everyday military practice, such as adversaries concentrating their weapons arsenals in the Italian areas of operations that were known for more lenient inspections and other operational activities (Ruffa, 2014: 217).

Rory Stewart (2006: 397–405) suggested an outcome in the opposite direction, even though his observation was not based so much on systematic research. As a former military practitioner, he happened to be able to compare British and Italian military-operational styles in Basra after the invasion of Iraq. After a year of leave he observed that the pro-active British style of operating in one part of the city had produced much less stability than the Italian policy of inaction in a neighbouring vicinity; the Italian approach had led to better results because it had forced Iraqis to take responsibility for their own affairs.

Conclusion

Emile Durkheim laid the foundations for many later sociological studies and theories, in France and all over the world. His work is still relevant today, as it has paved the way for fresher insights and studies that emphasize the importance of institutional culture and practices. This has proven to be particularly useful in the military. Durkheim also first demonstrated the importance of studying phenomena at a macro-collective level. He advocated the need for systematic comparisons of social phenomena at the societal and national level, and he elaborated methodologies for doing so.

Bibliography

Ben-Shalom, U., Z. Lehrer and E. Ben-Ari (2005) 'Cohesion during military operations: a field study on combat units in the Al-Aqsa Intifada'. *Armed Forces and Society* 32(1): 63–79.

Burk, J. (2008) 'Military culture'. In L. Kurtz (ed.), *Encyclopedia of Violence, Peace and Conflict*. Oxford: Elsevier, pp. 1242–1256.

Collins, R. (2008) *Violence: A Micro-Sociological Approach*. Princeton NJ and Oxford: Princeton University Press.

Coser, L. (1977) *Masters of Sociological Thought: Ideas in Historical and Social Context. Second Edition*, Long Grove, IL: Waveland Press.

Diken, B. and C. Bagge Laustsen (2005) *The Culture of Exception: Sociology Facing the Camp*. London and New York: Routledge.

Dobbin, F. (2009) 'How Durkheim's theory of meaning-making influenced organizational sociology'. In P.S. Adler (ed.), *The Oxford Handbook of Sociology and Organization Studies*. Oxford: Oxford University Press, pp. 200–222.

Durkheim, E. (1933 [1893]) *The Division of Labor in Society*. New York/London: Free Press.

Durkheim, E. (2013 [1895]) *The Rules of Sociological Method and Selected Texts on Sociology and its Method*. New York, etc.: Free Press.

Durkheim, E. (2006 [1897]) *Suicide: A Study in Sociology*. London and New York: Routledge.

Durkheim, E. (1976 [1912]) *The Elementary Forms of the Religious Life*. London: Allen and Unwin.

Durkheim, E. (1915) *L'Allemagne au-dessus de tout: la mentalité allemand et la guerre*. Paris: Armand Colin.

Durkheim, E. and E. Denis (1915) *Qui a voulu la guerre?* Paris: Armand Colin.

Giddens, A. (1971) *Capitalism and Modern Social Theory: An Analysis of the Writings of Marx, Durkheim and Max Weber*. Cambridge: Cambridge University Press.

Goldberg, C.A. (2008) 'Introduction to Emile Durkheim's "Anti-Semitism and Social Crisis"'. *Sociological Theory* 26(4): 299–323.

Greene, G. (1951) 'Malaya, the forgotten war'. *Life* 31(5): 51–65.

Griffith, J. and C.J. Bryan (2016) 'Suicides in the U.S, military: birth cohort vulnerability and the all-volunteer force'. *Armed Forces and Society* 42(3): 483–500.

Hajjar, R.M. (2014) 'Emergent postmodern US military culture'. *Armed Forces and Society*, 40(1): 118–145.

Harig, Chr. (2015) 'Synergy effects between MINUSTAH and public security in Brazil'. *Brasiliana – Journal for Brazilian Studies* 3(2): 142–168.

Heilbron, J. (2015) *French Sociology*. Ithaca NY and London: Cornell University Press.

Hoffmire, C.A., J.E. Kemp and R.M. Bossarte (2015) 'Changes in suicide mortality for veterans and nonveterans by gender and history of VHA service use, 2000–2010'. *Psychiatric Services* 66(9): 959–965.

Ingesson, T. (2016) 'The politics of combat: the political and strategic impact of tactical-level subcultures 1939–1995'. Ph.D. thesis, University of Lund.

Janowitz, M. (1960) *The Professional Soldier and Political Power: A Theoretical Orientation and Selected Hypotheses*. Ann Arbor: University of Michigan Press.

Joas, H. and W. Knöbl (2013 [2008]) *War in Social Thought: Hobbes to the Present*. Princeton NJ and Oxford: Princeton University Press.

King, A. (2006) 'The word of command: communication and cohesion in the military'. *Armed Forces and Society* 32(4): 493–512.

King, A. (2013) *The Combat Soldier: Infantry Tactics and Cohesion in the Twentieth and Twenty-first Centuries*. Oxford: Oxford University Press.

Malešević, S. (2010) *The Sociology of War and Violence*. Cambridge: Cambridge University Press.

Mastroianni, G.R. and W.J. Scott (2011) 'Reframing suicide in the military'. *Parameters*, Summer: 6–21.

Moelker, R. (2014) 'Being one of the guys or the fly on the wall? Participant observation of veteran bikers'. In J. Soeters, P. Shields and S. Rietjens (eds), *Routledge Handbook of Research Methods in Military Studies*. London and New York: Routledge, pp. 104–115.

Moskos, Ch. (1974) 'The American combat soldier in Vietnam'. *Journal of Social Issues* 31(4): 25–37.

Moskos, Ch. (2001) *Multinational Military Cooperation: Enhancing American Military Effectiveness* (unpublished mimeo).

Nagl, J. (2002) *Learning to Eat Soup with a Knife: Counterinsurgency Lessons from Malaya and Vietnam*. Chicago: Chicago University Press.

Riemer, J.W. (1998) 'Durkheim's "heroic suicide" in military combat'. *Armed Forces and Society* 25(1): 103–120.

Ruffa, Ch. (2014) 'What peacekeepers think and do: an exploratory study of French, Ghanaian, Italian and South Korean armies in the United Nations Interim Force in Lebanon'. *Armed Forces and Society* 40(2): 199–225.

Samet, E. (2014) *No Man's Land: Preparing for War and Peace in Post-9/11 America*. New York: Picador.

Schinkel, W. (2004) 'The will to violence'. *Theoretical Criminology* 8(21): 5–31.

Shils, E. and M. Janowitz (1948) 'Cohesion and disintegration in the Wehrmacht in World War II'. *Public Opinion Quarterly* 12: 280–315.

Soeters, J. (2005) *Ethnic Conflict and Terrorism: The Origins and Dynamics of Civil Wars*. London and New York: Routledge.

Soeters, J. (2013) 'Do distinct (national) styles of conflict resolution exist?' *Journal of Strategic Studies* 36(6): 898–906.

Soeters, J. (2018) 'Organizational cultures in the military'. In G. Caforio (ed.), *The Handbook of the Sociology of the Military*. Cham, Switzerland: Springer.

Soeters, J. and T. Szvircsev Tresch (2010) 'Towards cultural integration in multinational peace operations'. *Defence Studies* 10(1/2): 272–287.

Stewart, R. (2006) *The Prince of the Marshes: And other Occupational Hazards of a Year in Iraq*. Orlando, FL: Harcourt.

Vreÿ, F., A. Esterhuyse and Th. Mandrup (eds) (2013) *On Military Culture: Theory, Practice and African Armed Forces*. Claremont, CT: University of Connecticut Press.

Weick, K. and K.H. Roberts (1993) 'Collective mind in organizations: heedful inter-relating on flight decks'. *Administrative Science Quarterly* 38(September): 357–381.

Winslow, D. (1998) 'Misplaced loyalties: the role of military culture in the breakdown of discipline in peace operations'. *Canadian Review of Sociology and Anthropology* 35(3): 345–367.

Winslow, D. (1999) 'Rites of passage and group bonding in the Canadian Airborne'. *Armed Forces and Society* 25(3): 429–457.

Winslow, D. (2007) 'Military organization and culture from three perspectives: the case of army'. In G. Caforio (ed.), *Social Sciences and the Military: An Interdisciplinary Overview*. London and New York: Routledge, pp. 67–88.

Zerubavel, E. (1997) *Social Mindscapes. An Invitation to Cognitive Sociology*. Cambridge, MA. and London: Harvard University Press.

3 Karl Marx

Critical analyses of society and the military

Karl Marx (1818–1883) was a social and political theorist whose work has probably been more important outside than inside academia. His work has created the foundations of political ideologies that have been most influential in twentieth-century world history. He formulated ideas about class struggle and revolution that constituted the foundation on which the former Soviet Union, the People's Republic of China and their satellite states were based. With the demise of world communism today, Marx's thoughts might seem to have lost their influence in the world. That is a superficial observation, though. His work has retained much of its relevance in today's world.

Marx stressed the importance of studying social inequality and its consequences, which since then has turned out to be a major theme in sociology (e.g. Giddens, 1971). Many sociological studies have pursued Marx's thinking on social inequality and concentration of power, which – simply put – is about the differences between the 'haves' and the 'have-nots' in society. These differences occur inside and across nation-states. Even if social and economic inequality shows fluctuations within Western societies (e.g. Piketty, 2014), its disappearance on a worldwide scale is far from being realized. Citizens of Western nations are much wealthier than people in so-called developing countries, and their working and living conditions are correspondingly much better. Marx's work on social inequality and related topics such as revolutionary potential, exploitation and alienation remain tremendously important in a theoretical and practical sense. This applies to organization studies (e.g. Adler, 2009) as much as to something as recent as internet studies (Fuchs and Dyer-Witheford, 2012).

The relevance of his work for military studies will emerge in five themes, some of which will make a surprisingly fresh impression on today's discussions. In Chapter 6 on W.E.B. Du Bois we will encounter Marx's themes again, as we will discuss the connection between social inequality and race relations in the military. Before we set out, it may be interesting to point out that Karl Marx and his 'brother in arms' Friedrich Engels regularly authored newspaper articles on the military affairs of European nations and their colonies (Marx and Engels, 1961). These articles appeared in the national press of many countries, including Britain and the USA. This is another indication that the classical sociologists really were engaged in military affairs. How could they not have been in those nineteenth-century times when war and the armed forces dominated everyday news?

Military power elites

Marx's analysis of social inequality has given rise to numerous studies on power elites in all sorts of domains. Charles Wright Mills was one of the most prominent sociologists to study power elites in the US military and politics. For sure, Wright Mills was an engaged scholar (Barratt, 2014). He was, however, also a true sociologist, using Max Weber's concepts of economy and society, such as power, stratification, structure, bureaucratization and *Beamtenherrschaft*, the concentration of power in the hands of the bureaucrats (e.g. Moskos, 1974). After all, Wright Mills was the one who – together with his colleague Hans Gerth – made Max Weber's work known to the academy at large in America (Gerth and Wright Mills, 2009). But his social and political criticism, much like that of Marx, is difficult not to notice, and his work was a source of inspiration for the leftist movements of the time (Barratt, 2014).

In his famous work *The Power Elite*, Wright Mills (2000 [1956]) analysed the concentration of power at the disposal of those 'in command': in business, in the military and in politics. He argued that the increasing concentration of power in the hands of the few was the result of changes over the course of the twentieth century: the emergence of the large-scale firm, the expansion of the military and the growth of central government (Barratt, 2014: 256). The result of such a power concentration is that most people are excluded from government's decision making, even though periodic democratic elections provide the general direction of where a society is going. In non-democratic nations, the concentration of power in the hands of a few politicians, businesspeople and military officials is of course even more striking.

In addition to chapters on celebrities, chief executives, the 'very rich', the 'corporate rich' and the 'political directorate', Wright Mills devoted two chapters of his book to military power elites in the USA. In his first chapter on the military – 'The War Lords' – he points to the relatively minor threats that the USA faced in the days of its inception: wide oceans, weak neighbours, natives without much power. As a consequence, 'the sovereign United States [...] did not have to carry the burden of a permanent and large military overhead' (Wright Mills, 2000: 175). However, the influence of the military in government has gradually grown considerably more important. Many retired Civil War generals became president (Wright Mills, 2000: 177). Wright Mills gives lively descriptions of the average nineteenth-century general who experienced action in the Civil War and campaigns against Native Americans. He compares this type with the modern careerist colonels and generals who constitute the strategic apex of the military, from Mills' days till now.

Contrary to the old-time generals, who were good at handling weapons, riding horses and improvisations when in trouble, the top military experienced the Cold War and later became experts in planning, logistics and particularly policy making. Already at the time when Wright Mills published his analysis, policy formation in the fields of international diplomacy and foreign affairs had come to be dominated by military men, both in Washington DC and in America's embassies throughout the world. They have become experts in public relations to the extent of redefining international relations in such a way that the tremendous growth of military capabilities appears justified (Barratt, 2014). This has consequences. In Wright Mills' critical words (2000: 184): 'war or a high state of war preparedness is felt to be the normal and seemingly permanent condition of the United States'.

In the second chapter on the military – 'The Military Ascendancy' – he elaborates on the autonomy and large influence top military officials have among their political and economic colleagues. With this analysis he echoes the message of a famous, earlier article on 'The Garrison State', where the 'specialists in violence may run the state' (Lasswell, 1941: 457), that was influenced by events at the beginning of World War II.

Wright Mills' analysis pertains to the Cold War but is quite similar to Lasswell's. Its main message is that the military apex has become more predominant than it has ever been in the history of America's elite. This is no coincidence. Through their training, expertise and mindset top military people are seen as useful to 'lift the policy "above politics"' and they are 'needed men with the capacity for "making grave decisions"', without being 'openly identified with any private interests' (Wright Mills, 2000: 200).

As a result of increasing budgets, the military has become a major economic player in the nation. It also has a large stake in the spending of sizable budgets for research and development. And in adjacent sectors, such as disaster relief, it is an important factor as well, as the Corps of Engineers, for instance, demonstrated during the aftermath of Hurricane Katrina. Hence, strong economic–military links developed, which can be seen in 'an intense dependency on military contracts among some very large corporations' (Lieberson, 1971: 581). This became known as the 'military-industrial complex' (also: Moskos, 1974). So it is no surprise that many high-ranking officers, instead of merely retiring, go to sit on the boards of private companies. However, empirical research shows that these links do not fully dominate the general industrial state of affairs in the USA (Lieberson, 1971), or in other Western economies one may add.

Without any doubt, Wright Mills was quite critical of the military power elite, in a way Marx would have agreed with. This even led Mills to gloomily analyse 'the causes of World War Three' (Wright Mills, 1958). As he put it, 'the immediate cause of World War III is the preparation for it', and he blames the military power elites in both the USA and the Soviet Union for this (Wright Mills, 1958: 47). He went on to criticize 'the military metaphysic', 'the permanent war economy' and 'crackpot realism'. To prevent the worst from happening, he claimed that 'the only realistic military view is the view that war, not Russia, is now the enemy' (Wright Mills, 1958: 97). He also advocated negotiation and the allocation of military budgets to the economic aid and industrial development of underdeveloped countries, especially to India (Wright Mills, 1958: 101); this would need to happen under the aegis of the United Nations. There are many more guidelines in this book that, in Mills' view, could help prevent the outbreak of the next war, but too many to discuss here. The book ends with a discussion of the role of the intellectuals in all of this.

In hindsight, one could argue Charles Wright Mills has been much too gloomy and pessimistic: World War III has not occurred, and in the 1990s, when the Soviet Union collapsed, it seemed to many as if all problems had disappeared. As we all know, however, a number of wars and sizable military operations have occurred since that time, in Iraq, Afghanistan, Libya, Chechnya, Syria and smaller ones elsewhere. A lot of tension is still in the air in other places in the world. Decision making in this connection may indeed be influenced considerably by the military power elites, in the USA, the UK, France, Russia and many smaller nations. A lot of what C. Wright Mills had to say about the military power elite in the 1950s still seems to apply today, although probably not in all nations to a similar degree and in a comparable way as in the USA or other major military-oriented nations. We will turn to the issue of national differences in military affairs or strategic cultures in Chapter 11.

As to today's influence of the military power elite, one only needs to think of the three (retired) generals in US president Donald Trump's team at the time he was inaugurated in January 2017. Their appointment was a clear indication that generals are seen as highly valuable public servants who are experts in policy domains that are considered vital to America's interests. Undoubtedly, they influence the government's general direction in many ways, and will continue to do so for a long time.

The generals' roles?

Even though generals as representatives of the military power elite may be seen as instigators of military expenditures and action, things may also turn out differently. In the old days, presidents of the USA and in many other countries used to have explicit military experience. Today, after the abolition of the draft system, this is no longer warranted. Hence, presidents and political leaders enter the stage without any, or very much, military experience. This may lead to a reluctance to use violence, but the opposite may also occur. Political leaders without a lot of military experience may easily decide in favour of spending money on, and actually using, military means. President Trump's plans to expand military budgets at the expense of diplomacy and foreign aid led to a remarkable response. Over 120 retired generals and admirals urged Congress on 27 February 2017 'to fully fund U.S. diplomacy and foreign aid, saying such programs "are critical to keeping America safe"' (Reuters, 28 February 2017). Here military top brass, albeit retired, were less keen on propagating the military's direct interest, probably because they know what works well to prevent violence and conflicts.

Military coups

Revolutions play a large role in Marxist action theory, as they enable the poor and the deprived to gain power and obtain what they feel they are entitled to, says Marx. Applied to the military one may refer in this connection to military coups or 'coups d'état', as a special category of social event in organizations in general (Zald and Berger, 1978). Such events in organizations imply seizures of power from within, occurring outside normal channels. Yet, unlike the situation in ordinary organizations, such events in the military may have significant political and societal impact. In fact, one may use the concept of 'political armies' to indicate 'those military institutions that consider involvement in – or control over – domestic politics and the business of government to be a central part of their legitimate function' (Koonings and Kruijt, 2002: 1). Political armies, hence, are not likely to refrain from initiating military coups if they deem this necessary.

Such political armies and military coups in particular may seem like a phenomenon from the past and from regions far away, as Marx's own analysis of the rebellion in the British-Indian armed forces in the 1850s seems to illustrate (Marx and Engels, 1961 [1857]: vol. 12, 230–233). However, in the period between 1950 and 2000, military coups were numerous, particularly in Africa and Latin America, and they also occurred in Asia and even in Europe (Koonings and Kruijt, 2002). Notorious is the coup d'état in Chile in 1973 when president Salvador Allende was ousted by military action. The events in Turkey in the summer of 2016 show that the phenomenon of military coups has not disappeared at all, not even in the Western NATO alliance. The occurrence of military coups is connected to fundamental discussions in military sociology about controlling the military. This work has culminated in the so-called concordance theory (Schiff, 2009), which we will deal with in Chapter 9.

In an important study Naunihal Singh (2014) analyses the strategic logic of military coups and the determinants of their success or failure. Surprisingly enough he does not refer to Marx, but that is probably because he does not pay much attention to the motives of those who commit the coups: their grievances, frustrations and desire to defend and propagate their self-interests.

Singh conducted a study of six successful coups and four failed ones in one nation, Ghana, the first independent post-colonial nation in Sub-Saharan Africa. His theory is simple and it concurs with game-theoretical insights that are known as the 'coordination game' in collective action. In sociology, this aligns with the well-known 'sociological parable' illustrating the *self-fulfilling prophecy*: a run on the bank emerges when depositors believe – on the basis of newspapers, radio or rumours – that all others will withdraw their money from the bank, and correspondingly will do so themselves (Merton, 1968: 476). The behaviour of one actor is dependent on his or her belief about what the other actors will do. It does not matter whether the news is real or fake, these belief dynamics are likely to produce real outcomes.

If the actors' expectations and corresponding actions converge, collective action such as a run on the bank is likely to happen and, in the same way, a military coup is likely to succeed. The diffusion of the information is a matter of communication, in a meeting or, most likely, by broadcasting. Communication thus shapes expectations and produces collective action, because in such a way information, in this case about the coup, must be known to all relevant parties, but 'also has to be known to be known by all parties', and so on (Singh, 2014: 7). As such, attackers must 'make a fact'. Two attackers will lose if they don't know about each other's efforts; if they do know they will vanquish the one they deem to be the foe (Singh, 2014: 5–10). In the latter case, the coup will turn out to be successful. In order to prevent the coup from becoming successful, the government or the regime that is attacked will need to do the opposite. This is holding on to or seizing broadcasting facilities or driving the attackers from the broadcasting installations they occupy. This is exactly what the Turkish president Erdogan did when parts of the military rebelled during that summer night in 2016. Through radio broadcasting and social media he convinced the population that he was still in charge and mobilized the people to go into the streets and block the attackers' efforts to gain power. Hence the coup failed.

Coups that are staged by military people at the bottom of the institution are less likely to succeed compared to those initiated by generals or colonels because of the better resources the latter have at their disposal (Singh, 2014). In fact, the former are better known as mutinies, which phenomenon we will discuss in Chapter 11. There are various sorts of resistance from the lower levels of the organization that may have an impact on what is happening around and about. In general, one can say that soldiers deserting from military service (Bröckling and Sikora, 1998) or who revolt during operations (Cortright, 1975) can be seen as less well organized acts of resistance that may nonetheless have a big impact. It can easily be argued that the GI protest movement during the Vietnam War contributed to its final outcome of America's defeat and hasty departure from that country.

Wartime inequalities

One particular though important aspect of social inequality in the military regards the distribution of wartime casualties across socio–economic strata. This issue has attracted academic and media attention for a long time, particularly in the USA. It surely fits with a Marxian approach to military studies. Careful statistical research (Kriner and Shen, 2010: 47) has demonstrated that 'since the conclusion of World War II, socioeconomically disadvantaged communities have borne a disproportionate share of America's war casualties'. The reasons behind these findings relate to mechanisms that drive more young men and women with lower socioeconomic opportunities into the military. Simply put, there is inequality in who serves in the military.

In addition, there is an occupational assignment effect: enlisted personnel, who comprise the vast majority of combat deaths, come disproportionately from lower-income communities. Officers are less likely to die in combat and come disproportionately from higher-end communities (Kriner and Shen, 2010: 73). This phenomenon was particularly striking in the Vietnam War, where the GI resistance (Cortright, 1975) and the killing of officers by enlisted men that we noted earlier may be seen as an indication of the tensions in units that occurred as a result of such inequalities.

The finding that lower-income classes make up disproportionately more combat deaths has been quite persistent, even after a lottery draft system was introduced halfway through the Vietnam War. This lottery system was introduced because the inequality in dying had become so obvious and pervasive. The system helped to reduce the effect, but the skewed distribution remained nonetheless. Even after the conscript system was abolished, the connection between socio-economic status and the risk of dying in combat did not disappear. It is most likely that this phenomenon also occurs in other national armies.

In Israel, Yagil Levy (2006; 2010a) looked at what he called the 'hierarchy of military death'. He showed that middle-class conscripts are more capable of averting the risk of being deployed to life-endangering situations than conscripts from religious and peripheral groups. Religious soldiers accept the risks of dying in battle because of their religious and nationalist convictions. Because of their ethno-nationalist orientation, this applies in a more or less similar way to conscripts from peripheral groups. Yet, conscripts from peripheral groups also lack the social networks to object to such risks that middle-class conscripts and their parents are able to exploit. For citizens, this pattern applies even more as privileged citizens have the financial resources to move to another region should their own area come under attack. Citizens from peripheral groups, living closer to the borders, simply do not have the financial capacity to leave the vulnerable places they inhabit. These are often immigrants, in particular those from the former Soviet Union.

Again, there is no clearer way of demonstrating the relevance of Marx's ideas to military studies today than through this particular manifestation of social inequality.

Poor armies/rich armies

As the world divides between rich and poor countries, the same goes for armed forces. Legendary and notorious have been the poor but sometimes highly effective people's armies in colonial warfare that started immediately after the Second World War and finally ended in the late 1970s. Examples are the struggles of independence in the former Dutch East Indies, Algeria, Malaya, Kenya, Vietnam and Angola to name but a few (e.g. Greene, 1951; Oostindie, 2015; Caputo, 1999 [1977]). Those wars were fought against the Western rulers who had compartmentalized society between colonizers − or their representatives − and the colonized. These violent wars resulted from the rage of colonized people and they paved the path to liberation, as has been analysed so famously by Frantz Fanon in his book *The Wretched of the Earth* (2004 [1963]). This book came as a shock to many at the time. It still is an indispensable work for a correct understanding of the impact of inequalities in global dynamics.

After independence, memories developed. The many military museums in today's Vietnam do not display messages of resent about the country's various wars with respective intruders (France, USA, China). They are, however, quite triumphalist about the fact their people's forces expelled them. Much less technologically advanced than their enemies, the Vietnamese forces time and again turned out to be quite effective.

Armies of the poor during the Parisian insurrection of 1848

In June 1848 two irregular armies of the urban poor fought a four-day battle in the streets of Paris. The violence emerged after the government had planned to close down the so-called National Workshops that were created to provide work and a source of income for the unemployed. The violence that ensued has been characterized by Marx and Engels as a class-conscious movement of 'lumpenproletariat', consisting of unskilled and poor workers (Marx, 1973: 165ff). Careful research by the historical sociologist Mark Traugott (2002) and others, however, has revealed that skilled artisans, and not unskilled proletarians, stood at the forefront of the upheaval. The forces that defended the ruling regime were little different in occupational status. Hence, the lumpenproletariat thesis needed to be rejected. Traugott showed that class position creates no more than a diffuse political predisposition. In his view, other factors such as organizational subcultures, in particular the configuration of forces in terms of leadership, addressing rank-and-file grievances and the extent of isolation, should be given more explanatory weight in explaining the effectiveness during that particular urban battle (Traugott, 2002: xxxiv, 182–185). This point may apply more generally. Here one can see the need to connect Marx with Durkheim. Economic differences indeed do have an impact on the outbreak and development of violent conflicts, but only in combination with other factors, such as those that operate at the cultural or the 'mindset' level.

Today the distinction between poor and rich armed forces has implications for the composition of military missions that are conducted under the aegis of the United Nations. This participation is highly skewed: forces from nations from the so-called developing world substantially outnumber the contributions of forces from nations that belong to the so-called Western hemisphere. Armed forces from countries such as India, Pakistan, Nepal, Nigeria, Senegal, South Africa, Uruguay and Brazil contribute much larger numbers of troops than do countries from Europe. In addition, the UK and the USA have hardly participated in UN missions for several decades now. The reasons for this are partly professional and ideological, as Western forces prefer working in the more solidly organized environment of NATO operations. This preference has become much stronger after the disasters that American, Dutch and Belgian troops experienced while participating in UN missions in, respectively, Somalia, Bosnia and Rwanda, all in the 1990s. Also, Western militaries believe that they are more trained to do high-intensity combat operations; this conviction is particularly strong in Anglo-Saxon military environments. UN missions are usually more oriented towards peace-keeping, which for many Western soldiers is not perceived to be the military 'premier league'.

The other reasons for this skewed balance comes closer to what Marxist thinking would stress. For forces from developing nations the financial compensation by the UN and the opportunities for further professionalizing their troops and commanders provide ample reason to participate in UN missions. Because these troops are financially less well off, they profit from participating in such missions. Its flipside is that those forces have less technologically advanced systems at their disposal, such as helicopters or intelligence facilities. This, in general, is perceived to be a main limitation of those missions' effectiveness. On the other hand, one can argue that forces from developing countries are often culturally closer to the population groups in the conflict areas where they are dispatched. Many South African soldiers master Zulu or Xhosa as their native languages, which are Bantu-type tongues that are akin to the Swahili that is prevalent in large parts of the African continent. These advantages can also pertain to religious affinities, as we will see in Chapter 6. In this connection, the plea for so-called 'connected military sociologies' seems particularly relevant.

Commodification and alienation

Marx's work on the increasing commodification, or 'thing-ification', in everyday life has implications in the military as well. This element in Marx's thinking refers to his analysis of capitalism, in which commodities have a double nature: an economic value form shaped by exchange dynamics on the market and a natural form. A cupboard may be appreciated because of its natural properties (size, design, colour, material, comfort-in-use) but it can, and in the capitalist system always will, also be valued because of its worth in money terms (De Jong, 2007: 80). In pure capitalist thinking the economic value is more important than anything else. According to Marx this also applies to labour: at the end of the day a person sells their labour power and becomes a 'personified commodity' (e.g. Löwith, 1993: 110). What is more, the worker becomes an ever cheaper commodity, the more goods she creates (Giddens, 1971: 11).

This idea can be recognized in the history of the military, as two types of military labour may be distinguished: tributary and commodified soldierly labour (Zürcher, 2013). Since the introduction of the *levée en masse* during the French Revolution and the concomitant disappearance of mercenary armies, military work resulted from states obliging their young men to enlist as soldiers. This has become known as tributary soldierly labour, a system that was founded on a mixture of legal and moral coercion and which was accompanied by symbolic rewards such as the honour to fight for, and eventually to die for, the nation. This system persisted during many gruesome wars for more than 150 years, but gradually it showed severe insufficiencies. Particularly during the Vietnam War, it became evident that risks of being enlisted and being killed in action were not equally distributed, as we saw before. This not only led to the military's suboptimal performance and GI resistance in action, but also to large-scale public protests back home in America.

As a result, and in connection with the end of the Cold War, the draft, or conscription, system was abolished, first in the USA and later in many other Western nations. Instead of the citizen army, the all-volunteer force was introduced, which was a *market army* primarily based on material instead of symbolic rewards (Levy, 2007; 2010b); it was the start of the *commodified military* (Zürcher, 2013). The military job became 'just another job' as the famous phrasing by Charles Moskos goes. It was no longer a 'calling'; it developed quite rapidly into an 'occupation' (Moskos, 1977); an occupation with risks that had economic value, an occupation that had a price. Enter Karl Marx.

The development towards the *commodified military* has progressed since then. Following the path that had been paved in the business sector, the issue of outsourcing activities to the market came on the agenda of military organizations. Outsourcing military activities was deemed to be profitable because outsourced activities could, it was supposed, be done more efficiently under conditions of market competition. At the onset, only peripheral, non-operational activities, such as cleaning, cooking, laundry, maintenance, were outsourced following the recommendations that had previously been formulated by economic theory (Williamson, 1981). But quite rapidly the outsourcing of core operational activities ensued, which led to the rise of private military and security companies. During the Vietnam War in the 1960s and early 1970s the ratio between regular troops and contractors was 100:1, whereas it nowadays is close to 1.5:1 (Zürcher, 2013: 613–614; see also Heinecken, 2014: 629). This is a rapid and huge development enhanced by the missions in Iraq and Afghanistan, which has not reached a final stage yet. There are considerable differences in this regard between the armed forces of different nations, the USA having the lead in this regard, followed by the UK and Canada, whereas continental European nations are much more hesitant. Those differences are probably related to diverse conceptions of the military's role and varying ideological views (Cusumano, 2014; Cusumano and Kinsey, 2015).

Worth mentioning in this connection is the difference between contractors with a Western background and contractors from host nations who constitute the major part of contractors' work force (Heinecken, 2014: 629). The price of Western contractors and local national contractors differs, but the natural contribution of host national contractors is not necessarily less valuable even if it is much cheaper. Whereas Western contractors may deliver specialist knowledge or accomplish one-off tasks, host national contractors may, for instance, provide transport or language services with possible substantial consequences for the military in action (see Chapter 7 for further analysis of language mediators). Here, social inequality on a global scale is reflected in the price difference between Western and host-national contributors to military operations.

All these developments have led military organizations, particularly in the West, in the direction of business or public organizations in general. Economic value has become a main aspect of organizing military infrastructure and operations. This is not limited to Western militaries; the official military of the Democratic Republic of Congo (FARDC) raises money from the population, for instance at roadblocks, to provide protection against looting and ambushing by small-scale militias. In so far as they are successful in this, the revenue generation is seen as legitimate (Verweijen, 2013). In many countries across the globe armed forces derive revenues from their stakes in economic affairs. In Chapter 9 we will discuss this phenomenon in relation to civil–military relations. But there are more debatable aspects of the marketization of the military.

Loss of control, social inequality and former child soldiers

Gary Schaub and Ryan Kelty (2016: 341–367) argue that procuring security services from private actors in the market requires a different set of oversight and enforcement mechanisms than those used to control the armed forces. This turns out to be challenging, particularly when it comes to controlling the activities of private military contractors in the operational arena. Even if strict legal regulations are put in place, it appears to be difficult to hold private contractors' personnel responsible for criminal and aberrant behaviour outside of their home country. More generally, military commanders find it difficult to monitor private contractors' activities, to direct their behaviour or to enforce orders through the normal chain of command (Schaub and Kelty, 2016: 342). Harmonization of regulations concerning private military companies across nations is even more demanding.

Furthermore, private military contractors in the market may provide the opportunity for non-state actors, such as multinational corporations operating in unstable states, to hire military force for their own purposes. Also, political opponents in weaker nations may hire force from the market in order to overthrow their government. Given the idea that the state has the monopoly on violence, such situations are uncomfortable to say the least (Schaub and Kelty, 2016: 357–358). They reflect the security aspects of social and economic inequality, as poor people or corporations will not be able to hire private military companies for their own purposes.

Finally, there are questions related to the management of human resources. Private military companies are likely to pay higher wages, hence making it more difficult for the state's armed forces to retain their personnel. In addition, there are indications that private military companies seek to hire personnel from among former child-soldiers from Africa.

An interesting side aspect is that the increasing commodification of military activity is likely to lead to a more widespread occurrence of military unions (Bartle and Heinecken, 2006). There are considerable differences between nations in their tolerance of military unions. But given the increasing stress on economic aspects of the military, particularly in the field of labour relations (wages, retirement schemes, insurance policies), unions are likely to become increasingly more important. In some nations, such as the Netherlands, military unions are already stronger than unions in any other sector of the labour market.

But next to negotiating about the material rewards of soldiering, military unions will be confronted with an aspect that will close our discussion of Marx's relevance to the study of the military: *alienation* (Giddens, 1971). In Marx's thinking, alienation is a direct consequence of the commodification of labour. It refers to workers who have lost contact with the product of their own labour (through an extensive chain of division of labour), who are dominated by the organization they work for and by its machinery, who have become estranged from fellow workers because these are seen as competitors, and who – in sum – feel completely estranged from being a species of human per se (Erikson, 1986). In more general terms, alienation relates to feelings of powerlessness, meaninglessness, normlessness, isolation and self-estrangement (Seeman, 1959).

We have already seen parts of this reasoning in our discussion of Weberian bureaucracy and its potential failures as a result of either under- or over-bureaucratization. The tendency to outsource military activities may have an additional impact. South African scholar Lindy Heinecken (2014) pointed to the unforeseen consequences that outsourcing public security tasks may have for the military profession. As more and more of the military's activities are outsourced to market actors, she argues, this will mean a loss of the monopoly of knowledge and skills, a loss of autonomy, a loss of the sense of 'corporate-ness', and the erosion of the service ethic. In general, this tendency aligns with 'the degradation of the military profession as a whole' (Heinecken, 2014: 633). These are different words, but they can all be assembled under the heading of alienation. Although Heinecken does not explicitly refer to Marx, Marx would definitely agree. But nevertheless the impression emerges that this is romanticizing a past that is not likely to return.

Conclusion

The name of Karl Marx still is problematic for many because of its association with communism as practised in the former Soviet Union and its satellite states in Central and Eastern Europe, in China and Cuba and in a number of African nations. Those were not considered to be very successful or attractive regimes. The name Marx seems so contaminated that even scholars with a Marxist bent do not openly acknowledge this or are perhaps not even aware of Marx's influence on their work. However, the impact of his ideas is still fresh and relevant, as can be seen in many practical and academic discussions, in civil society and in the military.

Bibliography

Adler, P.S. (2009) 'Marx and organization studies today'. In P. Adler (ed.), *The Oxford Handbook of Sociology and Organization Studies: Classical Foundations*. Oxford: Oxford University Press, pp. 62–91.

Barratt, E. (2014) 'C. Wright Mills and the theorists of power'. In P. Adler, P. Du Gay, G. Morgan and M. Reed (eds), *The Oxford Handbook of Sociology, Social Theory and Organization Studies: Contemporary Currents*. Oxford: Oxford University Press, pp. 249–265.

Bartle, R. and L. Heinecken (eds) (2006) *Military Unionism in the Post-Cold War Era: A Future Reality?* London and New York: Routledge.

Blauner, R. (1964) *Alienation and Freedom: The Factory Worker and His Industry*. Chicago: University of Chicago Press.

Bröckling, U. and M. Sikora (eds) (1998) *Armeen und ihre Deserteure: Vernachlässigte Kapitel einer Militärgeschichte der Neuzeit*. Göttingen, Netherlands: Vandenhoeck & Ruprecht.

Caputo, Ph. (1999 [1977]) *A Rumor of War*. London: Pimlico.

Cortright, D. (1975) *Soldiers in Revolt: GI Resistance during the Vietnam War*. Chicago: Haymarket Books.

Cusumano, E. (2014) 'The scope of military privatisation: military role conceptions and contractor support in the United States and the United Kingdom'. *International Relations* 29(2): 219–241.

Cusumano, E. and Ch. Kinsey (2015) 'Bureaucratic interests and the outsourcing of security: the privatization of diplomatic protection in the United States and the United Kingdom'. *Armed Forces and Society* 41(4): 591–615.

De Jong, M. (2007) *Icons of Sociology*. Amsterdam: Boom.

Erikson, K. (1986) 'On work and alienation'. *American Sociological Review* 51(February): 1–8.

Fanon, F. (2004 [1963]) *The Wretched of the Earth*. New York: Grove Press.

Fuchs, Chr. and N. Dyer-Witheford (2012) 'Karl Marx @ internet studies'. *New Media and Society* 15(5): 782–796.

Gerth, H. and C. Wright Mills (eds) (2009 [1946]) *From Max Weber: Essays in Sociology*. Abingdon and New York: Routledge.

Giddens, A. (1971) *Capitalism and Modern Social Theory: An Analysis of the Writings of Marx, Durkheim and Max Weber*. Cambridge: Cambridge University Press.

Greene, G. (1951) 'Malaya, the forgotten war'. *Life* 31(5): 51–65.

Heinecken, L. (2014) 'Outsourcing public security: the unforeseen consequences for the military profession'. *Armed Forces and Society* 40(4): 625–646.

Koonings, K. and D. Kruijt (2002) *Political Armies: The Military and Nation Building in the Age of Democracy*. London and New York: Zed Books.

Kriner, D.L. and F.X. Shen (2010) *The Casualty Gap: The Causes and Consequences of American Wartime Inequalities*. Oxford: Oxford University Press.

Lasswell, H.D. (1941) 'The garrison state'. *American Journal of Sociology* 46(4): 455–468.

Levy, Y. (2006) 'The war of the peripheries: a social mapping of IDF casualties in the Al-Aqsa Intifada'. *Social Identities* 12(3): 309–324.

Levy, Y. (2007) 'Soldiers as laborers: a theoretical model'. *Theory and Society* 36(X): 187–208.

Levy, Y. (2010a) 'The hierarchy of military death'. *Citizenship Studies* 14(4): 345–361.

Levy, Y. (2010b) 'The essence of the "market army"'. *Public Administration Review* 70(3): 378–389.

Lieberson, S. (1971) 'An empirical study of military–industrial linkages'. *American Journal of Sociology* 76(4): 562–584.

Löwith, K. (1993) *Max Weber and Karl Marx*. London and New York: Routledge.

Marx, K. (1973, originally various publications) *Karl Marx on Society and Social Change*. Edited by N. Smelser. Chicago and London: University of Chicago Press.

Marx, K. and F. Engels (1961 [originally various publications]) *Werke*. Berlin, DDR: Karl Dietz Verlag.

Merton, R. (1968) *Social Theory and Social Structure*. New York: The Free Press.

Moskos, C. (1974) 'The concept of the military-industrial complex: radical critique or liberal bogey?' *Social Problems* 21(4): 498–512.

Moskos, C. (1977) 'From institutions to occupations: trends in military organizations'. *Armed Forces and Society* 4(1): 41–50.

Nyamuya Maogoto, J. (2006) 'Subcontracting sovereignty: the commodification of military force and the fragmentation of state authority'. *Brown Journal of World Affairs* 13(1): 147–160.

Oostindie, G. (2015) *Soldaat in Indonesië 1945–1950: Getuigenissen van een oorlog aan de verkeerde kant van de geschiedenis*. Amsterdam: Prometheus Bert Bakker.

Piketty, Th. (2014) *Capital in the Twenty-First Century*. Cambridge MA and London: Belknap Press of Harvard University Press.

Schaub, G.Jr and R. Kelty (eds) (2016) *Private Military and Security Contractors: Controlling the Corporate Warrior*. Lanham, MD: Rowman & Littlefield.

Schiff, R. (2009) *The Military and Domestic Politics: A Concordance Theory of Civil–Military Relations*. London and New York: Routledge.

Seeman, M. (1959) 'On the meaning of alienation'. *American Sociological Review* 24(6): 783–791.

Singh, N. (2014) *Seizing Power: The Strategic Logic of Military Coups*. Baltimore, MD: Johns Hopkins University Press.

Traugott, M. (2002) *Armies of the Poor: Determinants of Working-Class Participation in the Parisian Insurrection of June 1848*. New Brunswick NJ and London: Transaction Publishers.

Verweijen, J. (2013) 'Military business and the business of the military in the Kivus'. *Review of African Political Economy* 40(135): 67–82.

Williamson, O.E. (1981) 'The economics of organization: the transaction cost approach'. *American Journal of Sociology* 86(3): 548–577.

Wright Mills, C. (2000 [1956]) *The Power Elite*. New edn. Oxford and New York: Oxford University Press.

Wright Mills, C. (1958) *The Causes of World War Three*. New York: Simon and Schuster.

Zald, M.N. and M.A. Berger (1978) 'Social movements in organizations: coups d'etat, insurgency, and mass movements'. *American Journal of Sociology* 83(4): 823–861.

Zürcher, E-J. (ed.) (2013) *Fighting for a Living: A Comparative History of Military Labour 1500–2000*. Amsterdam: Amsterdam University Press.

4   Georg Simmel
Networks, conflict, secrecy and the stranger

Georg Simmel (1858–1918) was a German sociologist whose contributions to sociological thinking were no less influential than these provided by the famous three founding fathers we have already discussed. As a 'micro-scopist' he produced the first attempts to create a 'formal' sociology in which similarities between very different phenomena – based on numbers and positions – are discovered. He also wrote a study of money that is still well worth reading as it clarifies how the replacing of the barter system by the invention of money changed social life drastically.

His work, although originally written in German, swiftly became known in America. A number of his contributions appeared in the *American Journal of Sociology* during his lifetime (e.g. Simmel, 1902; 1904; 1906; 1909). Several young Americans studied at the university of Berlin following Simmel's lectures there, and they became the most fervent advocates of his work (Levine et al., 1976). His work continues to be relevant also, and perhaps especially, to today's military. This discussion of Simmel vis-à-vis the military comes in four parts. It will show that his work has been amplified in more recent sociological contributions, even if the authors themselves are not always aware of Simmel's influence. His views will also prove relevant to the chapters devoted to W. E. B. Du Bois and Erving Goffman (Chapters 6 and 7).

Positions and numbers in networks

In the first place, Simmel's theorizing on the position of individuals in larger entities (groups, networks) has invaluable significance for military organizations and their performance. Simmel (1902) was the first to explicitly point to the importance of numbers, positions, group size and group affiliations in the explanation of human behaviour. He stressed that the size and form of relations impact largely on human behaviour, irrespective of the personalities involved and the content of the interaction. The sheer number of people involved in an interaction works as a principle of division of the group, both vertically and horizontally. This idea can be recognized in Durkheim's work as well. The insight has proved to be important in the further development of the analysis of networks and organizational dynamics (Scott, 2009).

Simmel analysed the rather different dynamics occurring in small groups consisting of two or three people – dyads and triads. We will encounter the consequences of these small-group dynamics, particularly triads, for military interactions, in Chapter 7. Simmel also pointed to the multiple group affiliations that have emerged in modern times; this leads for instance to a situation where a person in Hamburg or even in New York or New Delhi could be a fan of Germany's leading soccer club Bayern Munich. Multiple group affiliations are a result of, but in turn also lead to, cosmopolitanism, differentiation, secrecy, individualism, conflict and competition (Moss Kanter and Khurana, 2009; Simmel, 1902; 1955).

These ideas have, moreover, implications for diversity issues, such as the integration of members of minority groups in military units, as we will see in Chapter 6. But they are also important to understand larger problems related to collaboration with other services or national forces, or with host national actors when operating abroad. In this connection the relevance of the work on 'strong' and 'weak ties' by Mark Granovetter (1973; 1983) and on 'structural holes' by Ronald Burt (1995) is undisputed (e.g. Scott, 2009), for military practice at home, but even more so in missions abroad. Here is why.

In military operations, such as in Iraq and Afghanistan, Western forces need to seek partnerships with host national parties that through their local resources, information and competences can help them achieve their goals. The question then is how to select such partners. In general, Western forces tend to seek partnerships with host nationals that (a) are in close geographical proximity, (b) who are like them, and (c) whom they correspondingly like and who reciprocally like them (Bollen and Soeters, 2010: 178–180). These processes evolve rather implicitly and they are the consequence of basic and 'universal' social-psychological dynamics. A main point is that Western forces tend to develop partnerships with organizations that have compatible organizational cultures, whose employees have studied in the West, or at least have mastered the English language (Bollen and Soeters, 2010). The results of these processes are displayed in Figure 4.1.

This figure shows that through these dynamics closely connected, dense networks are likely to develop. This is not wrong in itself; on the contrary such 'strong ties' are seen as comfortable, easy and even cost-effective. The negative consequences, however, are not so apparent. The problem is that such condensed networks are not particularly good at diffusing information to and from, and actually reaching out to all potential relevant partners in the area of operations.

This can be seen in the comparison of the networks that are displayed on the left and the right side of Figure 4.1. On the left side, the military organization has close and multiple connections – 'strong ties' – with some partnering organizations, but none with others. From an information perspective, two of the three ties the military have developed are redundant; since the three ties are interconnected in one dense network, one tie would have sufficed, strictly speaking. An additional consequence is that the military has no ties with other

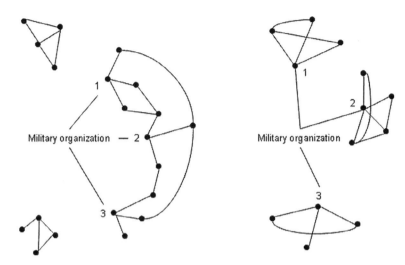

Closely connected and disconnected networks

Loosely connected networks with "structural holes"

Figure 4.1 Military organization seeking partnerships in one closed, dense network or in more disconnected networks
Source: Adapted from Burt, 1995; reprinted from Bollen and Soeters, 2010: 179.

possible partners and may even be unaware of their existence or their potential value. On the right side, the military organization is connected to all potential partners, albeit with 'weak' and single ties. These ties enable the organization to develop possibilities to get information from, and to reach out to all potential partners in the area, who otherwise would remain disconnected. That is because those contacts are non-redundant and have 'structural holes' between them.

The consequences for military practice are noticeable, albeit perhaps not that clearly at first sight. Sarah Chayes (2006), a US citizen living at the time of the ISAF mission in the Afghan city of Kandahar, described how the American military needed to find host national partners in the area of operations to assist them in construction and security jobs, transport and comparable logistic activities and hiring local personnel for linguistic services. Over time Americans favoured only one regional, political leader and his tribe to do business with, which was in Chayes' eyes the Americans' major mistake of the operation. This outcome matches with the left side of Figure 4.1. The result was multifold: there was no longer a level playing field in the region because one partner was given preference all the time at the expense of other potential partners (tribes, political factions). This led Chayes (2006: 182) to conclude that 'it seemed to most Kandaharis that the primary mission of U.S. troops in Kandahar was to service Gul Agha Shirzai (the regional leader with whom the Americans partnered/JS) and his Barakzai tribe'. As a consequence, a feeling of resentment against the US troops developed and grew over time. Besides, all relevant information was controlled by this one and only partner, excluding others who were likely to become increasingly hostile. The mission's general legitimacy in the region declined as a result (Bollen and Soeters, 2010: 180), rendering the whole operational situation even more difficult than it had been before. There are more examples as the following shows.

Strong ties among special operations forces

Belgian military sociologists Delphine Resteigne and Steven van den Bogaert (2017) analysed how special operations forces in the Afghanistan mission have been working together and sharing information since the beginning of this century. This has been in an unprecedented positive way, even though those special operators come from different nations.

The special operations force created their own HQ in Kabul, which had an atmosphere that was rather different from the mission's main HQ in the same city. Strikingly distinct was the easier access to the commander, the emphasis on communication from below, the less bureaucratic way of developing and executing plans based on creativity and out-of-the-box thinking, and the higher degree of role specialization, all of which made the special operators confident about themselves. The level of mutual trust among them was high. Being led by US commanders, there was a strong tendency to assimilation in the HQ. The professional commonalities outweighed the national differences among special operations personnel in the SOF HQ in Kabul. Clearly, their mutual ties were very strong.

However, the location of the HQ was kept secret, and even though the SOF community was keen on keeping relevant Afghan colleagues involved, it seemed their connection to the conventional, Western troops in the area was less well developed. The SOF's mutual bonding was much stronger than their contact with conventional troops. The fact that they wanted to have their own HQ, enabling them to go their own way and not be disrupted by conventional troops' plans and actions, illustrates the 'weakness of strong ties', as Mark Granovetter (1973) famously put it. This may have operational consequences for the mission at large. It is, however, unclear whether the positive consequences, i.e. not being disturbed, prevail over the negative ones, i.e. one 'hand', the conventional troops, not knowing what the other 'hand', the SOF, is doing.

Conflict

Unlike many other sociologists since, Simmel, like Marx, always stressed the importance of studying competition and conflict. After all, both scholars lived in conflictual societies. This renders their work all the more relevant for the military. We already saw that in the case of Marx; now it is time to pay attention to Simmel's thoughts on conflicts.

Simmel (1904; 1955) starts with the notion that conflict, *Der Streit*, is an ordinary phenomenon in societies; there is nothing special about it. It has positive sides, as it works as an integrative force in the group that is involved in a conflict; it pulls the group members tightly together. It is often said that political leaders who face criticism at home start developing conflicts with their neighbours abroad for this reason. Conversely, the unity of a group is often lost when it no longer has an opponent, as the example of the fragmentation of Protestantism reveals after its opponent, the Catholic Church, lost much of its relevance and power (Simmel, 1955: 97–98). Another, connected observation is that conflict also centralizes the group and its decision making, for which reason 'the organization of the army is the most centralized among all organizations [...]. The army is the organization in which the unconditional rule of the central authority excludes any independent movement of the elements' (Simmel, 1955: 89).

Furthermore, Simmel observed that the transition from war to peace constitutes a more serious problem than does the reverse, and consequently he examines carefully the various motives and processes for ending a conflict. He analyses (1955: 109ff) the termination of a conflict and sees a number of reasons why it might come to an end. A conflict may cease through the disappearance of its object, because of the discovery that the whole process was irrational anyway, because of the exhaustion of one's strength, because one has won, or because one has settled the issue through compromise or conciliation. At the end of his theorizing of conflicts he also pays attention to the drama of irreconcilability after the conflict has ended.

A specific implication of Simmel's work pertains to the emergence of alliances of groups that get involved in a conflict. Next to pulling members inside a group together, conflicts may bring persons and groups together which have otherwise nothing to do with each other (Simmel, 1955: 90). Such alliances may be stable, but more often they emerge on an ad-hoc basis to unite in a single, temporary action (war, conflict). Groups make alliances for a number of reasons. Basically, those reasons are that in a conflict with others one cannot be choosy about one's friends, that the conflict itself often lies beyond the allies' immediate interests, that the possible gains of a victory can be quick and intensive, that specific personal elements often recede, and that allies can reciprocally stimulate among each other the feelings of hostility towards the adversaries (Simmel, 1955: 106–107).

This Simmelian thinking is 'old stuff' from the beginning of the twentieth century (1904), but it is still useful, perhaps more useful than people are aware of. In fact, it may be an useful idea to connect these Simmelian ideas with the famous insights provided by von Clausewitz (1989 [1832]) about the triad between the people, the military and politics. There is more recent work, though. Randall Collins (2011), a specialist in the sociology of violence, elaborated conflict dynamics, including processes of escalation and de-escalation, in basically a similar way to Simmel but in a more analytical and comprehensive manner. Without referring to Simmel explicitly, Greek-American scholar

Fotini Christia (2012) conducted extensive studies in Bosnia and Afghanistan on alliance formation in civil wars. Having mastered the host national languages of Serbo-Croat and Farsi, she conducted fieldwork during the military operations of Western troops in those respective areas. Her fieldwork was based on extensive interviews with local stakeholders, i.e. politicians and other government authorities, generals, war lords, mujahedin and even convicted war criminals. She also used existing data, such as wartime declarations, ceasefire agreements, fatwas, memoirs, archival documents and propaganda material. All of this she did independently, as a single researcher, albeit with the help of host nationals, colleagues and friends. From all this material she compiled an extensive data base which would later lead to important findings.

Christia discovered that each group seeks to form wartime intergroup alliances that constitute minimum winning coalitions that ensure a victory, the gains of which need to be shared with the least number of allies. Such alliance formations are highly dependent on perceptions of relative power distribution, and they tend to be instable as warring groups switch all the time and may often be susceptible to fractionalization. Hence, there are vicious cycles of alliance shifts and fractionalization in civil wars. According to Christia (2012: 240), alliance formation is not based on identity politics, even though politicians, journalists, military people and scholars often advance this as an important factor. Christians have aligned with Muslims in Bosnia, as much as Sunnis can befriend Shiites now and fight them later, as she put it. First and foremost it is about power and improving one's chances of winning it through alliances with others. These findings, based on Christia's sophisticated scholarly work, very much resemble Simmel's insights, and they are highly useful for military people in action today. The opponent is not usually a single, stable party, and will consist of various, constantly shifting groups that may ally themselves with anyone, even foreign militaries. As long as those foreign militaries do not inadvertently advance one group at the expense of others in the region (as we saw above in the Kandahar example), the military may profit from this insight and use it in their tactics. Most of all it is important that the military knows about these dynamics, as not knowing is costly.

Theory of supercooperators

Simmel's work on number distributions, network dynamics, conflicts and group affiliations have laid the foundation for mathematical and experimental research in the social and political sciences. This type of 'game theory' started with the work of Theodor Caplow, whose elaboration of triads, 'in praise of Georg Simmel' (Coser, 1977: 187), has been important in this regard. Particularly significant has been the work by Robert Axelrod, a mathematical political scientist who demonstrated in the 1980s that there is a system in the way cooperation or its opposite, conflict, starts and extends. Axelrod developed the idea of the 'tit-for-tat' strategy, indicating the ways in which conflicts develop and how to intervene to prevent bad, or worse, events following. This type of game theory has been influential in developing policies of deterrence and the avoidance of real hostilities during the Cold War. Martin Nowak (2011), a professor of mathematics at Harvard, may be considered Axelrod's successor; he extended his work through simulation studies and experimental work in many places throughout the world. As a general conclusion of his highly valued works he criticized punishment as a method of gaining cooperation. If used at all, sanctions and retaliations should be mild for a first violation and stricter should violations be repeated; besides, sanctions should not be predictable. Problems and conflicts are more likely to be solved by cooperation, positive interaction, generosity and occasional forgiveness, which contributes to the positive reputation of the one who can let bygones be bygones (e.g. Soeters, 2013). The continuing relevance of this work for policies in the international security arena is evident. Simmel was among the first to see the significance of numbers and positions for social and political dynamics, even though he himself used mathematical symbols and notations only rarely.

Secrecy, the military and intelligence

Simmel (1906) first published a long and rich exposé on the sociology of secrecy and secret societies in the *American Journal of Sociology*. Here again he shows his affinity with abstract thinking, even though the article is illustrated with numerous real-life examples. Simmel starts with the notion that secrecy – and one of its derivatives, lying – in itself can be sociologically understandable, even though this may be considered despicable from a moral point of view. Even within a marriage secrets exist, and it is important that secrets remain just that, because in absence of 'reciprocal discretion, on the side of receiving as well as of giving, many marriages are failures' (Simmel, 1906: 462). As a consequence, because of its protective nature 'secrecy [...] is one of the greatest accomplishments of humanity' (ibid.). Simmel further points to one of the main sociological dimensions of secrecy, which is the delineation between those who are included and those who are excluded from the secret; 'secrecy sets barriers between men, but at the same time offers the seductive temptation to break through the barriers by gossip or confession' (Simmel, 1906: 466). Secrecy, hence, comes along with other group dynamics pertaining to inclusion, exclusion, gossip, lying and hiding. Secrecy, silence and denial are very sociological phenomena as they require the cooperation of many (e.g., Zerubavel, 2006).

From there on, Simmel starts analysing secret societies, such as 'a conspiracy, or a band of criminals, a religious conventicle, or an association of sexual extravagances' (Simmel, 1906: 470). Here a number of sociological aspects come to the fore:

- the confidence the members have in the secret group as well in each other;
- the centralized and strictly hierarchical nature of the group's structure ensuring that only a few know everything and others know little, about which they also must keep silence;
- the importance of usages, formulas and rituals;
- the autonomy the secret society strives for, i.e. the 'tone of a freedom' because the general rules and norms of the surrounding society do not apply; and finally
- the feeling of being aristocratic, an elite, which is implicitly acknowledged by the others through 'their enmity and jealousy'; secrecy promises status and prestige from in- and outsiders (Simmel, 1906: 470–487; Scott, 2009).

Simmel analyses this phenomenon without any negative value judgements, much in the way Max Weber analysed the bureaucracy and advocated the way sociology should be practised, which is *sine ira et studio*, i.e. without anger and partiality.

Simmel's work on secrecy is unquestionably relevant and applicable to the military in general and intelligence agencies in particular. Information sharing, or not, is one of the main themes that intelligence communities struggle with, and reading Simmel may help them to come to appropriate decisions in this connection. First, it is important to realize that in the field of military and security operations numerous incidents have occurred in which the lack of information sharing, or information hoarding, led to dramatic events. The attack on the Twin Towers in New York and government buildings in Washington DC on 11 September 2001 and the many terrorist attacks in Europe and elsewhere in the years thereafter are the most striking examples. In all these tragic events, at least some of the (national) intelligence services possessed elements of information that if properly shared and combined could have prevented those events.

The main criticism, with the benefit of hindsight, was that those agencies were acting too much on their own, precisely because of their striving for secrecy. Indeed, many of Simmel's characteristics of secret societies seem to apply to such intelligence agencies, including in these particular cases. This includes the desire to hold on to their autonomy, because secrecy-based autonomy seems best to protect one's self-interest and power position. Secrecy helps to nourish elitist ambitions to make others envy you, and overall it is a smart strategy if one wishes to maintain or even expand budgets and jobs. In general, one can contend that not sharing information preserves the privileges of those who have the information (Moore and Tumin, 1949). Even though Simmel himself was neutral about this as we saw before, such analyses have incurred severe criticism from politicians and academics. Already in the 1960s and 1970s, sociologists had gone out of their way to demonstrate the negative consequences of secrecy in the context of security systems (Coser, 1963; Lowry, 1972), criticisms which came to a peak in the years immediately following 9/11 (Turner, 2006).

Why secret intelligence fails

In analysing the events that led to the disastrous attacks on 9/11, Michael Turner, following others including state-led investigations, pointed to the high degree of decentralization and fragmentation in the US intelligence community. The many military and civilian agencies display mission-specific myopia (because of an unshakable devotion to one's agency's mission), and a 'can-do' attitude that requires risk-taking, leading to poorly conceived actions. In addition, mandates are ambiguous, the inter-service competition and bureaucratic rivalries are intense, and the separation of intelligence from policy is strict because of the wish to be as objective as possible. In the same way, the separation between intelligence and law enforcement is clear-cut as the American system of checks and balances tries to minimize the risks of the growth of a 'Gestapo' or a 'KGB'. All of this results in duplication of efforts, overlap and waste, contributing to slow decision making, and it prevents the full consideration of information (Turner, 2006: 17–42). Because of these characteristics – 'bureaucratic pathologies' in Turner's words – the 9/11 attackers were able to remain undetected, even though aspects of their whereabouts were known to at least some of the relevant intelligence agencies. To Turner this has not changed a lot since then, although the budgets and law enforcement regulations have been considerably increased.

It is too easy and surely unjustified to simply discredit intelligence agencies' striving for secrecy. For one, organizations in general do not change that much over time. 'Structural inertia' typifies certain organizations that possess relatively fixed repertoires of highly reproducible routines, which they have and maintain for good reasons (Hannan and Freeman, 1984). Intelligence agencies need to be careful about what they disseminate to others. As the saying goes, 'loose lips may sink ships', or put the other way around, many victories have been won by the advantage of surprise; one only needs to think of the Trojan Horse in ancient Greek military history. Hence, there is virtue in secrecy (Dufresne and Offstein, 2008). Secrecy makes one less vulnerable, and therefore information sharing is only deemed acceptable when done with others whom one can trust.

In today's militaries one can see such caution – suspicion perhaps – in the way the so-called 'Five Eyes' (USA, UK, Canada, Australia and New Zealand) share all kinds of information on military issues, and exclude others, for instance Germany, even if they belong to the same NATO alliance (whereas Australia and New Zealand do not). Here one can clearly recognize Granovetter's and Burt's analyses regarding selective partnerships combined with Simmel's thinking about secret societies. If nations share the same language, i.e. English, and a common history, i.e. of the British Commonwealth or colonialism, they tend to trust one another and consequently work more closely together. Obviously, this has many advantages, but it militates against the opportunity to distribute information to, and tap information from, others that are more distant but potentially useful. One can think of Germany because of its greater knowledge and different view of Russian politics, or nations in the Middle East who may provide militarily relevant information that is usually hidden from Western eyes. For today's military intelligence organizations and militaries in general, it is important to strike a balance between being too secrecy-oriented and selective or even biased, and being too loose in disclosing information to just anyone. Simmel's analysis of secret societies demonstrates that both extremes, being closed on the one hand and naïve on the other, are orientations that intelligence and military organizations can ill afford to have.

The stranger

Finally, Simmel's writing about the role of the 'stranger' (Levine, 1977) is relevant to the military. It is related to the topics we have discussed above. The 'stranger' is someone who is not quite part of the community they visit and, hence, is able to observe it from a distance and with some independence. They question what seems unquestionable, because they have a feeling for the incoherence and inconsistency of the in-group's behaviour, interaction and culture (Schuetz, 1944). A classic example would be the trader or salesperson who travels from region to region or from business to business. A sociologist would be another example, as a sociologist is someone who by training is likely to view everyday social life with some distance (Dahrendorf, 1968: 93–94). A more recent example would be today's migrant workers who not only bring skills and knowledge with them, but also their different background that may or may not be understood and appreciated. Also, the nature of the stranger's stay – for instance a visit or more permanent residence, on invitation or accepted with reluctance – plays a role in the interaction between the host community and the stranger (Levine, 1977: 23).

Simmel's view of the stranger stresses the positive side. The 'stranger' is able to carry messages between groups, communities or businesses that would otherwise remain unconnected. Because he or she is only partially involved, the 'stranger' can attain a different, more distanced view of what is happening around and about. As a result, strangers can more easily provoke social change and innovation than could insiders. Besides, being distant and close at the same time, having one foot inside and one foot outside, the 'stranger' may often be called on as a confidant and as a judge between conflicting parties because he or she has no stake in the emotions that flow around the community or group (Coser, 1977: 182; Moss Kanter and Khurana, 2009: 295).

The social type of the 'stranger' is relevant to the military in many ways. In Chapter 7 we will meet military interpreters who – acting between host nationals and foreign militaries – surely have all the characteristics of the 'stranger'. Representatives of ethnic minority groups may act as such too, as we will see in Chapter 6. Here another example may illustrate how much good 'strangers' can do in the military, and in military operations specifically. British military scholar Theo Farrell (2010) described how British operations in the Afghan province of Helmand evolved over time. He saw the different rotating troops engage in hard combat with the Taliban, following an established repertoire of core military competences that even go back to the Second World War (also: King, 2010). Even though the British position gradually improved because of large losses among adversary troops, the real improvement came when a newly formed (the 52) brigade entered the arena. As this former reserve brigade had recently been expanded, augmented by military personnel from other backgrounds, it was less committed to conventional military practices. Its commanding officer had been involved in two earlier missions of a non-combat nature. He had been deployed on a mission to reform Iraq's military police, and on another to rearrange the Lebanese army. Both tasks had made him aware of the importance of influencing the host national population by taking their interests seriously. As such, he and other personnel of the newly formed brigade were 'strangers' because of the different impact they had experienced while travelling between many military and non-military groups and communities throughout their careers. And they were successful in applying those various experiences during their deployment to Helmand; they turned out to be genuine innovators.

There are more examples of strangers making their appearance in and around military organizations. Of particular notice is Schuetz's account of the homecoming veteran. This article was published in 1945 when large numbers of American soldiers were soon to be discharged from active duty at the end of World War II. Analysing the veterans' position, Schuetz first points to the structured environment in the armed forces and the reputation of being a uniformed person that soldiers experience while in the military. Upon returning home, the veteran is likely to find a civilian environment that is much more 'anomic' than the military; besides, without the uniform the obvious special status disappears. The whole situation is 'strange'. Therefore, not only the veteran but also the welcoming society needs to prepare for the mutual adjustment. The veteran needs to understand civil society again and society needs to learn 'that the man whom they await will be another and not the one they imagined him to be' (Schuetz, 1945: 376). This lesson is as relevant and timely today as it was more than 70 years ago.

NVA officers in the Bundeswehr

German Sociologist Nina Leonhard (2016) used Schuetz's perspective of the stranger and the homecoming veteran in a fascinating study of the integration of the East German Nationale Volksarmee (NVA) and the West German Bundeswehr after the country's unification in 1990. She studied the experiences and memories of NVA officers once they had been integrated in the larger Bundeswehr. Their stories about the uncertainty regarding their new positions and ranks, including the possibility of degradation, the evaluation of their past (political) behaviour by their new superiors, the ambivalent but often thankful relations with officers from the Bundeswehr, and the alienation from previous comrades illustrate how much the NVA officers were strangers in their new military environment. For sure, this often occurs in other situations where political and military systems undergo drastic change.

Conclusion

Simmel's work may have been somewhat underestimated for a long time, but now the implications of his analytical thinking have become clear in many societal, institutional and organizational fields (e.g. Scott, 2009). As such his contribution to sociology is indisputable. There is something else, though. Like Max Weber and Emile Durkheim, Georg Simmel witnessed towards the end of his life the outbreak of the First World War in August 1914 and the dramatic events that ensued. He wrote essays and gave speeches about these events referring to the '*Augusterlebnis*', with an optimistic and apologetic twist – supportive of the German point of view – that nowadays seems difficult to accept (Joas and Knöbl, 2013: 134–137, 153; De Jong, 2007). Simmel took a stance comparable to Weber's (and other German authors) vis-à-vis these events. It shows that the thinking of famous sociologists, no matter how advanced in an analytical, 'universal' way this may be, is also time- and context-dependent. The larger part of their thought remains valid and extremely useful; some of it, however, much less so.

Bibliography

Bollen, M. and J. Soeters (2010) 'Partnering with "strangers"'. In J. Soeters, P.C. van Fenema and R. Beeres (eds), *Managing Military Organizations: Theory and Practice*. London and New York: Routledge.

Burt, R.S. (1995) 'The social structure of competition'. In N. Nohria and R.G. Eccles (eds), *Networks and Organizations: Structure, Form and Action*. Cambridge, MA: Harvard University Press.

Chayes, S. (2006) *The Punishment of Virtue: Inside Afghanistan after the Taliban*. London: Penguin Books.

Christia, F. (2012) *Alliance Formation in Civil Wars*. Cambridge: Cambridge University Press.

Collins, R. (2011) 'C-escalation and D-escalation: a theory of the time-dynamics of conflict'. *American Sociological Review* 77(1): 1–20.

Coser, L. (1963) 'Peaceful settlements' and the dysfunctions of secrecy'. *Journal of Conflict Resolution* 7(3): 246–253.

Coser, L. (1977) *Masters of Sociological Thought: Ideas in Historical and Social Context*. 2nd edn. Long Grove, IL: Waveland Press.

Dahrendorf, R. (1968) *Pfade aus Utopia: Arbeiten zur Theorie und Methode der Soziologie*. Gesammelte Abhandlungen 1. Munich: Piper & Co. Verlag.

De Jong, M. (2007) *Icons of Sociology*. Amsterdam: Boom.

Dufresne, R.L. and E.H. Offstein (2008), 'On the virtues of secrecy in organizations'. *Journal of Management Inquiry* 17(2): 102–106.

Farrell, Th. (2010) 'Improving in war: military adaptation and the British in Helmand province, Afghanistan 2006–2009'. *Journal of Strategic Studies* 33(4): 567–594.

Granovetter, M. (1973) 'The strength of weak ties'. *American Journal of Sociology* 78(6): 1360–1380.

Granovetter, M. (1983) 'The strength of weak ties: a network theory revisited'. *Sociological Theory* 1(1): 201–233.

Hannan, M.T. and J. Freeman (1984) 'Structural inertia and organizational change'. *American Sociological Review* 49(2): 149–164.

Joas, H. and W. Knöbl (2013 [2008]) *War in Social Thought: Hobbes to the Present.* Princeton NJ and Oxford: Princeton University Press.

King, A. (2010) 'Understanding the Helmand campaign: British military operations in Afghanistan'. *International Affairs* 86(2): 311–332.

Leonhard, N. (2016) *Integration und Gedächtnis: NVA-Offiziere im Vereinigten Deutschland.* Cologne: Herbert von Halem Verlag.

Levine, D.N. (1977) 'Simmel at a distance: on the history and systematics of the sociology of the stranger'. *Sociological Focus* 10(1): 15–29.

Levine, D., E.B. Carter and E. Miller Gorman (1976) 'Simmel's influence on American sociology. I'. *American Journal of Sociology* 81(4): 813–845.

Lowry, R.P. (1972) 'Toward a sociology of secrecy and security systems'. *Social Problems* 19(4): 437–450.

Moore, W.E. and M.M. Tumin (1949) 'Some social functions of ignorance'. *American Sociological Review* 14(6): 787–795.

Moss Kanter, R. and R. Khurana (2009) 'Types and positions: the significance of Georg Simmel's theories for organizational behavior'. In P.S. Adler (ed.), *The Oxford Handbook of Sociology and Organization Studies: Classical Foundations.* Oxford: Oxford University Press, pp. 291–306.

Nowak, M. (with R. Highfield) (2011) *Altruism, Evolution, and why We Need Each Other to Succeed.* New York: Free Press.

Resteigne, D. and S. van den Bogaert (2017) 'Information sharing in contemporary operations: the strength of SOF ties'. In I. Goldenberg, J. Soeters and W. Dean (eds), *Information Sharing in Military Operations.* Cham, Switzerland: Springer International.

Schuetz, A. (1944) 'The stranger: an essay in social psychology'. *American Journal of Sociology* 49(6): 499–507.

Schuetz, A. (1945) 'The homecomer'. *American Journal of Sociology* 50(5): 369–376.

Scott, A. (2009) 'Georg Simmel: the individual and the organization'. In P.S. Adler (ed.), *The Oxford Handbook of Sociology and Organization Studies: Classical Foundations.* Oxford: Oxford University Press, pp. 268–289.

Simmel, G. (1902) 'The number of members as determining the sociological form of the group'. *American Journal of Sociology* 8(1): 1–46.

Simmel, G. (1904) 'The sociology of conflict. I'. *American Journal of Sociology* 9(4): 490–525.

Simmel, G. (1906) 'The sociology of secrecy and secret societies'. *American Journal of Sociology* 11(4): 441–498.

Simmel, G. (1909) 'The problem of sociology'. *American Journal of Sociology* 15(3): 289–320.

Simmel, G. (1955, originally various publications) *Conflict and the Web of Group-Affiliations.* New York: The Free Press.

Soeters, J. (2013) 'Odysseus prevails over Achilles: a warrior model suited to post-9/11 conflicts'. In J. Burk (ed.), *How 9/11 Changed Our Ways of War*. Stanford, CA: Stanford University Press.

Turner, M.A. (2006) *Why Secret Intelligence Fails*. Revised edn. Washington, DC: Potomac Books.

Von Clausewitz, C. (1989 [1832]) *On War*. Princeton, NJ: Princeton University Press.

Zerubavel, E. (2006) *The Elephant in the Room: Silence and Denial in Everyday Life*. Oxford: Oxford University Press.

5 Jane Addams

From peace activism to pragmatic peacekeeping

Jane Addams (1860–1935) may have been less a scholar than a social activist. However, she published a large number of essays, speeches and books on pragmatism and social policies that have been neglected for too long but have ample relevance today. Those publications, including these published in the *American Journal of Sociology*, helped her ideas survive and gradually made her reputation as one of sociology's founders.

It may seem odd to include Jane Addams in this book on sociology and military studies since she won the Nobel Prize for Peace in 1931. Coming from 'mundane' activities in the field of household work and community and city development in Chicago, she gradually turned into a feminist peace broker and activist. She ceaselessly stressed the need to seek positive peace instead of negative peace, the latter simply being the negation of war. This made her conclude that solutions to conflicts, even truly violent conflicts, are too often approached with blunt military means. Paradoxically, this may be a valuable message for the military, as it pertains to its operational practices, policies and general conduct. Instead, perhaps in addition, she offers the alternative of working closely together with local communities to 'weave peace' into their societies, a concept coined by Patricia Shields (2017: 38–40). This may be achieved by developing strategies in the realm of public administration, safety, health and community development. This is what positive peace is about. Even though some of Addams' thinking may seem naive at a first glance, it may have ample implications for many sectors of society (e.g. Wozniak, 2009), including today's peace missions in conflict-ridden regions.

Jane Addams was not the first to point to the importance of 'mundane' matters such as household and community development and the improvement of living conditions in urban neighbourhoods. About half a century earlier, Harriet Martineau (Giddens and Sutton, 2013: 19) introduced sociology to Britain, insisting that an analysis of a society must include an understanding of women's lives. Accordingly, she paid attention to previously ignored issues such as marriage, children, the sick, domestic and religious life, and race relations. She had observed the challenges faced by those who wanted to improve race relations during her travels to America, a topic which we will turn to in the next chapter. Martineau became an advocate of both women's rights and the emancipation of slaves. With Jane Addams she was one of the women founders of sociology and social theory (Madoo Lengermann and Niebrugge-Brantley, 1998).

From city improvements to peace activism

In Chicago, Addams began an active life after her father passed away. He had left her an inheritance that enabled her to purchase a somewhat dilapidated house that was soon to become known as Hull House. In this house, which today is a museum, she and her friend Ellen Gates Starr co-founded a social settlement to improve the lives of the poverty stricken, disease ridden, dirty, smelly, contentious immigrant community (Shields, 2017: 5–13; Deegan, 2007). She and her friend established a kindergarten, organized reading parties and other educational activities, provided shelter to the homeless, built public showers and a gymnasium, created an atmosphere that was particularly advantageous to young women and their children, and received high profile speakers such as Theodor Roosevelt, George Herbert Mead, W. I. Thomas and W. E. B. Du Bois, the Afro-American sociologist who we will meet in the next chapter. She also initiated early work in social studies; she organized surveys in the immigrant neighbourhoods and on the basis of these data developed coloured nationality and employment urban maps. This work proved to be fertile ground for the growth of the later 'Chicago School' of urban sociology. She also advocated that the 'city as household' metaphor should replace the militaristic view of the 'city as citadel' (Addams, 2007 [1907]).

Addams wrote and presented many speeches – including to the American Sociological Society – which subsequently appeared in her sociological and general magazine articles and influential books (e.g. Addams, 1896; 1899; 1905; 2002; 2007). Among the many issues she addressed she particularly fought against the idea that poverty could be traced back to the moral 'failings' of individuals. Due to economic downturns, families can quickly fall into poverty through no fault of their own, as she never ceased to make clear (Shields, 2017: 47). She stressed that *sympathetic understanding* (Hamington, 2009) is needed to see others' positions and interests and the burdens they often have to carry. She had the ability to see multiple perspectives, she advocated cultural pluralism, and she was committed to action instead of mere theorizing (Shields, 2017). This proved to be the basis of her feminist pragmatist ideas.

Her activities in Chicago did not only have a social and educational character. In the neighbourhoods surrounding Hull House the immigrant groups from different nations and regions (Italy, Poland, Germany, Jewish people from the diaspora, African-Americans from the segregated South) were frequently at war with one another, civil war so to speak. Religious and racial differences and disparities in interests, property and market position were motives for violent crime, mafia-type encounters and street killings. Addams observed that conflicts lessened and sometimes ended when opposing groups worked together to resolve a shared problem (Shields, 2017: 11). Unlike Marx, she saw cooperation and not conflict as the solution to poverty, destitution, inequality and criminality. She actively tried to turn her ideas into practice. In those years, Addams was lauded across the nation as a 'good woman' (Deegan, 2007) and a 'full-fledged citizen' (Deegan, 2010).

This would change, however, with the outbreak of the First World War in 1914. Addams started to take a position when the USA prepared to intervene in the gruesome hostilities that took place on the battlefields of Belgium and France. In 1915 she presided at a women's peace conference in The Hague in the Netherlands, which had managed to stay neutral, and she proclaimed the need to seek mediation as a path to peace. This was the first time that women had organized to protest against war and the exclusion of women from decision making. The conference resolutions made clear that women were also affected by war and that women should have a place in all aspects of government and administration, including decision making about war and peace. In this way the movement for women's rights and peace-making were connected. The Women's International League for Peace and Freedom (WILPF) is still a major network more than 100 years since it was founded by Addams and her associates.

Accompanied by a delegation from the conference, Addams subsequently visited heads of states in the belligerent nations, citizen groups and wounded soldiers to convey the conference's message (Shields, 2017: 12). When the USA entered the war she continued to press for peace. This altered her image and standing among the general public and the popular press rather suddenly. From being a 'good woman', she suddenly became a villain and a social pariah, abandoned by friends, colleagues and, remarkably enough, other sociologists (Deegan, 2007: 6). This culminated in 1919 when she was targeted by the US government as the most dangerous person in America. This change of fate drove her from the sociologists' stage for decades to come. However, she gradually resumed her position of public leadership after the war, among other things by joining a US humanitarian effort to provide food relief to victims in Belgium and France. In her eyes, the idea of women as bread-givers endorsed the need for social responsibility. All this work eventually gained her the Nobel Peace Prize in 1931.

Shields and Soeters (2017) have reconstructed her ideas on peace development and applied them to contemporary challenges for today's security organizations. Addams (2007) argued that prospects for peace were often undermined by residuals of militarism and colonialism. She criticized the survival of the attitude of the conqueror toward 'inferior people' who at her time in Chicago were mostly immigrants. She also targeted military-type responses to 'adversaries' such as striking unions or protest movements. Militarism – 'friend-or-foe-thinking' – in her eyes prevented the capacity to weave the complex social fabric of communities and cities together. She argued that social equity and city government-as-household would be conducive to the development of positive peace and the dissolution of violent conflicts.

More particularly, she introduced a number of characteristics that underlie peace weaving. These are:

- maintaining harmonious relationships throughout society;
- the absence of rigid moralism, fixed belief systems and stereotyping of others;
- the value of sympathetic knowledge;
- a community of inquiry focusing on shared problems and everyone's participation; and
- lateral progress, redefining progress such that it encompasses the advancement of all, including the truly vulnerable.

The ideas developed and advocated by Addams have current relevance with respect to policies towards immigrants seeking refuge in the West. This topic will be dealt with in Chapter 8, when we will try to understand border control dynamics following the ideas developed by Michel Foucault. Jane Addams' 'peace weaving' idea applies to the remainder of this chapter, which deals with the use of military resources in UN peacekeeping (Shields and Soeters, 2017). This obviously stands in contrast to the better known military capabilities that are geared towards warfare, counterterrorism and special operations.

UN peacekeeping

The world has become so interconnected that some sort of world governance has become inevitable. The foundation of the United Nations (UN) at the end of the Second World War is a manifestation of this development. It is the supra-national institution that oversees – and acts on – global problems, be they climate-, poverty-, cultural heritage- or conflict-related. The idea of the late German sociologist Ulrich Beck (2006) that the world has become a *world risk society* is strongly connected to the UN's existence. Risks are no longer localized as they are in principle omnipresent; the risks cannot be calculated because they are unknown to some extent; and supra-national risks can no longer be compensated for and controlled by individual nation-states. What nation-states can do is discuss the state of affairs in supra-national institutions such as the European Union (EU), the African Union (AU) or the United Nations (UN), and then act, no matter how imperfectly.

One category of such actions is the deployment of UN peacekeeping missions, next to non-UN peacekeeping missions mostly initiated by the EU or the AU (Sandler, 2017). Such missions are conducted by combinations of civilian and uniformed personnel (e.g. Junk et al., 2017). The phenomenon of UN missions has shown a substantial increase of personnel over the last decades, as Figure 5.1 displays with respect to personnel in uniform (i.e. military and police). Apparently, peacekeeping missions are necessary and most likely successful, at least some of them to a certain degree. Over the last few decades UN peacekeeping missions were deemed successful in Namibia, El Salvador, Mozambique, Eastern Slavonia and East Timor, whereas the operation in Cambodia in the 1990s was considered a mixed success (Howard, 2008: 9). The results of thorough statistical analyses of the effect of peacekeeping operations are unequivocal. Considering

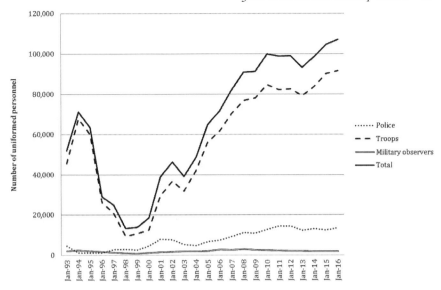

Figure 5.1 Surge in uniformed personnel in UN missions since 1993
Based on data from www.un.org/en/peacekeeping/resources/statistics/conbributors_a
rchive.shtml, accessed 24 August 2017, compiled by Jacqueline Heeren-Bogers.

that peacekeepers are sent to more difficult situations, statistics show that intervention by the international community helps maintain peace. Such interventions tend to foster peace in the short term, limit casualties, make peace more likely to last and to last longer (Page Fortna, 2004: 288; Sandler, 2017: 19).

Criticism of UN operations has been voiced since their very inception, nonetheless. The nature of these comments is quite comparable to the kind and intensity of the reproaches that Addams faced when she advocated her ideas on peace development. UN missions have been considered chaotic and based on organized hypocrisy, among other things, because there are gaps between commitments and resources needed to meet them and because much needed reforms are likely to fail (Lipson, 2007). UN missions are very often deemed to be toothless or even impotent because of limited resources and because soldiers in those missions, particularly Western soldiers with a nationalist bent, may not be sufficiently willing or prepared to fight and protect host nationals (Blocq, 2010). As we all remember, a lack of robustness contributed to three notorious atrocities during UN missions in the 1990s, i.e. those in Somalia, Rwanda and Bosnia. The multi-cultural and multi-linguistic composition of UN missions, and the corresponding tension between national belonging and allegiance versus membership of a multinational framework (Ben-Ari and Elron, 2001), are not easy to transform into effective performance. And finally, the over-representation of forces from poor nations that we saw earlier (e.g., Sandler, 2017) implies that such missions' technological equipment on average does not match the capabilities of, for example, NATO or Russian operations.

Unintended consequences of peacekeeping

Given all this criticism it is a bit of a romantic illusion to think that peace-keeping missions only produce positive results. In fact, a well-known volume edited by Chiyuki Aoi, Cedric de Coning and Ramesh Thakur (2007) revealed a number of what have become known as negative 'unintended consequences' of peacekeeping. A long time ago, Robert K. Merton (1936) systematically analysed the phenomenon of unintended consequences of purposive social action in general. He pointed at the impact of errors and the role of complexity and failing knowledge to understand and react to it. He also paid attention to the influence of interests, which are 'instances where the actor's paramount concern with the foreseen immediate consequences excludes the consideration of further or other consequences of the same act' (Merton, 1936: 901) – this matches with functional versus substantial rationality, as we saw before. And finally, he observed that intentions of doing good may turn into the opposite, for example democratic elections may bring undemocratic parties to power.

As far as UN peacekeeping is concerned, unintended consequences are mainly seen in the field of gender relations (prostitution, trafficking, sexual harassment by UN personnel, the spread of diseases such as HIV/AIDS, and local women and children being left behind). Most of these occurrences are due to extreme poverty among host national women and girls. Furthermore, there are consequences for the local economy and the emergence of a dual economy as new standards develop in the area of operations. There may be a rise in general price levels, and because some people are able to profit more from the UN's presence than others, salary disparities and inequalities in standards of living will increase. Besides, there may be a 'brain-drain' flowing from the local civil service to the UN. Finally, as women may be treated with preference by the UN mission, resentment in the host national community against women may develop.

In a similar vein, Séverine Autessere (2012) pointed to unintended consequences of well-intentioned international efforts to bring the violence in DR Congo to an end. She noticed that 'narratives' about the main causes and consequences of the violence overshadowed other factors, for instance, one category of victims getting much more attention and funding than others. This led to the continuation of the problems instead of their solution, despite all good intentions. Some authors refute the claim that UN missions are a neutral, let alone benign activity (Higate and Henry, 2009: 157).

All this criticism, however, may be balanced by the consideration that the results of UN peacekeeping, intended and unintended, may be also encouraging; in fact they often are. We have previously referred to the, at least moderately, positive results of empirical research in this connection (Page Fortna, 2004; Howard, 2008; Sandler, 2017).

The most cautious remark one could make is that anything is better than nothing. What is more, organized hypocrisy – decoupling talk from action, which is not doing what you say or not saying what you do – may reconcile pressures that otherwise could lead to a state of being incapable of any effective action at all (Lipson, 2007). Besides, Lise Howard's thorough and realistic analysis of a number of UN missions (2008: 8–20) demonstrated that in some missions indeed, mechanisms of organizational learning could be found (alas, in others this was not the case). These were the missions that proved successful. Organizational learning was revealed at the level of the mission itself, consisting of integration of the mission with the host national environment, as well as between missions involving the learning and evaluating processes at the Department of Peacekeeping Operations at UN HQ in New York. Addams' ideas resonate in Howard's following words: 'peacekeeping is at its best when the peacekeepers – both military and civilian – take their cues from the local population [...]' (Howard, 2008: 2). In fact, the odds for peacekeeping are highest when the peacekeepers learn from the host nationals, and the host nationals learn from the peacekeepers (also: Williams and Mengistu, 2015).

Then, there is the duration of peacekeeping missions. A number of them have lasted for more than half a century: the mission in Cyprus (UNFICYP), studied by Charles Moskos (1976), and the missions in Southern Lebanon (UNIFIL) and the Democratic Republic of Congo (MONUSCO and predecessors) are the most notable examples. This long duration is often seen as problematic, because those missions require large contributions of manpower and resources. In addition, not finishing the job seems equal to being unproductive. This contrasts with the general much shorter duration of 'traditional' military missions, such as the ones by NATO in Iraq, Afghanistan and Libya. In these three missions, the duration of operations was much shorter, ranging from several months (Libya) to some fifteen years in Iraq and Afghanistan. America's and other nations' labours in the latter two operations still continue, but only in a limited way. This coincides with the observation that professional soldiers like wars and operations that are 'clean, short and decisive' (Teitler, 1977). However, as much as this seems acceptable in classical hostilities and wars, it seems less adequate with today's wicked problems that consist of intra-national frictions, hunger- and poverty-related tensions, failing governments and waning security institutions.

The paradox here is that high-intensity military operations of a short length may make things worse instead of better. The dictator Muammar Kaddafi was toppled rapidly during the air campaign over Libya in 2011, which from a democratic perspective may be seen as a good result in itself. Yet the outcome at the end of that short intervention was the complete devastation of Libya's political, social, economic and security fabric. The resulting migration crisis produced considerable problems for Europe which have so far proved to be difficult to manage and solve. Some authors argue that previous to the air campaign, international support for Libyan civil society's non-violent actions to end the regime would have been more effective and less devastating (Chenoweth and Stephan, 2014). This is not just an opinion; it is an insight related to in-depth empirical research that convincingly shows the power of non-violent action in conflicts in general (Stephan and Chenoweth, 2008).

In conclusion, UN missions' long duration in so-called 'frozen' conflicts is not what Westerners like to see as they are inclined to value short-term results. However, such drawn-out missions seem inevitable under certain conditions. In fact they may be considered good practice, as ending them before tensions are resolved would be irresponsible. One could even argue that short military interventions, leaving the mess for the host nationals to clear up, are counter-productive. This is certainly something that Addams would agree with. Peace weaving takes time, a lot of time, she would contend.

Pragmatism and peacekeeping

It has been mentioned several times: Jane Addams' ideas were grounded in a pragmatist, action-oriented philosophy to which among others the American philosopher John Dewey contributed prominently (Schneiderhan, 2011: 595). Pragmatism is based on the idea that thinking and experiencing are inextricably intertwined. In this view, there should be less emphasis on given and fixed means and ends, but more on 'ends-in-view' that emerge from experience itself, i.e. from the situation within which action unfolds. It does not only make sense to improve one's skills to achieve a goal, but also to set and develop targets to improve one's capacities. Hence the significance of process dynamics, or more precisely experimentation in action, which should be more than just trial-and-error, and also based on cooperation with other city groups and institutions (Gross, 2009: 87). Such cooperative experiments should be founded on what Dewey calls a 'careful survey' involving 'examination, inspection, exploration, [and] analysis' (Schneiderhan, 2011: 597). Amidst these processes one should be open to insights that break with convention; there should always be room for 'perplexity', as Addams put it (Schneiderhan, 2011: 596). Thinking should never be excluded from action; it should be aim and fire, aim and fire, aim and fire … not just aim, aim, aim; nor just fire, fire, fire.

All of this can be recognized in the activities that Addams and her colleagues conducted at Hull House. Their social work was different from the usual practices in the field of charity in Chicago at that time, which was replete with economist thinking, suspicion of potential fraud and the wish to weed out the lazy (Schneiderhan, 2011: 599). Addams and her friend Ellen Starr actively tried to understand the particularities of poverty and social provision, seeking to solve the mismatch between the services of the benevolent citizens at one end of the city and the situation of impoverished citizens at the other. This way they provided immaterial as well as material services (teaching and playing as well as shower facilities).

Pragmatism has gained appreciation in many fields of scholarly and practical work, such as management and organization studies and public administration (e.g. Shields, 2008). This way of approaching problems is seen as a way to meet the challenges of a dynamic and complex world (Farjoun et al., 2015). It also has implications for the military, as can be recognized in the ideas about the constabulary force that were developed by Morris Janowitz (see Chapter 9). More particularly, Addams' ideas can be directly connected to peacekeeping. Shields and Soeters (2013) have applied a simple conceptual framework of pragmatism to the successive peacekeeping missions in DR Congo. This framework has been formulated by the American psychiatrist David Brendel and consist of four Ps, all indicating important elements of pragmatism. These concepts, decribed below, may help in analysing the content and results of peacekeeping, including possible flaws and room for improvement (Shields and Soeters, 2013). They also may serve as a wrap-up of the many features of pragmatism we discussed above.

Practical

First, peacekeeping missions should be as practical as possible, much in the way Addams and her colleagues provided practical services to the needy, such as public baths and showers. This first aspect is something the UN could seriously improve. In DR Congo the greater share of the available budget is spent on the mission itself (salaries, infrastructure, transport). The budget for quick-impact projects in Congolese society and for training and professionalizing the official armed forces is only a very small portion of the total. Also, the UN troops have often not been very good at providing shelter and security to the host nationals against the militias that are strolling and plundering around. Besides, stressing the importance of abstract values such as human rights and good governance often comes at the expense of practical issues such as repairing roads and schools (also: Autessere, 2012).

Pluralistic

UN peacekeeping missions are pluralistic per se. They consist of military and civilian personnel, they include troops from a wide variety of countries, and they employ host national personnel. As such, the pluralism of peacekeeping missions is appreciated by the host nationals, as it reflects the 'whole experience'. It clearly makes a different impression than an all-Western or 'white' mission, which could possibly awaken not-so-positive memoirs of old colonial times. However, as we saw before, this pluralism or international diversity of the mission's composition also creates problems in communication and operational effectiveness. What is more, the civilians and military are sitting in two separate trains, so to speak, going in the same direction. Civil–military interaction in UN missions needs to be improved substantially. Finally, and this connects clearly to what Addams advocated all along, there is a need for more women in

UN peace missions. This may be beneficial to mission effectiveness because women help improve interactions with female host-nationals, but most likely there are further advantages in that a gender-balanced peacekeeping force is likely to generate more trust among the host population (Bridges and Horsfall, 2009).

Participatory

Community participation, inclusion, democratic decision-making and the development of good relations belong to the main features of pragmatism, and also to Addams' view and deeds. As said, UN missions – also in DR Congo – hire substantial numbers of host national personnel, which means that the local population can take part in the mission's direction and successes. This is good. However, host nationals are mostly hired for mundane, housekeeping and cleaning jobs that are important in themselves but preclude participation in higher decision-making. In DR Congo there are hardly any Congolese employees among the mission's top staff, although it is true that a number of Congolese work in the mission to broadcast radio programmes in Lingalese and other native languages. Local people are often hired for language mediation (e.g. Pouligny, 2006), as we will discuss in Chapter 7. Nonetheless, however important these language mediators may be, their contribution is often side-lined by higher-ranking personnel. Besides, as we saw before, there may be a bias towards those from the host national population who are hired, possibly creating tensions, envy and anger among those who have less chance of being employed and earning a living from the UN.

Provisional

The final aspect of pragmatism stresses the significance of experimentation and developing targets-in-action next to advancing skills to achieve given goals. This is certainly an element that needs upgrading in UN peacekeeping, even though Howard (2008) revealed a number of missions that have been successful both operationally and in terms of organizational learning. UN's peacekeeping missions in general, however, are large bureaucracies that consist of stove-pipes or elevators that have too little horizontal interaction and too limited leaning to organizational learning and experimentation (e.g. Williams and Mengistu, 2015). They still produce an 'engineering-style' of planning and an external, expert, top-down view of what needs to be done. They are oriented towards end-goals, and less to intermediate goals and results that may emerge during the process and that should be used to decide upon the next steps to be taken. As such, UN missions are likely to resemble the military parent-organizations they stem from. Addams would suggest that such things be done differently, although she would agree that changing common and traditional practices and structures is not an easy job. It is not impossible, though.

Empowering women in Afghanistan

In a large-scale experiment in the framework of the National Solidarity Program (NSP), 250 randomly selected villages and small towns in Afghanistan were mandated to elect gender-balanced councils – hence, including female participation – in order to obtain funds for development projects. In the control group of another 250 comparable villages and small towns no such policy interventions occurred. With the help of a large array of research instruments it was shown that in the treatment group there was more acceptance of female participation in local governance. Even though there were no changes in women's roles in household decision-making or in broader society, there was a change in male and female attitudes to women and their role in community life. The researchers concluded that even in societies where women are subject to discrimination, change through policy intervention is possible (Beath et al., 2013: 555–556). Addams would be happy to know about these results that fully endorse her line of thinking.

Conclusion

Jane Addams' work has often been overlooked. Joas and Knöbl's grand overview of war in social thought (2013) does not mention her, or her work, at all. In general, her work – even though some of it appeared in the *American Journal of Sociology* – has not been widely acknowledged in sociological academia. She was famous in American society though, until she started criticizing that country's involvement in the First World War. That made her position problematic, but she managed to survive the antagonism and be awarded the Nobel Peace Prize towards the end of her life. Gradually, her ideas won acclaim, first among female activists and scholars, more recently in much broader spheres. She can be rightly recognized as a founding mother in the domain of sociology and military studies. But she is also a mother whose lessons have not yet been learned clearly enough.

Bibliography

Addams, J. (1896) 'A belated industry'. *American Journal of Sociology* 1(5): 536–550.

Addams, J. (1899) 'Trade unions and public duty'. *American Journal of Sociology* 4(4): 448–462.

Addams, J. (1905) 'Problems of municipal administration'. *American Journal of Sociology* 10(4): 425–444.

Addams, J. (2002 [1922]) *Peace and Bread in Times of War*. Urbana and Chicago: University of Illinois Press.

Addams, J. (2007 [1907]) *Newer Ideals of Peace*. Urbana and Chicago: University of Illinois Press.

Aoi, Ch., C. de Coning and R. Thakur (2007) *Unintended Consequences of Peacekeeping*. Tokyo, New York and Paris: United Nations University Press.

Autessere, S. (2012) 'Dangerous tales: dominant narratives on the Congo and their unintended consequences'. *African Affairs* 111(443): 202–222.

Beath, A., F. Christia and R. Enikolopov (2013) 'Empowering women through development aid: evidence from a field experiment in Afghanistan'. *American Political Science Review* 197(3): 540–557.

Beck, U. (2006) 'Living in the world risk society'. *Economy and Society* 35(3): 329–345.

Ben-Ari, E. and E. Elron (2001) 'Blue helmets and white armor: multi-nationalism and multi-culturalism among UN peacekeeping forces'. *City and Society* 13(2): 271–302.

Blocq, D. (2010) 'Western soldiers and the protection of local civilians in UN peacekeeping operations: is a nationalist orientation in the armed forces hindering our preparedness to fight?' *Armed Forces and Society* 36(2): 290–309.

Bridges, D. and D. Horsfall (2009) 'Increasing operational effectiveness in UN peacekeeping: toward a gender-balanced force'. *Armed Forces and Society* 36(1): 120–130.

Chenoweth, E. and M.J. Stephan (2014) 'Drop your weapons: when and why civil resistance works'. *Foreign Affairs* (July–August): 94–106.

Deegan, M.J. (2007) 'Jane Addams'. In J. Scott (ed.), *Fifty Key Sociologists: The Formative Theorists*, London and New York: Routledge.

Deegan, M.J. (2010) 'Jane Addams on citizenship in a democracy'. *Journal of Classical Sociology* 10(3): 217–238.

Farjoun, M., Chr. Ansell and A. Boin (2015) 'Pragmatism in organization studies: meeting the challenges of a dynamic and complex world'. *Organization Science* 26(6): 1787–1804.

Giddens, A. and P.W. Sutton (2013) *Sociology*. 7th edn. Cambridge: Polity Press.

Gross, M. (2009) 'Collaborative experiments: Jane Addams, Hull House and experimental social work'. *Social Science Information* 48(1): 81–95.

Hamington, M. (2009) *The Social Philosophy of Jane Addams*. Urbana and Chicago: University of Illinois Press.

Higate, P. and M. Henry (2009) *Insecure Spaces: Peacekeeping, Power and Performance in Haiti, Kosovo and Liberia*. London/New York: Zed Books.

Howard, L. Morjé (2008) *UN Peacekeeping in Civil Wars*. Cambridge: Cambridge University Press.

Joas, H. and W. Knöbel (2013 [2008]) *War in Social Thought: Hobbes to the Present*. Princeton NJ and Oxford: Princeton University Press.

Junk, J., F. Mancini, W. Seibel and T. Blume (eds) (2017) *The Management of UN Peacekeeping: Coordination, Learning, and Leadership in Peace Operations*. Boulder, CO: Lynne Rienner.

Lipson, M. (2007) 'Peacekeeping: organized hypocrisy?' *European Journal of International Relations* 13(1): 5–34.

Madoo Lengermann, P. and J. Niebrugge-Brantley (1998) *The Women Founders: Sociology and Social Theory 1830–1930*. Boston: McGraw-Hill.

Merton, R.K. (1936) 'The unanticipated consequences of purposive social action'. *American Sociological Review* 1(6): 894–904.

Moskos, Ch. (1976) *Peace Soldiers: The Sociology of a United Nations Military Force*. Chicago: University of Chicago Press.

Page Fortna, V. (2004) 'Does peacekeeping keep peace? International intervention and the duration of peace after civil war'. *International Studies Quarterly* 48(2): 269–292.

Pouligny, B. (2006) *Peace Operations Seen from Below: UN Missions and Local People*. Bloomfield, CT: Kumarian Press.

Sandler, T. (2017) 'International peacekeeping operations: burden sharing and effectiveness'. *Journal of Conflict Resolution* 61(9): 1875–1897.

Schneiderhan, E. (2011) 'Pragmatism and empirical sociology: the case of Jane Addams and Hull House, 1889–1895'. *Theory and Society* 40: 589–617.

Shields, P. (2008) 'Rediscovering the taproot: is classical pragmatism the route to renew public administration?' *Public Administration Review* 68(2): 205–221.

Shields, P. (ed.) (2017) *Jane Addams: Progressive Pioneer of Peace, Philosophy, Sociology, Social Work and Public Administration*. Cham, Switzeland: Springer.

Shields, P. and J. Soeters (2013) 'Pragmatism, peacekeeping, and the constabulary force'. In S.J. Ralston (ed.), *Philosophical Pragmatism and International Relations: Essays for a Bold New World*. Lanham, MD: Lexington Books.

Shields, P. and J. Soeters (2017) 'Peaceweaving: Jane Addams, positive peace, and public administration'. *American Journal of Public Administration* 47(3): 323–339.

Stephan, M.J. and E. Chenoweth (2008) 'Why civil resistance works: the strategic logic of nonviolent conflict'. *International Security* 33(1): 7–44.

Teitler, G. (1977) *The Genesis of the Professional Officer's Corps*. Thousand Oaks, CA: Sage.

Williams, A.P. and B. Mengistu (2015) 'An exploration of the limitations of bureaucratic organizing in implementing contemporary peacebuilding'. *Cooperation and Conflict* 50(1): 3–28.

Wozniak, J.F. (2009) 'C. Wright Mills and higher immorality: implications for corporate crime, ethics, and peacemaking criminology'. *Crime, Law and Social Change* 51: 189–203.

6 W. E. B. Du Bois

Race, diversity and inclusion, in society and the military

W. E. B. Du Bois (1868–1963) has been proclaimed to be 'the first sociologist of race', and even though race relations in earlier times were much worse than they seem to be today, it may be safe to say that race continues to be a problem in societies all over the world (Nkomo, 2009). There are many examples to underline this contention. The racial background of many of today's tensions between the population and the police – in the USA and elsewhere – is just one of them. In the armed forces this may not be different, although Charles Moskos and others have contended that the US military organization works as a 'race equalizer', providing social mobility to African-American personnel that was absent in other sectors for too long. Even so, there is a long history of painful – and hopeful! – events since multi-racial integration began to develop in the military, in the USA and certainly also elsewhere in the world.

But first, let's turn to the life and works of W. E. B. Du Bois himself (e.g. Blackwell and Janowitz, 1974; Nkomo, 2009; Morris and Ghaziani, 2005; Morris, 2015). At the end of the nineteenth century Du Bois was among the first scholars in the USA to start working on something called sociology. Trained in the humanities and history in particular, he soon developed a penchant for modern social sciences, including the accompanying methodologies. This change in professional orientation was enhanced by his two-year stay in Berlin, where he studied under Gustav Schmoller and other famous professors and where he became a friend of Max Weber. He maintained friendly relations with Weber until the latter's untimely death in 1920; during this friendship he influenced Weber's thinking about race and ethnicity (Morris, 2015: 149–167).

Being black, it would have been difficult, not to say impossible, for Du Bois to acquire academic positions at the top-level research universities in the USA, despite the fact that he had obtained a Ph.D. from Harvard. He became a professor at Atlanta University in Georgia, where he founded the Atlanta Sociological Laboratory. This department turned out to be highly productive in studying African-American issues of all kinds, often with the help of volunteer researchers and field workers. Throughout his life Du Bois was endlessly looking for research funding that was often denied.

Shortly before he went to Atlanta he had been working on a study of the black community in Philadelphia (Du Bois, 1996 [1899]). Influenced by British examples and Jane Addams' work on urban neighborhoods in Chicago, *The Philadelphia Negro* is currently seen as the first true empirical sociological work, using mixed methodologies, on urban communities. It was published some twenty years before the famous *Polish Peasant* study of Polish immigrants appeared (Coser, 1977: 533). Interestingly, every sociology student is familiar with the latter study and most likely not with Du Bois' seminal study. Not surprisingly, Du Bois is not even mentioned once in Lewis Coser's *Masters of Sociological Thought* (1977; see also Morris, 2015: xv). It indicates the marginal and neglected role Du Bois was granted throughout his life and beyond, despite his academic achievements. Only rather recently has attention to his work been surging. So, what are these achievements?

His insights and contributions relate to general sociology, the sociology of race and more specifically to the sociology of the black – in today's phrasing African-American – community (Morris and Ghaziani, 2005: 51). He advocated that sociology should be developed on the basis of thorough field work using multiple methods instead of general theorizing that at best relies on quick observations from a 'car window'. Long before Merton, he pointed at the relevance of developing sociological theories of the middle range rather than pursuing grand abstract theories (Morris, 2015: 29).

As to the sociology of race, his main argument – now generally accepted, but certainly not received wisdom at the time – was that race is a socially constructed and dynamic category, and not something which is biologically defined and determined. Hence, he fought against implicit and explicit racism in society at large, but also against racist bias in the smaller world of sociologists themselves. Indeed, it is quite astonishing to identify the – at least implicit – racism in many sociologists' works of the early times. Next, Du Bois pointed at the 'color line' or *veil* that divides oppressed from dominant groups, which brings him close to Karl Marx's lines of thought. However, where Marx only had an eye for the horizontal line dividing the classes, Du Bois also saw a vertical fissure, a separation of classes by race, cutting across the economic layers that Marx had revealed (England and Warner, 2013: 963). The black community is in his view rooted in a diverse class structure and, hence, cannot be seen as an undifferentiated mass in a way Marx would indicate (Morris and Ghaziani, 2005: 51). The color line as coined by Du Bois could be seen in American society as well as on a global scale, particularly in the many nations under colonial rule and under the apartheid regime that was emerging at the time in South Africa (Du Bois, 1901; 1998; 1944).

Du Bois never tired of rejecting the idea of black inferiority, a common and persistent idea at the time. On the contrary, African-Americans possess unique gifts and cultural messages for the world, as he emphasized for instance in *The Souls of Black Folk*, a collection of his essays published as a book in 1903. The essays are about rural sociology, leadership, religion, education and of course race relations. A special essay in this small book is devoted to the 'Sorrow Songs', 'some echo of haunting melody from the only American music which welled up from black souls in the dark past' (Du Bois, 1969: i). It shows Du Bois is interested in music as a social phenomenon, as Max Weber was, but differently (Kemple, 2009).

These essays sharply contrast with a most critical essay he published as *The Souls of White Folk* (Du Bois, 1999 [1920]: 17–29), in which he condemned the assumed superiority of whites over others (Nkomo, 2009: 384). Given these features, the end goal for the black community is not assimilation – becoming similar to the dominating white people – but social development and emancipation (Morris and Ghaziani, 2005: 51).

Further points of attention in Du Bois' work are the intersection of race, class and gender, and his idea of the so-called *double consciousness* that black people are confronted with. With this concept Du Bois referred to

> a peculiar sensation, this double-consciousness, this sense of always looking at one's self through the eyes of others, of measuring one's soul by the tape of a world that looks on in amused contempt and pity. One ever feels his twoness, – an American, a Negro; two souls, two thoughts, two unreconciled strivings; two warring ideals in one dark body.
>
> (Du Bois, 1969 [1903]: 2)

Even though the tone is more dramatic (for understandable reasons!), it is not difficult to connect this analysis with the idea of the 'stranger' that was coined by Georg Simmel at roughly the same time.

Du Bois on the military

Du Bois did not often mention race issues in the military. However, he authored a monumental work on the historical events immediately following the Civil War that led to the official – even though in practice not complete – freeing of the slaves. The focus of this study was on 'the efforts and the experiences of the Negroes themselves' (Du Bois, 1998 [1935]: preface). The study was criticized by historians because of its factual errors and interpretive hyperbole, but it was also a pioneering study that 'can never be ignored' (Du Bois, 1998 [1935]: xv). The military naturally emerges in this study because of the Civil War itself. In the balance of power between the forces of the Northern and the Southern states as well as in the war's final outcome, the (former) slaves played an important role. Colonel Higginson's account of his leading the regiment of the first black soldiers – 'the first slave regiment' – during the latter part of the conflict gives an idea of their role and how it was perceived by a white officer who himself had been active in the Abolitionist movement (Wentworth Higginson, 2012 [1869]).

One more particular event deserves special mention. During the First World War, after the United States had decided to engage in the hostilities in Europe, the US government sought the consent and cooperation of the African-American community and its leadership. For this purpose a conference was organized to which leaders from the black community, including Du Bois, were invited. This cooperation was not self-evident because at that time the mob-lynching of blacks had reached a peak. Du Bois, who as we know was quite critical about race relations in his country, argued in a lead editorial comment to 'forget our special grievances and close our ranks shoulder to shoulder with our own white fellow citizens and the allied nations that are fighting for democracy' (Allen Jr, 1979: 25). This statement stood in sharp contrast to the resolution of the conference that called for a 'minimum of consideration' with respect to the grievances of the black community. Both positions had been penned by the same, ambivalent person: W. E. B. Du Bois (Allen Jr, 1979: 32).

Race relations in the US military

The history of race relations in the US military is a long one. Black soldiers participated in US military organizations from the nation's very beginning, and even before its inception (Nalty, 1986; Sibley Butler, 1988). During the Revolutionary War against the British over 5,000 black men served with the American troops. As we just saw, former slaves played an important role in the Civil War as well. Nearly 180,000 blacks fought on the side of the Union, in 120 separate army units named the 'United States Colored Troops' (Sibley Butler, 1988: 118). In the ensuing wars with Native Americans (the 'Indian Wars'), the war on Cuban soil, via the First World War to the Second World War, black soldiers carried large shares of the burden, always in segregated units. In the intervening periods, when peace reemerged, the number of black soldiers diminished considerably, which in a Duboissian sociology could be seen as a manifestation of discrimination.

During World War II the number of black soldiers rose to 900,000 enlisted men. In this war the forces had their first experiences of racial integration. During the Battle of the Bulge in the Belgian Ardennes in the weeks around Christmas 1944, the army asked for volunteers from black support units that were located in the immediate surroundings. Thousands of them responded and volunteered for the front line. The ensuing battle demonstrated black soldiers' excellent combat performance, without serious friction in cooperating with the white troops. These interactions have been studied in *The American Soldier*, the giant research project to which we will turn in Chapter 9 on Morris Janowitz (Stouffer et al., 1949). The so-called 'Tuskegee Airmen' were another famous example of black military men's superior combat performance in the Second World War, in this case the African-American pilots who escorted bombers deep into Germany (Moskos, 2007: 15–16). Until the beginning of the war many white Americans believed blacks were not capable of performing a difficult task such as flying a plane. The biological thinking about races that Du Bois condemned so furiously was still alive in the years preceding the Second World War. Only real experience could prevent the consequences of the Thomas theorem that is so famous in sociology: 'If men define situations as real, they are real in their consequences' (Coser, 1977: 521).

If decision makers and policy makers are convinced blacks are not capable of flying a plane, they will not be allowed to undergo pilot training and hence will not fly a plane. Black 'inferiority' is a social construction, as Du Bois argued. Yet, this social construction ended in World War II.

In 1948 President Truman decided to desegregate the armed forces; this new policy was tested during the Korean War. The experiences with racial integration were favourable, but this racial peace ended in the 1960s. Over the course of the Vietnam War, white–black polarization increased, with clashes occurring throughout the services all over the world (Moskos, 2007: 16). Resistance to orders among enlisted men and even (quasi-) mutinies occurred on a fairly broad scale, and black soldiers were among the most rebellious (Cortright, 1975: 39, 201, and further). African-American soldiers were militant leaders of the GI resistance, which could be seen as a response to perceived discrimination and unequal opportunities for minority service-men. The resistance was not confined to political and social dynamics inside the military. World boxing champion Muhammed Ali was the most famous conscientious objector, and he declared that he 'ain't got no quarrel with them Viet Cong', while in the same statement referring to the denigration of 'so-called Negro people' in his home country. We will delve somewhat deeper into the issue of rebellion during the Vietnam War in Chapter 11 on Cornelis Lammers.

Obviously, this could not continue, and the Vietnam War turned out to be a watershed experience. Since the 1980s, after the all-volunteer force had been introduced, race relations have generally been more positive. The number of black soldiers in the US forces has increased over the years, even leading to a degree of over-representation as compared to the black population in American society at large (Janowitz and Moskos, 1974). Survey studies conducted among US military personnel in Somalia, Bosnia and Iraq showed that interracial cooperation is 'stronger in the field than in garrison, stronger on duty than off, stronger on post than in the world beyond the base' (Moskos, 2007: 16–17). What is more important, African-Americans have been successful in climbing the military hierarchy up to the highest levels (Moskos and Sibley Butler, 1996). As Charles Moskos famously put it: 'The armed forces are the only place in American society where whites are routinely bossed around by blacks' (Moskos, 2007: 17). W. E. B. Du Bois might be satisfied, at least to a certain degree. However, despite the progress that has occurred, James Burk and Evelyn Espinoza (2012) discovered that there still is racial bias and institutional racism in three aspects of personnel relations in the US military. These pertain to officer promotions, administering military justice and care for wounded minority veterans, the latter because of barriers blocking entry into the veterans' health care system. No evidence could be found either in the case of entry into the military or in the risk of death in combat (Burk and Espinoza, 2012: 414).

Apparently, there are still tensions that also appear at the intersection of race and gender, a point that Du Bois often referred to.

Graduation at West Point

A picture of African-American female junior officers finishing their studies at the US Army Academy at West Point in the spring of 2016 shows them holding up their fists in a way that seems to refer to historical black protest movements in the United States. It has been argued there may be a symbolic connection with the Black Power protest during the Olympic Games in 1968, and others have related the picture to Beyoncé's endorsement of the 'Black Lives Matter' movement at her Super Bowl performance a couple of months earlier in February. The picture of the West Point graduates raised a discussion as some veterans and others argued that it was an expression of a 'divided army'. But then it may be good to go back to World War II, where African-American soldiers helped obtain the victory over the Nazis through participation in direct combat. Brenda Moore (1996) described in her beautiful book the story of the only African-American members of the Women Army Corps (WAC) stationed overseas during World War II. That is a story of success but also of the discrimination women faced because of their race and gender. The book provides indications of the members' united front in their long struggle for equal rights, while they were actively supporting the operations to drive out the Nazis from Europe.

It should be kept in mind that African-Americans are not the only minority group in American society and the American military. In particular Hispanics (Americans of Latin-American descent), but also Asian-Americans and Native Americans constitute considerable proportions of the US military's work force (Rohall et al., 2017). At the end of this chapter we will see one example of how Native American 'warriors' have contributed to success in American military history.

Minority relations in other armed forces

Challenging race and group relationships is obviously not limited to the United States and its armed forces. For centuries, European nations such as the United Kingdom, France, Spain, the Netherlands, Germany and Belgium have colonized other parts of the world, which led to the creation of colonial forces or the integration of soldiers from colonized nations into the European militaries. This was based on what may be called the 'ethnic draft', which was based on either coercion, ideology and/or contract (Peled, 1994). Ethnic groups in the colonized areas were differentiated by their usefulness and reliability for the colonizers. Some were considered less valuable and trustworthy than others, whereas some groups were believed to be 'martial races' (e.g. Enloe, 1980).

Like the African-American soldiers, these 'ethnic' soldiers have often carried large burdens in battle. A famous example is the role played by Algerian and Senegalese soldiers siding with the French troops – their colonizers – on the battlefields of the First World War in France and Belgium. Other colonial troops – for example the Nepalese soldiers – the Gurkhas – who formed part of the British army – were involved in those battles as well (Koller, 2008). The huge sacrifices made by these minority soldiers are not often acknowledged. And they repeatedly encountered the same sort of racism, though sometimes characterized as 'benign', that African-American soldiers faced in the US forces (Lunn, 1999; Wentworth Higginson, 2012 [1869]). Du Bois himself regularly pointed out the similarities between the problematic race relations in America and those in European colonies all over the world, in Africa, Asia and Latin America.

A striking example pertains to today's armed forces in the former Spanish colonies in Latin America. In Bolivia and Ecuador, the integration of previously marginalized indigenous populations into state institutions in general and the military in particular, has been one of the main challenges to democratic governance (Selmesky, 2007). Since these nations became independent in the early nineteenth century, recruitment of native men for the armed forces has not been self-evident. Given the great diversity of the indigenous populations themselves, the groups that were deemed trustworthy were recruited, whereas those believed to be a potential state security threat once they had been trained as soldiers were excluded or marginalized (Selmesky, 2007: 50). If enlisted, *Indigenas* were not always been given equal treatment, also because of racial prejudices. Admission to officer training for native men was difficult until the 1950s and even after that time indigenous recruits faced unpleasant experiences during their time at military college. To mention just one aspect, indigenous cadets felt often pressed to change their Indian names to Spanish ones, as a sort of 'cultural camouflage' (Selmesky, 2007: 58). The result has been – at least until 2003 – that the conscripts were mostly from indigenous groups whereas the officers were predominantly of European descent. From the 8th to the 17th of October 2003, during 'La Guerra del Gaz' in Bolivia, this situation culminated in a crisis whereby the army killed tens of indigenous protesters – comparable to the 'Bloody Sunday' killings in Northern Ireland of 1972. The orders had come from the officers who were predominantly not of indigenous descent (Radio Pachamama, 2003). Since then the situation has changed, also politically, as the civil rights of the indigenous people have improved considerably and their position in the military has been enhanced.

On a global scale there are many such stories to tell. Among them, the establishment of integrated armed forces in South Africa in the post-apartheid period deserves special mention. As said before, Du Bois rightly compared the race relations in the USA to the tensions in countries colonized by Europeans. In South Africa Dutch citizens and British troops had colonized large territories and fought bitter wars with each other, at the cost of the living opportunities of the indigenous populations. This led to the apartheid regime, which was abolished as recently as 1991. One of the consequences of the events in 1991 was a total overhaul of the South African military. It had been a white minority conscript force, where blacks were permitted to serve in separate ethnic battalions but were not conscripted nor permitted to become officers. This composition and the army's fight inside the country against the resistance to apartheid created a large distance vis-à-vis the native population groups; the armed forces were increasingly seen as the enemy. The policies put in place after the abolition of apartheid led to the integration of all the different forces that had been engaged in the resistance, the so-called revolutionary forces. The end of apartheid also produced a policy of affirmative action, valuing and supporting people from the non-white communities. But there were – and still are – serious problems. The diversity of the population groups in this large country is significant (there are eleven languages) and affirmative action may lead to a kind of politicization of the armed forces that may hinder the maturation of their professional-bureaucratic character that aims to emphasize qualification, experience and merit (e.g. Heinecken and Soeters, 2018).

A final example may be the ethnic composition of the Russian armed forces that has shown remarkable developments over time (Curran and Ponomareff, 1982). Russia and the former Soviet Union included a number of non-Russian population groups such as those in the Baltic republics and in the Caucasus. During World War II the Red Army was officially composed of ethnically integrated units but because of manpower shortages the formation of national units in, among others, Estonia, Lithuania and Latvia, was allowed. However, these were considered unreliable. Also, reserve units, such as in Ukraine, were almost entirely composed of ethnically homogeneous host nationals who were admitted in order to do their military duty close to their home environment. In general, non-Russian units were present on a number of important fronts, but their reliability and effectiveness remained uncertain. After the war, national units survived until the 1950s when they were disbanded and replaced by fully ethnically integrated units. The reason was that native Georgian troops refused to fire on their own population at the time of the Tbilisi uprising in 1956. Today Russia has become much less ethnically diverse after the fall of the Soviet Union. Nonetheless, all citizens irrespective of their origin, religion or other background characteristics are assigned to integrated units outside their own territories.

The benefits of cultural diversity.

Du Bois ceaselessly argued that African-Americans were not inferior to the whites who occupied the dominant positions in America's social and economic life. He pointed out that black people had unique gifts and cultural messages for the world (*The Souls of Black Folk*, Du Bois, 1969). This is a point that today's militaries need to keep in mind, as it does not apply only to African-Americans. Today's militaries all over the world can benefit a lot from paying attention to diversity and inclusion policies (e.g. Kümmel, 2012). There are a number of reasons why forces that consist of both men and women, or people differing in colour, religion, regional origin, language group, age and sexual orientation, would do better than 'mono-composed' forces that do not reflect such diversity (Van der Meulen and Soeters, 2007).

In the first place, diversity and inclusion policies help to close the gap between the military and the society at large, given the fact that society at large in most nations is increasingly becoming diverse in composition. This contributes to a force's legitimacy and reputation. In today's world the military simply cannot afford to be disregarded, to be seen as of secondary importance, let alone to be perceived as the enemy of the people or the enemy of a part of the population. The so-called 'civil service issue' – some population groups dominating others in governmental institutions, such as the military – is at the heart of most civil upheaval across the globe. To help prevent this, the military needs to align with (increasing) diversity in society, as we saw in the chapter on Max Weber discussing the necessary bureaucratic nature of the military. Second, diversity and inclusion policies are conducive to filling the need for military manpower that in many nations no longer can be recruited via a conscript system. In an all-volunteer system newly enlisted men and women need to be recruited in an open labour market, in competition with other employers. It is in the military's own interest to draw from a pool of potential recruits that is as large as possible. Third, increasing the diversity of the armed forces may well help to boost their effectiveness, as the example of the Navajo code talkers during the battle of Iwo Jima during World War II shows. These were Native American, Navajo soldiers of the US Marine Corps, who devised a complex code derived from their own language. The messages communicated in this code could be relayed within minutes, but could not be deciphered by the Japanese military. It helped the Americans win that battle (Durrett, 1998).

There are also other, more recent examples that illustrate the benefits of a diverse workforce in military operations.

Dutch Muslim soldiers on deployment in Muslim societies

Over the last few decades, Western militaries' operations have been conducted in societies with a partially or predominantly Islamic population: Bosnia, Iraq, Afghanistan, Mali and elsewhere. As the social and cultural distance between Western soldiers and the host population in those regions is quite large, it may help to have military men and women 'on board' who are less distanced from the locals. An exploratory study among Dutch Muslim soldiers on deployment in Muslim societies gives some indication of how this works in practice (Bosman et al., 2008). Those soldiers did not indicate that they had to struggle with multiple identities. First and foremost they were Dutch professional military people. Nonetheless, they sometimes experienced confrontations with friends or relatives who questioned their loyalty when fighting 'Muslim brothers'. In the area of operations, different types of encounter with host nationals could be distinguished, ranging from the positive encounter occurring because of the Muslim soldiers' intimate knowledge of (religious) habits and language expressions to the outright hostile encounter, in which surviving is the main logic of action. The overall contribution was more than constructive. In the main, one can argue that the connection between in-ranks' cultural diversity and cross-cultural competence is likely to be beneficial to the outcome of an operation (Also: Hajjar, 2010).

Faits divers

In line with the insights regarding group dynamics provided by Georg Simmel, one can say that number distributions in units create specific behavioural and social dynamics that are relevant to diversity and inclusion policies. Rosabeth Moss Kanter (1977: 206–242) made clear that very small minorities in skewed groups (so-called 'tokens') face special attention and pressure at work because they are more visible, they contrast more with the overwhelming majority, and they are more easily stereotyped. Despite these characteristics those tokens are also more accepted because they do not pose a threat to the majority as long as their views and actions are in line with the ideas of the established group. This may alter when more balanced subgroups and large minorities (35–65 per cent, 40–60 per cent or 50–50 per cent) develop, as these could become strong enough to be a competitor to the other majority group. Identity clashes could develop as a consequence.

If 'tokenism' or competitive subgroup dynamics occur, it is important to notice this and to be aware that diversity policies are not necessarily the same as inclusion policies. There are three variants. If the members of the minority groups are urged to conform with the dominant culture (Bolivian cadets taking Spanish names, for instance), one speaks of *assimilation*. If the minority members are just valued because of the contribution they make, but are not seen as insiders (host nationals who are hired as interpreters in military operations without being granted military status), one speaks of *differentiation*. *Inclusion* only occurs when members of minority groups in organizations are treated as insiders and valued because of the contribution they bring and when they are at the same time allowed and even encouraged to retain their uniqueness within the organization (Shore et al., 2011: 1266). One can clearly see the connection with the typology we saw in the chapter on Emile Durkheim when we discussed the three ways to organize multinational military cooperation: assimilation, separation (= differentiation) and integration (= inclusion).

Finally, it needs to be acknowledged that next to benefits, uncomfortable issues that are associated with diversity may also arise in the military. If 'the power of identity' (Castells, 1997) inside the organization becomes too great, the autonomy of commanders to decide and operate as they see fit from an operational point of view may decline. Yagil Levy (2014) analysed how this phenomenon occurs in the Israeli Defence Force since religious soldiers – expressing their own ideas about how things should be done – have entered the combat units in larger numbers. Following Simmel and Kanter, such changes in numbers may create considerable subgroup tensions with operational consequences. In addition, members of very small minority groups ('tokens') may begin to feel so stereotyped and pressured when they are not capable of adapting to the dominant group that they may start using violence against their colleagues. In the US forces there have been such incidents, but fortunately very rarely. Sometimes diversity is a mixed blessing at best.

Conclusion

Today's race- and diversity relations seem to be much less challenging than at the time W. E. B. Du Bois developed his insights. The integration and inclusion of minorities in the workforce are at the top of the policy agendas of most work organizations, including the police and the military. However, racist bias and tensions in society at large and in organizations have not disappeared, as so many incidents all over the globe continuously show. Besides, the *color line* or the *veil* may still exist in more subtle forms. They may be hidden in personality tests, profiles and even sociological analyses that intend to be objective but may inadvertently create new divisions. 'Sorry, but you did not pass the test.' 'Sorry, but you do not fit into the profile for this position.' The *veil* may then turn out to be 'discrimination with a smile' (England and Warner, 2013). Du Bois' work continues to be relevant.

Bibliography

Allen, E.Jr (1979) '"Close ranks": Major Joel E. Springarn and the two souls of Dr. W. E.B. Du Bois'. *Contributions in Black Studies – a Journal in African and Afro-American Studies* 3(art. 4): 25–38.

Blackwell, J.E. and M. Janowitz (eds) (1974) *Black Sociologists: Historical and Contemporary Perspectives.* Chicago and London: University of Chicago Press.

Bosman, F., F. Ait Bari and J. Soeters (2008) 'Dutch Muslim soldiers during peace operations in Muslim societies'. *International Peacekeeping* 15(5): 695–705.

Burk, J. and E. Espinoza (2012) 'Race relations in the U.S. military'. *Annual Review of Sociology* 38: 401–422.

Castells, M. (1997) *The Power of Identity: The Information Age: Economy, Society and Culture.* Vol. II. Malden MA and Oxford: Blackwell.

Cortright, D. (1975) *Soldiers in Revolt: GI Resistance during the Vietnam War.* Chicago: Haymarket Books.

Coser, L. (1977) *Masters of Sociological Thought: Ideas in Historical and Social Context.* 2nd edn. Long Grove, IL: Waveland Press.

Curran, S.L. and D. Ponomareff (1982) *Managing the Ethnic Factor in the Russian and Soviet Armed Forces.* Santa Monica, CA: Rand Corporation.

Du Bois, W.E.B. (1996 [1899]) *The Philadelphia Negro: A Social Study.* Philadelphia: University of Pennsylvania Press.

Du Bois, W.E.B. (1901) 'The relation of the negroes to the whites in the South'. *Annals of the American Academy of Political and Social Science* 18: 121–140.

Du Bois, W.E.B. (1969 [1903]) *The Souls of Black Folk.* New York: Signet Classic.

Du Bois, W.E.B. (1999 [1920]) *Dark Water: Voices from within the Veil*. Mineola, NY: Dover.

Du Bois, W.E.B. (1925) 'Worlds of color'. *Foreign Affairs* 3(3): 423–444.

Du Bois, W.E.B. (1998 [1935]) *Black Reconstruction in America, 1860–1880*. New York: Free Press.

Du Bois, W.E.B. (1944) 'Prospects of a world without race conflict'. *American Journal of Sociology* 49(5): 450–456.

Durrett, D. (1998) *Unsung Heroes of World War II: The Story of the Navajo Code Talkers*. New York: Facts on File.

England, L. and W.K. Warner (2013) 'W.E.B. Du Bois: reform, will, and the veil'. *Social Forces* 91(3): 955–973.

Enloe, C. (1980) *Ethnic Soldiers. State Security in Divided Societies*. Athens, GA: University of Georgia Press.

Hajjar, R.M. (2010) 'A new angle on the U.S. military's emphasis on developing cross-cultural competence: connecting in-ranks cultural diversity to cross-cultural competence'. *Armed Forces and Society* 36(2): 247–263.

Heinecken, L. and J. Soeters (2018) 'Managing diversity: from exclusion to inclusion and valuing difference'. In G. Caforio (ed.), *The Handbook of the Sociology of the Military*. Cham, Switzerland: Springer.

Janowitz, M. and C. Moskos (1974) 'Racial composition in the all-volunteer force'. *Armed Forces and Society* 1(1), 109–123.

Kemple, Th. (2009) 'Weber/Simmel/DuBois: musical thirds of classical sociology'. *Journal of Classical Sociology* 9(2): 187–207.

Koller, Chr. (2008) 'The recruitment of colonial troops in Africa and Asia and their deployment in Europe during the First World War'. *Immigrants and Minorities* 26(1/2): 111–133.

Kümmel, G. (ed.) (2012) *Die Truppe wird Bunter: Streitkräfte und Minderkeiten*. Baden-Baden, Germany: Nomos.

Levy, Y. (2014) 'The theocratization of the Israeli military'. *Armed Forces and Society* 40(2): 269–294.

Lunn, J. (1999) '"Les races guerrières": racial preconceptions in the French military about West African soldiers during the First World War'. *Journal of Contemporary History* 34(4): 517–536.

Merton, R. (1968) *Social Theory and Social Structure*. Enlarged edn. New York: Free Press.

Moore, B. (1996) *To Serve My Country, To Serve My Race: The Story of the Only African American WACs Stationed Overseas during World War II*. New York: New York University Press.

Morris, A.D. (2015) *The Scholar Denied: W.E.B. Du Bois and the Birth of Modern Sociology*. Oakland: University of California Press.

Morris, A. and A. Ghaziani (2005) 'DuBoisian sociology: a watershed of professional and public sociology'. *Souls* 7(3–4): 47–54.

Moskos, C. (2007) 'Diversity in the armed forces of the United States'. In J. Soeters and J. van der Meulen (eds), *Cultural Diversity in the Armed Forces: An International Comparison*. London and New York: Routledge.

Moskos, C. and J. Sibley Butler (1996) *All That We Can Be: Black Leadership and Racial Integration the Army Way*. New York: Basic Books.

Moss Kanter, R. (1977) *Men and Women of the Corporation*. New York: Basic Books.

Nalty, B.C. (1986) *Strength for the Fight: A History of Black Americans in the Military*. New York: Free Press.

Nkomo, S. (2009) 'The sociology of race: the contributions of W.E.B. Du Bois'. In P.S. Adler (ed.), *The Oxford Handbook of Sociology and Organization Studies*. Oxford: Oxford University Press, pp. 375–398.

Peled, A. (1994) 'Force, ideology and contract: the history of ethnic conscription'. *Ethnic and Racial Studies* 17(1): 61–78.

Radio Pachamama (2003) *Para que el Tiempo No Borre la Memoria … No a la Impunidad*. CD recordings of radio reports.

Rohall, D.E., M.G. Ender and M.D. Matthews (eds) (2017) *Inclusion in the American Military: A Force for Diversity*. Lanham, MD: Lexington Books.

Selmesky, B.R. (2007) 'Indigenous integration into the Bolivian and Ecuadorian armed forces'. In J. Soeters and J. van der Meulen (eds), *Cultural Diversity in the Armed Forces: An International Comparison*. London and New York: Routledge.

Shore, L.M., A.E. Randel, B.G. Chung, M.A. Dean, K. Holcombe Ehrhart and G. Singh (2011) 'Inclusion and diversity in work groups: a review and model for future research'. *Journal of Management* 17(4): 1262–1289.

Sibley Butler, J. (1988) 'Race relations in the military'. In Ch.C. Moskos and F.R. Wood (eds), *The Military: More than just a Job?* Washington, DC: Pergamon-Brassey's.

Stouffer, S.A., E.A. Suchman, L.C. DeVinney, S.A. Star and R.M. Williams (1949) *The American Soldier: Adjustment during Army Life*. Princeton, NJ: Princeton University Press.

Van der Meulen, J. and J. Soeters (2007) 'Introduction'. In J. Soeters and J. van der Meulen (eds), *Cultural Diversity in the Armed Forces: An International Comparison*. London and New York: Routledge.

Wentworth Higginson, Th. (2012 [1869]) *Army Life in a Black Regiment*. Cambridge, MA: Riverside Press.

7 Erving Goffman

Total institutions, interaction rituals, street-level bureaucrats

The Canadian sociologist Erving Goffman (1922–1982) is not very well known for his contributions to the study of the military. His work refers to many sectors of society, but not the military. Nevertheless, it is useful for a better understanding of some of the dynamics within the armed forces, as will become clear in this chapter. Goffman uses a dramaturgical perspective, focusing on the concrete interactions between people who are 'on stage', which means they perform in an organizational context (e.g. Turner, 1991; Burns, 1992; Manning, 2014).

His work is important from an academic sociological point of view, as it shows the strengths of observations of everyday life, and it paved the way to the study of emotions in organizations. We will meet this phenomenon when we discuss the work of Arlie Russell Hochschild in Chapter 12. But Goffman's work has also gained considerable influence among the public at large, particularly when it comes to understanding the organizational dynamics of closed organizations, i.e. organizations where the inmates are not supposed or allowed to leave. The comedy-drama film *One Flew over the Cuckoo's Nest* about the experiences of patients in a mental health institution helps bring Goffman's analysis very much alive. The military relevance of this work and his interaction analysis is unquestionable, as we are about to see.

Admission to the military

Goffman's analysis (1991 [1961]) of the closed world of mental health institutions, homes for the aged, boarding schools, prisons, or monasteries, reminds us of Simmel's analysis of secret societies that we discussed earlier. These are worlds with 'high walls', whether physical, symbolic or both (Scott, 2009: 278). This analysis has been immediately recognized as being of ultimate importance to the military. Goffman's concept of the *total institution* and the way new recruits are socialized, assimilated and controlled in such institutions has remarkable applications to military academies, garrisons, bases, warships and gated camps in deployments abroad. True, there may be some relaxation of rules and practices in these institutions nowadays, but the general idea still applies.

As we saw before in the analysis of military culture, the military tends to work and live on islands in wider society, islands that are very well guarded against outsiders. This happens for reasons of security – no one would want to see a terrorist enter a garrison – but particularly to develop and maintain the military culture and its various manifestations. Here Goffman connects with Durkheim's work on the *conscience collective*, i.e. the collective mindset or institutional culture of societies, or in this case military communities.

In these closed communities, a small supervisory staff plays a dominant role. Unlike the inmates, the staff employees are allowed to leave the institution after working hours. They teach new recruits the armed forces' *rules of the game* from the moment the newcomers have stepped into the military world. Newcomers who appear not to fit into the organization's regime are excluded, formally or informally, or they exclude themselves in the very first period after having entered the military organization. This *rite de passage* is a high-pressure process of selection and self-selection, which culminates in a 'baptizing' ceremony. All of it very much resembles the practices that all 'total institutions' use to incorporate, assimilate and discipline new inmates, as Erving Goffman described and analysed so famously.

Goffman distinguishes the following steps in the process of admission, in creating the conditions through which recruits are able to internalize the specificities of military culture:

- The process starts with the supervisory staff stripping away the support of the social arrangements of the recruits' home world, including their clothing which is replaced by institutional clothing (uniforms), and new haircuts; within hours a certain de-personalization takes place; this first stage is characterized by complete isolation, in which the recruit is forbidden to communicate with people from the outside world including their families; in many of today's armed forces the recruits must hand in their mobile phones during the first period of basic training (also: Arkin and Dobrofsky, 1978).

- This first period furthermore consists of admission procedures such as photographing, fingerprinting, assigning numbers and listing personal possessions for storage; this period is accompanied by series of abasements, degradations and humiliations by the supervisory staff; the process is referred to as 'the welcome' or as 'mortification of the self' and in fact it is a 'clean break with the past' (Goffman, 1991: 24ff; Dornbusch, 1954). Even the recruits' names may be dropped as they can be changed into nicknames, replaced by the family names only, or altered into completely new names that refer to dominant groups, as we saw in the case of the Bolivian army (see Chapter 6); in this first stage the recruits are deprived of all sorts of privacy.

- Gradually the new recruits become ready to start living by the rules of the house and they learn to speak the institution's lingo, which provides new anchors in life. Rewards or privileges – having a coffee break, an evening out – are held out in exchange for obedience to the staff (Goffman, 1991: 51ff).

- A more or less formal end of this period is the 'baptizing ceremony'; during a well-defined period of days or weeks the senior inmates, who have been through all this before, take over the role of the supervisory staff (even though staff personnel keep an eye on what is going on) in first degrading and subsequently re-installing the recruits into their new military roles.
- In the same period, both a feeling of fraternization among the recruits develops as well as a sort of social differentiation among the recruits through which 'right guys and girls' are distinguished from recruits with less status; hence, cliques among inmates start to develop.
- Individual recruits may develop various sorts of adaptations: from 'situational withdrawal' – reducing participation to a minimum – or rebellion against the staff, to preferring institutional life over the outside world and playing the role of the perfect 'inmate', hence becoming better than the staff. The more usual reaction, however, is 'playing it cool', which is the opportunistic and calm combination of all kinds of reactions dependent on the situation at hand (Goffman, 1991: 60ff); this coping style is likely to lead to successfully passing basic training and corresponding military initiation rites.
- The 'survivors' among the recruits have gradually learned how to behave themselves and they are regarded with corresponding respect, even by the supervisory staff. They have also learned the 'art of silence' to protect the organization's secrecy (Simmel, 1906: 474). The organization of annual ceremonies by the inmates illustrates their new status and position vis-à-vis the supervisory staff, the lower ranking ones in particular. They were the ones who made life so difficult in the beginning of their military career. Higher-ranking officers remain out of reach in all of this.

Even though Goffman applied these process characteristics to all sorts of total institutions, it is likely that there is a differentiation among the various types of such institutions. As Mouzelis (1971) stressed, young monks may experience head shaving in a different way to military cadets. Monks are likely to perceive this as a heavenly experience, whereas cadets may perceive such a haircut to be alienating or even degrading. Other refinements, pertaining to power distribution and other organizational characteristics, may help to better analyse variations in admission and initiation processes in different national armed forces and services. Despite the many similarities derived from a common supranational military culture, there are also differences between the initiation rites of for example the French and the American military academies (e.g. Weber, 2012). Special operations forces have their own peculiarities in initiating new recruits that differ from other services' practices.

There is also a time-related aspect. For sure, today's human resources policies in the military, reflecting wider society's concerns, contribute to open up training and educational institutions and align their initiation practices with what is nowadays accepted in society at large. Total institutions in the military therefore tend to become 'quasi total institutions' (Soeters, 2018). Initiating practices in the military are no longer as severe and degrading as they once were, which may be seen as another manifestation of Norbert Elias' process of civilization that we will discuss later. Debates about the legitimacy of these practices remain, most likely due to this civilizing process.

Military 'duties' in the Russian barracks

Belgian military sociologist Joris van Bladel (2003) analysed the process of new recruits becoming part of the informal culture in a Russian barracks. In this analyses he used Goffman's ideas about the total institution. In general, he saw similar patterns to Goffman in his construction of the inmate's world. However, there are differences.

In the Russian armed forces the system of the *dedovshchina* is important. It refers to an informal hierarchical structure primarily based on seniority among the conscript soldiers themselves. 'The rule of the grandfathers' is an involuntary process of fraternization. The longer the period one has been in the military (during a 2-year conscription period), the higher ranked one is and the more power one has. Seniority goes together with authority, which in fact is a very common aspect of military bureaucracies. The dynamics are essentially similar to what happens in other militaries but they are more severe.

Being senior may include the power to steal from the younger ones or make them beg for money that they correspondingly have to hand over. In the Russian army scarcity of (luxury) food, beverages and cigarettes is a fairly persistent phenomenon. That is what makes these 'power games' so unavoidable, often leading to violence among the conscripts themselves. Those conscripts who are physically strong and know how to use their fists may escape from the seniors' practices. Also, self-organization among the conscripts based on regional bonding may hinder the impact of the seniority system among the soldiers.

A way to reduce the impact of this system is to improve communications between soldiers and the corps of NCOs and officers. Conscripts who feel threatened in barracks should have the opportunity to talk confidentially with their formal superior.

Interaction rituals and language mediation

Next to his work on asylums, Goffman's theories about the presentation of self in everyday life and the corresponding interaction rituals (Collins, 2004) have proven to be valuable (Giddens and Sutton, 2013). They are particularly useful in analysing how military personnel interact with host nationals when on missions abroad. This goes from top-level commanders dealing with host national authorities such as mayors, governors and ministers, to infantry soldiers on patrol trying to talk to and have fun with kids on the streets. In Chapter 4 we have seen how the selection of people with whom we interact is decisive with regards to the effectiveness of that interaction. Simmel and followers showed how, in choosing whom we interact with, the 'strength of weak ties' should be balanced with the 'weakness of strong ties'. Through Goffman's work we can now better understand how the interaction itself determines what results are achieved while interacting with the other(s).

A main point in Goffman's analysis is that individuals will try to control interactions; they will try to control the responses made by the other(s). All participants in an interaction play their own game and all players have their own particular interests. Hence, interactions between people are usually 'strategic interactions' (Burns, 1992; Hoedemaekers and Soeters, 2009). Information and expressive behaviour can be manipulated, distorted or concealed by one party and uncovered or extracted and interpreted or misinterpreted by the other (Burns, 1992: 59). Interactions always contain combinations of trust and control between people. Goffman uses these notions particularly in relation to what has been written about espionage, smuggling and criminal conspiracies. Not only is the connection of these activities to military intelligence not that distant, but the relevance may be closer to everyday military practices – particularly while on mission abroad – than one would think at first sight.

Before we get to this point, it is important to note one more element of Goffman's work: his face theory (Goffman, 1967: 5–46). Goffman (1967: 5) defines *face* as: 'an image of self delineated in terms of approved social attributes'. In *face keeping*, people attempt to protect or save their own or some else's face or image. In an interaction, people do not want to lose face, which implies that it is not appropriate to say whatever comes to one's mind in any situation. Sometimes for reasons of deference it is even required to state something in a special way ('Dear Excellency'). That is because harming an individual's face could lead to harming one's own face, and this could create feelings of embarrassment and discomfort (Goffman, 1956). This is more likely to happen in situations of high social pressure, where self-restraint in the Eliasian meaning of the word is a prerequisite (Kuzmics, 1991). Politeness, therefore, is a valued feature in such interaction. *Face threatening acts* should be avoided or mitigated as much as possible. This applies all the more in collectivist cultures in the Middle East and Asia, where losing face is considered a serious and pervasive problem, more so – as it appears – than in the West (Hoedemaekers and Soeters, 2009).

All of this is relevant when studying the interaction between Western military people on mission and host nationals, military or civilian. These interactions are difficult enough by themselves, but they are even more complicated for linguistic reasons. One cannot expect host nationals to speak a Western language – English usually – in an appropriate manner, and it is almost inconceivable that a Western soldier would speak Arabic, Pashtun, Farsi, Swahili, Hindi or Urdu, for example; even expressing oneself in French, which is the lingua franca of many African nations, or Spanish, the dominant language in Latin America, is usually asking too much.

This implies that interpreters or military linguists enter the field of operations (also: Hajjar, 2017). Military linguists come in three categories. They may be Westerners who have studied relevant non-Western languages at home; those from host nations who migrated in an earlier period to the Western country and became citizens of that country; or host nationals recruited in the area of operations itself. Obviously these three categories are quite different in terms of rank and position in the military organization.

Host nationals who are recruited in the area of operations generally do not have a formal rank inside the military organization, which means that they can be seen as 'involved outsiders'. More than anyone else they are 'strangers' in the Simmelian sense. Such interpreters are likely to be trusted and mistrusted at the same time, both by the military who hire them and by the host national community from which they originate and in which they live. The problem generally does not emerge in the interaction with military people with whom they work closely (e.g. Hajjar, 2017); rather, the average soldier is likely to treat the local interpreters with indifference, sometimes giving them the cold shoulder because they are seen as competitors. On the other hand, the people to whom they belong may start seeing them as traitors (Pouligny, 2006: 95) and threaten to retaliate. Interpreters' personal lives may therefore be in danger, which is why they often hide the fact that they do this job; the people in their communities, including their own family, are not supposed to know they work for the foreign military. All of this is nicely summarized in an old English proverb: 'he who speaks two languages is a knave' (Simmel, 1955: 141).

Hence, ties with both sides may develop into 'torturing ties', as the interpreter is linked to two groups or cliques that are not connected or even averse to one another (see Figure 7.1). The problem is that each group requires the

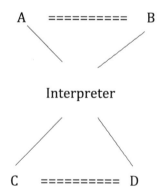

Figure 7.1 Simmelian ties, indicating that A and B belong to one group or clique and C and D to another
Source: Adapted from Krackhardt, 1999: 190.

intermediary, in this case the interpreter, to conform to its own norms. These cross-pressures tend to tear the intermediary apart; hence, the relations with both sides are 'torturing ties' (Krackhardt, 1999). This is the most tragic situation.

There are also other roles and positions, however. In accordance with Simmel's analysis the interpreter may also play the role of the mediator, the *tertius iungens*, the one who makes the opposite sides join and helps them to engage in common innovations (Obstfeld, 2005). The intermediary, in this case the interpreter, may also hold the two groups together, as a child may prevent a marriage from falling apart. He or she may also be the very opposite, i.e. the troublemaker, or be the *tertius gaudens*, the 'laughing third one' who profits from both sides and is able to manipulate them (Coser, 1977; Moss Kanter and Khurana, 2009). In analysing these different outcomes it matters whether the triad is a permanent, a temporary or an ending constellation. In general, however, as Simmel pointed out, the triad is rather different from the dyad as it indicates transition, conciliation and the absence of absolute contrast (De Jong, 2007: 151).

Perhaps because of this variety of roles that the 'third one' may play, people want to be interpreters. Even if the stressful, 'torturing' impact of the job is high, some people choose to act as interpreters for the military for a number of reasons. They may simply want to make a living with their language skills; they may have ideological reasons in endorsing the military's stated objective to bring freedom and prosperity to their country and want the two parties – host nationals and foreign military – to remain on speaking terms; and sometimes they simply want to do a good language mediation job. For the military, it is important to be and remain aware of the various Simmelian roles that interpreters may play, and make use of them in an advantageous way without harming them. After all, the 'third one' may be quite vulnerable.

This brings us back to Goffman. Analysing the interactions between military personnel and host nationals mediated by interpreters in the Afghanistan mission, Hoedemaekers and Soeters (2009) were able to recognize three communicative roles that Goffman once distinguished in his analysis of 'radio talk' (1981: 197–327). These were: the *animator* who simply reproduces, memorizes or recites the words of others; the *author* who puts together or scripts the lines that are being uttered, staying within the theme of the conversation; and the *principal* who takes the initiative and is free to formulate new text.

The interpreter performs all three roles, dependent on the discretionary space he receives from the one(s) he works for. First, he – usually the interpreter is a 'he' – is a 'translation machine', producing a literal translation of what is being said, in both directions. But he may also add something extra by giving a little advice to the hearer about what the speaker means or by reformulating the utterances in order to make them better understandable. Finally, the interpreter may speak for himself, for example, if he raises a question in the conversation. This may be very helpful to avoid misunderstanding or to fill a gap in the information flow. Hajjar (2017: 11) in a similar, more recent study found that interpreters can be apt at noticing when somebody is hiding something, which they have subtly revealed while the other speaker has not been paying attention. All in all, it turns out that interpreters switch continuously between the three communication roles that Goffman identified.

Interpreters are important as well when it comes to face protection. They try to smooth the interaction and avoid problems, by using markers such as 'sister' or 'brother' to show they belong to the same host national group. They thus create an environment of trust. The interpreter will apologize even when the military spokesman would not think any excuse to be necessary, and will usually start with small talk in order to align with the rituals that are common in many non-Western nations, for instance in Afghanistan. Using metaphors is another helpful, indirect way of communicating that Westerners are not used to; this conversation style is important in a non-Western environment. Interpreters also advise Western military on handling gender and religious matters.

Obviously, conversations between Western military people and host nationals, mediated by interpreters, are strategic interactions par excellence. Western military personnel are interested in intelligence and gaining support for their mission; host nationals may have an interest in gaining money for infrastructure in their communities; whereas an interpreter is concerned with doing a good job for the military while protecting his own safety (Hoedemaekers and Soeters, 2009). The latter factor is particularly important, as we have seen. Interpreters act strategically, and they do so by manipulating, distorting or concealing what is being said, at least to some extent. Given their position between two opposing or at least disconnected parties, interpreters are indispensable, which makes them vulnerable and powerful at the same time. Put most simply, interpreters are needed to improve communication processes in military operations abroad, as communication is military business too.

The 'polymetis' soldier

The American anthropologist James Scott (1998) has criticized the many failed attempts by governments to improve the human condition in their states. He pointed at policies of collectivization in the former Soviet Union, the planning of high modernist cities such as Brasilia, and the taming of nature by the planting of large-scale forests and farms all over the world. He ascribes these failures to 'state simplifications': abstract state-created knowledge, technical/functional rationality of presumed universal application, as well as centralized steering and authoritarian intervention. He does not apply this criticism to military operations, but it does not require a lot of imagination to do so.

Instead of such 'blueprint' policies, Scott advocates approaches that take advantage of local experience and practical knowledge, which is necessary to respond to a constantly changing natural and human environment. Referring to Greek mythology, he invokes the concept of 'metis', which implies being smart in a practical way, being able to be patient and to renounce and suppress one's own emotional and ferocious impulses. Again, Scott does not direct this plea to the military, but that could be done easily.

This would imply that schemes of state simplification in military affairs ('with us or against us'; 'invade and win') should be avoided and that military personnel should be trained to become 'polymetes' soldiers. That would imply that they would be trained to communicate with host nationals, to rely on small steps, favour reversibility, plan on using surprise and presume human inventiveness (Scott, 1998: 345; Soeters, 2013; also Hajjar, 2014). Of course, learning how to make proper use of local interpreters, and treat them with respect, would be part of such an approach.

Street-level bureaucrats

On-stage behaviour is highly interesting, as we just saw, and it should be distinguished from back-stage behaviour in back offices, police stations, garrisons or HQs. In other theorizing – in line with Goffman and Weber of course – this distinction has led to the concept of 'street-level' bureaucrats (Lipsky, 2010 [1980]). With this concept Lipsky (2010) had police officers, social workers and teachers in mind. Later applications pertain to customs inspectors and other law enforcement agents, such as border guards or labour inspectors. This concept has not often been applied to the military. The concept is interesting, though, and contributes to an understanding of soldiers' conduct on the streets.

Lipsky (2010) used the concept to point to the dilemmas that individuals in public services face. Street-level bureaucrats are confronted with pressures from both their managers back-stage and their clients on-stage, i.e. during 'street encounters'. Hence, like the interpreters we saw before, they are bound by Simmelian ties, making their working lives not so easy. Street-level bureaucrats' jobs are characterized by constant time pressures and insufficient resources ('too much work'). They are also confronted with ambiguous working goals, making it uncertain whether a job has been properly done and rendering performance evaluation difficult. Besides, the demand for their services often is unpredictable, which is at odds with one of the essential features of Weberian bureaucracy. Finally, there are physical as well as psychological strains, and sometimes even threats from clients who typically act from a non-voluntary position. Today, their behaviour is open to public scrutiny as their actions may be filmed by the public on their cellphone cameras. Police officers' violence may result in general outrage if footage of it is posted on the internet.

As a result, street-level bureaucrats often experience a fair degree of alienation, a concept we already encountered in the chapter on Karl Marx. Alienation is likely to occur because street-level bureaucrats work on only one aspect of a client's conduct (legal position, educational progress, health status), because they cannot control the input nor the outcome of their work, and because, as said before, they cannot control the pace of their work. Police officers may feel seriously frustrated if they are criticized in social media by people who were not on the scene.

As a counter-strategy – remember, Goffman taught that every human interaction is strategic interaction – street-level bureaucrats develop practices to create discretionary space and autonomy for themselves and to control the job and its consequences (Lipsky, 2010: 117ff). In interacting with clients they will usually engage in 'civil inattention', which is what people in the streets unconsciously do: recognizing other people's presence but avoiding any gesture (gazing, coming too close, touching) that might be taken as too intrusive (Giddens and Sutton, 2013: 302).

But street-level bureaucrats are in a powerful position as they shape and determine the conditions for explicit interaction (in terms of time, place and content). They define when, how and where an action takes place. In particular, the setting in which the interaction takes place is chosen to impress the client and make them feel dependent (school, hospital, court room, police station). For sure, street-level bureaucrats, often uniformed, display a considerable degree of 'impression management', to use another of Goffman's famous expressions (1959). If possible, they also make sure that their clients are isolated from one another, and they present their services as benign; actions affecting clients are always 'taken in their best interest'. In coping with the managing – back-office – bureaucrats' strategies the street-level bureaucrats tend to lean towards favouring what is being measured by performance evaluation. That simply is in their own interest.

Given these practices it may come as no surprise that street-level bureaucrats are said to 'make policy' on the streets. This of course is only partially true. General laws and policies constitute the general framework in which street-level bureaucrats need to function. However, street-level bureaucrats do have opportunities to interpret these laws and policies in ways that conform to their own convictions and interests, and act accordingly. This may go in many ways: right or wrong and everything in between, as stipulated by the societal definitions of that moment. In terms of Chapter 6 on race and discrimination, ethnic or racial profiling, namely police officers stopping people of colour more frequently, may have been more or less legitimate twenty years ago, whereas it now creates enormous public upheaval.

It is not difficult to apply all of this to military personnel on mission. If soldiers are not fully engaged in combat, they will often be in the position of street-level bureaucrats. This particularly applies to UN missions and other post- or semi-conflict situations in which the military finds itself, which tend to be more frequent than real combat situation. In fact, during the so-called security-gap when no police officers are available, the military often finds itself in a position where they need to conduct policing instead of military tasks (e.g. Neuteboom and Soeters, 2017). This is difficult because they are not explicitly trained to do this. Without proper preparation, commanders need to understand the dynamics on the streets in missions abroad that are likely to occur in the way Lipsky (2010) described. Understanding these dynamics may prevent the possible misconduct of military personnel, such as power abuse or other biases. Soldiers may also act too passively. Comprehending these dynamics may enable commanders to sympathize with their troops who may feel vulnerable, alienated and frustrated with the position they find themselves in on the streets.

So it may make sense to adopt some of the advice that Lipsky (2010: 227) offered in summary: the need to establish a clear mission, to set specific goals for each individual, team or unit, to monitor performance, and as a commander to be personally involved in what is happening. The distance between the back-office military in the camps or HQs, and personnel on the streets should never be very large, and back-office military should know about what is happening in the streets, preferably through previous experiences of their own. In this connection, it may be added that military 'impression management' – sunglasses, combat gear, heavy vehicles – may look appropriate at first sight, but may in the end turn out to be more counter-productive than beneficial. The distance between the street-level bureaucrats and their 'clients' on the streets may grow too large.

Military violence in non-combat situations

Scholars have been preoccupied with the behaviour of soldiers in combat. However, many military missions pertain to peacekeeping, patrolling, manning checkpoints, seeking information and searching for suspects, for instance by interrogating people. These activities look a lot like policing, and in conducting these activities soldiers are the 'street-level bureaucrats' Lipsky (2010) referred to. However, perhaps more than ordinary 'street-level bureaucrats', such soldiers may feel alienated and vulnerable because they may be targeted by terrorists and other opponents among the general public. After all, their presence indicates the presence of tensions and threats on the streets. The situation along Israel's borders may be a case in point. In line with Collins' micro-sociological work on violence (2008), Gazit and Ben-Ari (2017) showed how soldiers may have a penchant to use violence in such non-combat situations. Based on their fieldwork at Israel's borders, they discerned (a) planned and staged violence such as arresting suspects using violence that is clearly visible (grabbing, hitting, pushing) or shooting around without aiming, (b) the display of violence as a diversion, as enter-tainment, because 'it is fun', and (c) bullying and showing disrespect to others, often to show off their masculinity. It is part of a commander's job to prevent this behaviour from getting out of control, particularly by preventing the 'violent few' to trigger the violence.

Finally, Pilster et al. (2016) have demonstrated a phenomenon that shows that soldiers' behaviour in action on the streets is related to the way their force's organization is structured. Based on theoretical reasoning and statistical analysis, they demonstrated that ill conduct of armed forces is less likely to occur if these armed forces are built up in more differentiated military, para-military and police organizations. This differentiation guarantees that biases of local organizations will be compensated for or mitigated by the other forces that have no connection with a specific local situation. In the eyes of these scholars, India, which has since its independence built up a large but differentiated structure of paramilitary and defence forces, is an enlightening example.

Conclusion

Erving Goffman's dramaturgical perspective brought a number of insights that served later scholars to develop their own work, particularly in the field of emotion work and everyday interaction between people. The practical implications of his work – also in the military – are numerous, as we have seen. They provide commanders with insights and tools that are difficult to neglect. We will encounter some other practical implications in Chapter 12 on Arlie Hochschild. Emotions at work may include joy and enthusiasm, but also sorrow and frustration.

Bibliography

Arkin, W. and L.R. Dobrofsky (1978) 'Military socialization and masculinity'. *Journal of Social Issues* 34(1): 151–168.

Burns, T. (1992) *Erving Goffman*. London and New York: Routledge.

Collins, R. (2004) *Interaction Ritual Chains*. Princeton, NJ: Princeton University Press.

Coser, L. (1974) *Greedy Institutions: Patterns of Undivided Commitment*. New York: Free Press.

Coser, L. (1977) *Masters of Sociological Thought: Ideas in Historical and Social Context*. 2nd edn. Long Grove, IL: Waveland Press.

De Angelis, K. and M. Wechsler-Segal (2015) 'Transitions in the military and the family as greedy institutions: original concept and current applicability'. In R. Moelker, M. Andres, G. Bowen and Ph. Manigart (eds), *Military Families and War in the 21st Century: Comparative Perspectives*. London and New York: Routledge.

De Jong, M. (2007) *Icons of Sociology*. Amsterdam: Boom.

Dornbusch, S.M. (1954) 'The military academy as an assimilating institution'. *Social Forces* 33(1): 316–321.

Gazit, N. and E. Ben-Ari,(2017) 'Military violence in its own right: the micro-social foundations of physical military violence in non-combat situations'. *Conflict and Society: Advances in Research* 1(3): 189–207.

Giddens, A. and P.W. Sutton (2013) *Sociology*. 7th edn. Cambridge: Polity Press.

Goffman, E. (1956) 'Embarrassment and social organization'. *American Journal of Sociology* 62(3): 264–271.

Goffman, E. (1959) *The Presentation of Self in Everyday Life*. New York: Anchor Books.

Goffman, E. (1967) *Interaction Ritual: Essays on Face-To-Face Behavior*. New York: Pantheon Books.

Goffman, E. (1981) *Forms of Talk*. Philadelphia: University of Pennsylvania Press.

Goffman, E. (1991 [1961]) 'On the characteristics of total institutions'. In E. Goffman, *Asylums: Essays on the Social Situation of Mental Patients and other Inmates*. London: Penguin, pp. 13–115.

Hajjar, R.M. (2014) 'Military warriors as peacekeeper-diplomats: building productive relations with foreign counterparts in the contemporary military advising mission'. *Armed Forces and Society* 40(4): 647–672.

Hajjar, R.M. (2017) 'Effectively working with military linguists: vital intercultural intermediaries'. *Armed Forces and Society* 43(1): 92–114.

Hoedemaekers, I. and J. Soeters (2009) 'Interaction rituals and language mediation during peace missions: experiences from Afghanistan'. In G. Caforio (ed.), *Advances in Military Sociology: Essays in Honor of Charles C. Moskos, Part A.* Bingley, UK: Emerald, pp. 329–352.

Krackhardt, D. (1999) 'The ties that torture: Simmelian tie analysis in organizations'. *Research in the Sociology of Organizations* 16: 183–210.

Kuzmics, H. (1991) 'Embarrassment and civilization: on some similarities and differences in the work of Goffman and Elias'. *Theory, Culture and Society* 8(2): 1–30.

Lipsky, M. (2010 [1980]) *Street-level Bureaucracy: Dilemmas of the Individual in Public Services.* New York: Russell Sage Foundation.

Manning, P.K. (2014) 'Organizational analysis: Goffman and dramaturgy'. In P. Adler, P. Du Gay, G. Morgan and M. Reed (eds), *The Oxford Handbook of Sociology, Social Theory and Organization Studies: Contemporary Currents.* Oxford: Oxford University Press, pp. 266–298.

Moss Kanter, R. and R. Khurana (2009) 'Types and positions: the significance of Georg Simmel's theories for organizational behavior'. In P.S. Adler (ed.), *The Oxford Handbook of Sociology and Organization Studies: Classical Foundations.* Oxford: Oxford University Press, pp. 291–306.

Mouzelis, N.P. (1971) 'Critical note on Total Institutions'. *Sociology* 5(1): 113–120.

Neuteboom, P. and J. Soeters (2017) 'The military role in filling the security gap after armed conflict'. *Armed Forces and Society* 43(4): 711–733.

Obstfeld, D. (2005) 'Social networks: the Tertius Iungens orientation, and involvement in innovation'. *Administrative Science Quarterly* 50(1): 100–130.

Pilster, U., T. Böhmelt and A. Tago (2016) 'The differentiation of security forces and the onset of genocidal violence'. *Armed Forces and Society* 42(1): 26–50.

Pouligny, B. (2006) *Peace Operations Seen from Below: UN Missions and Local People.* Bloomfield, CT: Kumarian Press.

Scott, A. (2009) 'Georg Simmel: the individual and the organization'. In P.S. Adler (ed.), *The Oxford Handbook of Sociology and Organization Studies: Classical Foundations.* Oxford: Oxford University Press, pp. 268–289.

Scott, J.C. (1998) *Seeing Like a State: How Certain Schemes to Improve the Human Condition Have Failed.* New Haven CT and London: Yale University Press.

Segal, M.W. (1986) 'The military and the family as greedy institutions'. *Armed Forces and Society* 13(1): 9–38.

Simmel, G. (1906) 'The sociology of secrecy and secret societies'. *American Journal of Sociology* 11(4): 441–498.

Simmel, G. (1955, originally various publications) *Conflict and the Web of Group-Affiliations.* New York: Free Press.

Soeters, J. (2013) "Odysseus prevails over Achilles: a warrior model suited to post-9/11 conflicts". In: J. Burk (ed.) *How 9/11 Changed Our Ways of War.* Stanford Ca.: Stanford University Press.

Soeters (2018) "Organizational cultures in the military". In: "Caforio, G. (ed.) (2018) *Handbook of the Sociology of the Military.* Cham, Switzerland: Springer.

Turner, J.H. (1991) *The Structure of Sociological Theory.* Belmont, CA: Wadsworth.

Van Bladel, J. (2003) 'Russian soldiers in the barracks: a portrait of a subculture'. In A.C. Aldis and R.N. McDermott (eds), *Russian Military Reform 1992–2002*. London and Portland OR: Frank Cass.

Weber, Cl. (2012) *À genou les hommes, debout les officiers: la socialisation des Saint-Cyriens*. Rennes: Presses Universitaires de Rennes.

8 Michel Foucault

Discipline and surveillance in and
by the military

French social philosopher and sociologist Michel Foucault (1926–1984) has
published a remarkable collection of writings, some of which have less or
almost nothing to do with the military, but some have – among them a series
of lectures at the Collège de France on the need to defend society (Foucault,
2003 [1975/6]). Foucault authored important publications about socio-medical
issues from a historical perspective, including the development of medical
institutions and the approach to mental illness and sexuality (e.g. Foucault,
2006 [1961]). From these works theoretical insights emerged that have widely
recognized implications, across professions, sectors and nations. Foucault's work
shares a number of themes with Max Weber (e.g. O'Neill, 1986; Szakolczai,
1998; Dandeker, 1990), but also with Emile Durkheim, Karl Marx, Erving
Goffman and Norbert Elias, the last of whom we will meet later (Van Krieken,
1990). Foucault provides perspectives that are new and original, with, however,
a pessimistic undertone that not all appreciate or agree with. Some of his
writings are quite difficult to understand because of their abstract theoretical
character.

Discipline, surveillance and that other famous Foucauldian word, 'governmentality', are all about *conducting the conduct* of the other(s), and this phenomenon has wide consequences. Foucault's work (1991a) on discipline and the
origin of the prison system has immediate implications for the military, as has
been argued by Christopher Dandeker (1990). The idea of military surveillance
originally pertains to monitoring the external border and observing the internal
order. In a contemporary context, surveillance of others may apply to the
military in at least two ways: by surveillance of population groups and their
potentially hostile capabilities in the mission area, including the homeland, and
through surveillance of one's own troops. Of course, the implications can be
even more directly observed with respect to intelligence agencies and communities. There is a clear connection with today's fight against terrorism.
Applied to the current security context, Foucault's work has gained considerable
importance because of the refugee crisis in Europe and its immediate
surroundings. The issue of border control, and the role of (para-)military and
police agencies in this field, including Frontex and Europol, is one that
demands more attention.

Discipline, surveillance and the panopticon

In what is perhaps his most sociological book, *Discipline and Punish*, Foucault (1991a [1975]) contends that over the past centuries a development has taken place in the way society deals with people who committed crimes or were deviant in whatever way. Until some 250 years ago, public torture and executions were part of the way authorities in Europe and elsewhere handled criminals and other offenders, as evinced by Foucault's description of a public execution in Paris in 1757 (Foucault, 1991a: 3–5). Only 'eighty years later' (Foucault, 1991a: 6) the penal system had changed completely, not only in France but all over Western Europe. From cruel public executions that had existed for centuries – crucifixion, decapitation, and drawing and quartering – a penal system had evolved in which professional judges judged the individual person, not the crime. The aim of the new system was to provide a cure, to 'treat' the criminal, in a prison system with strict regulations and procedures. From a public spectacle, punishment had become the most hidden part of the penal process (also: Smart, 1985: 71ff).

As an essential element of this prison system, Foucault borrowed an idea from the British philosopher Jeremy Bentham, who in the late eighteenth century had designed what he called the panopticon, an institutional building in which literally everything ('pan') can be seen ('opticon'). It is based on a construction principle that consists of

> at the periphery, an annular building; at the centre, a tower; this tower is pierced with wide windows that open onto the inner side of the ring; the peripheric building is divided into cells [...] that have two windows, one on the inside [...], the other, on the outside [...]. All that is needed, then, is to place a supervisor in a central tower, and to shut up in each cell a madman, a patient, a condemned man, a worker or a schoolboy. By the effect of backlighting, one can observe from the tower, standing out precisely against the light, the small captive shadows in the cells of the periphery. [...] Each individual [...] is securely confined to a cell from which he is seen from the front by the supervisor; but the side walls prevent him from coming into contact with his companions [in the adjacent cells/JS]. He is seen, but he does not see; he is the object of information, never a subject in communication. The arrangement of his room [...] and the divisions of the ring, those separated cells, imply a lateral invisibility. And this invisibility is a guarantee of order.
>
> (Foucault, 1991a: 200)

In consequence, 'in the peripheric ring, one is totally seen, without ever seeing; in the central tower, one sees everything without ever been seen' (Foucault, 1991a: 202).

This design 'automatizes and disindividualizes power' (Foucault, 1991a: 202), and the inmates, or the workers, the patients, the schoolboys internalize the idea that they are being kept under constant surveillance, even if they – at any given moment – are not. It makes the inmates comply with the rules of the game, whether or not they are actually being watched; the fact that they always may be being watched is enough. Despite the description of its construction features, the panopticon does not need to be an architectural design, a physical building. It is a sociological metaphor for meticulous immaterial and material systems of surveillance and the internalizing thereof; it is the sociology of the *gaze of power* (e.g. Fox, 1998: 416). Preventing and controlling deviance, obedience to the rules, and conducting the conduct of men are the aims of the game.

This idea is of course reminiscent of the 'Big Brother' character that novelist George Orwell coined. More academically, it reminds us of the idea of the 'double consciousness' that W. E. B. Du Bois wrote of with respect to the position and corresponding mindset of African-Americans: always internally dealing with the idea of being watched and judged by others, in this case by white Americans. For Foucault this dynamic applies to all 'human–system' relations. Of course, the connection with the social inequality theme that Karl Marx stressed is strong, and no wonder: Foucault became famous in the revolutionary milieux of the 1960s and 1970s (e.g. Heilbron, 2015). The idea also resembles Durkheim's socialization dynamics, but where Durkheim focused on cultural internalizing in general, Foucault stressed the internalization of power relations in particular. Of course, power and culture are interrelated, but there is a striking difference in emphasis between the two scholars. As we will see later, Norbert Elias, with a similar historical-sociological research approach, pointed to the same phenomenon of declining public cruelty and violence and the increasing self-constraint of individuals internalizing the judgements of others. However, whereas Elias underlined the positive implication of this finding, Foucault broadened the focus and attributed a certain pessimism to it. In particular, he descibed the wider dynamics of processes of surveillance, discipline and self-discipline.

In the quotation above, Foucault already aligned the position of the encapsulated 'madman, patient, condemned man, worker or schoolboy'. They are all kept under surveillance, in reality or at any possible moment. He could have added soldiers, as military men and women undergo similar sorts of treatment in garrison, which we already saw in the previous chapter on Erving Goffman's analysis of (quasi-) total institutions. Soldiers are intensively trained to internalize and comply with the rules, the procedures, the skills and drills that the military organization prescribes, which we have already discussed in the chapter on Max Weber. This enables them to act according to the intentions of the organization in a disciplined manner. If according to the rules using violence is necessary, it should happen in such a way that it does not get out of control. Foucault uses a term in this connection that is somewhat pejorative as it reminds us of how the comportment of horses is mastered: soldiers' work – like many other people's work – is subject to *dressage*, i.e. disciplining and training (Jackson and Carter, 1998).

The commander's *gaze* at the soldiers pertains to direct, interpersonal commanding but it also relies on more bureaucratic practices of writing, grading and examining. In fact, one could argue – as Weber did – that the military exported these practices into the market sector and hence laid the foundation of modern business in America.

The origin of business practices and the West Point connection

The British accounting scholars Keith Hoskin and Richard Macve (1986; 1988) have studied how the development of educational practices made possible the near-universal adoption of accountancy standards in business. The introduction of writing in an alpha-numerical system (words connected to numbers) including the 'double-entry' technique led to the acceptance of standards that control and discipline the behaviour of workers. The American military academy at West Point laid the foundations for this development. At the academy, strict procedures based on standards, averages and norms were introduced, dividing the cadets into classes according to their skills and intelligence. All aspects of performance, academic and behavioural, were constantly measured, evaluated and recorded in a joint numerical-linguistic language. Major decisions were communicated via written messages, which made the system even more impersonal and seemingly 'objective'. Fully in accordance with Foucault's analysis of the power of 'panoptic' gazing, this system had a strong disciplinary character among the officer cadets.

Graduates of West Point, particularly from the engineering department, were among the first to help weapons manufacturers and railway companies increase their workers' performance by introducing these techniques outside the military. As such, the disciplinary character of military practices stood at the origin of new business practices in industry and trade.

This example demonstrates that personal and spatial surveillance is complemented and often supplanted by statistical or actuarial surveillance and normalization. Collecting, publishing and ranking performance indicators of public organizations – schools, universities or hospitals – is a strong manifestation of constant visibility and governance *from a distance*, with attention to detail (Sauder and Nelson Espeland, 2009: 69–72). It leads to a process of normalization that consists of comparison, differentiation, hierarchizing, homogenization and exclusion (Foucault, 1991a: 183; Sauder and Nelson Espeland, 2009: 72ff). Normalization is an instrument of power as it coerces people's conduct in one direction. Through surveillance and normalization, public organizations are compared with one another, as they are differentiated from the ideal and placed in a hierarchy starting with the top-performing organizations. The whole set of public organizations under scrutiny (e.g. universities) is homogenized because those organizations that do not conform are publicly punished, scandalized and finally excluded from the 'league'. This creates anxiety and uncertainty, but may also result in resistance, leading to a condemnation of the rankings by university authorities. However, discussing the validity of the rankings will most likely lead to better, more refined rankings, making their disciplinary impact in due course even stronger. Another category of resistance refers to 'gaming' the system: manipulating variables that play a role in the rankings without really addressing the dynamics that have led to a poorer ranking; for instance, by not allowing lower performing students to enter the university programmes under scrutiny (Sauder and Nelson Espeland, 2009; De Bruijn, 2007).

All this concerns newspaper or journal articles reporting on the ranking of public organizations and firms – e.g.'The Best Company to Work For' – for whom ranking is a relatively new phenomenon. However, as said, this process was preceded by earlier internal organizational practices that made the emergence of accounting, the quantification of the performance of units and their workers inside organizations, possible (Mennicken and Miller, 2014: 25–27). Accounting makes the 'incomparable comparable by distilling substantively different kinds or classes of things into a single financial [or statistical/JS] figure' (Mennicken and Miller, 2014: 26).

This can be recognized in the military. In the Vietnam War a kind of managerialism guided the decision making in operations, in which the numbers of weapons seized and the areas 'cleared' of Vietcong were important statistics (McCann, 2017). An important indicator of progress was the so-called 'body count', the number of losses among the Vietcong due to American (or allies') military actions. It was a quantitative measure to compare the 'productivity' of units and actions in different time periods. However, next to the dubious moral elements of this statistic – inciting to kill – this measurement turned out to be counter-productive as there was a tendency to inflate the numbers, which led to over-optimism and even to misjudgements about the progress of the war (Mueller, 1980). The American public had grown most critical about this way of indicating (alleged) success. This gross statistic did not return in later operations, but the desire to measure progress in military action did not disappear (e.g. McCann, 2017).

Rietjens et al. (2011) studied the process of 'measuring the immeasurable' concerning the military actions in Afghanistan. These measurements were imposed by the politicians who ordered the mission and who wanted to be informed on the progress made. The measurements revealed many flaws with respect to the validity and reliability of the indications of progress. Some authors tend to speak about 'fictionalized' management based on such data (McCann, 2017: 505). In addition to other problems, the measurements were based on proxy operationalization of vague concepts (security, safety). Besides, the number of performance indicators often changed, as they were too detailed and elaborate and not aligned among the national contingents and operational areas. Furthermore, the connection between the various hierarchical layers was often missing. 'Our metrics suck', as one commander lamented. Most striking, however, was the controversy among the military themselves about military leadership ideally being driven by either the intuition and the charisma of the commander or by statistical assessments. Some people, particularly high ranking commanders, were quite critical about the statistics and said these could not contribute to better insights; judgements were best left to the intuition of the commanders. Those views can be seen as acts of resistance to the system of surveillance and normalization that external actors − in this case politicians ordering the military operations − impose on the military. Politicians, on behalf of the larger society, desire to reduce commanders' autonomy and render them more controllable than the latter would consider acceptable.

This study of how to assess the effectiveness of military operations shows that Foucault's analysis has considerable value, in the military as much as outside. The idea of the panopticon is a highly attractive and strong concept. This is certainly so in times where on every street corner, office building, construction site or transportation vehicle, camcorders and sensors register whatever takes place; they collect, store and process information with unlimited capacity. Nobody passes by or can work without being seen (Koskela, 2002; Sofsky, 2008), even though the surveillance is impersonal and indirect (Dandeker, 1990: 196). The same applies to the use of the internet by individual people − cookies! − that is, they are constantly being registered from a distance. Finally, mobile phones and the ability to upload recordings via social media puts everyone under scrutiny. Nobody goes unwatched these days, at least potentially.

The same happens in areas of operations where drones monitor inhabitants' moves and actions without interruption, as we will see in Chapter 14 on Bruno Latour's work on science and technology. Correspondingly, soldier modernization programmes introduce technological devices such as camcorders and sensors that will make virtually every event, every move and every sound of the individual soldier in action, able to be monitored from a distance. This information is useful for evaluation and training purposes but it also provides the basis for legal action in case a possible violation of rules and procedures has occurred.

Nonetheless, it has also been argued that the concept of the panopticon should be abandoned (Boyne, 2000). As we saw before, attempts to see and judge everything also elicit resistance from workers, including soldiers, and even more so when they climb the hierarchical ladder. This can be interpreted as commanders' resistance to politicians as we saw above, but there is also another aspect. A more elaborate use of performance indicators may render the commanders' performance also more visible for the soldiers and sailors throughout the whole organization. Today's world not only permits the few to keep the many under surveillance (as the original panopticon idea implies), but also that the many (the soldiers) may watch the few (the commanders). The surveillance machinery is now potentially serving the crowd as much as it serves the top brass (Boyne, 2000: 301). One can also include the general public that may observe and film how police or soldiers act on the streets, as we saw in the previous chapter.

In addition, in ordinary society there are limits to surveillance because of civil rights and privacy concerns. One consequence is that one overlooks potential terrorists while they are preparing and coming close to actually executing their deeds. Politicians and ordinary citizens have frequently wondered why terrorists have been known to the intelligence agencies but were not prevented from carrying out their attacks. The major reason is usually that information was not shared with other agencies or that priorities in task allocation were not set adequately. This often gives the impression that those responsible for the surveillance anticipate what may be called 'normal damage'. Panoptical control at the micro-level seems impossible and even unwanted (Boyne, 2000: 302).

As to military operations abroad (Iraq, Afghanistan), one can conclude that total control of the host population, including their hostile elements, is virtually impossible, despite massive numbers of boots on the ground or continuous surveillance by drones. Today's military presence abroad, but also the military presence during colonial times, is almost always temporary and geographically limited, covering only segments of society, never the whole of it. Hence, a great deal of military action – in uncovered areas, after the operations, and in segments out of sight – is beyond the reach of a military panopticon.

This puts Foucault's analysis, however valuable, in a somewhat different perspective. Goffmann's total institutions also lost some of their all-pervasive character, as we saw in the previous chapter, becoming quasi total institutions at best. Despite increasing capabilities, total control of others is unlikely and not accepted, even if this means the loss of the idea of total safety.

Governmentality and international relations

Next to making clear the power dimension in surveillance, Foucault (1991b [1978]) has become famous through the concept of *governmentality*. This idea contains the words 'government' and 'rationality' but it may also refer to 'government' and 'art' (Gordon, 1991) and even to 'government' and 'mentality' (Merlingen, 2003). Government is about how to govern: who governs, who is governed, by whom one accepts to be governed, how does governing exactly take place? Governmentality is about the rationalities and techniques of power, traditionally at three levels, i.e. by people themselves, in the family, and in the realm of the state (Foucault, 1991b: 91).

Working with this concept in the field of international security relations, Michael Merlingen (2003; 2011) made interesting contributions. He applied the concept of governmentality by focusing on governing by International Governmental Organizations (IGOs) and by the EU in the context of the Common Security and Defence Policy (CSDP). More specifically, he pointed at the international socialization of societies and states by IGOs, exercising 'a molecular form of power that evades and undermines the material, juridical and diplomatic limitations on their influence' (Merlingen, 2003: 362). He illustrated this Foucauldian thesis by studying the ways in which the Organization of Security and Cooperation in Europe (OSCE) has managed to induce former communist nations in Central and Eastern Europe (Poland, Hungary, etc.) into modes of behaviour that were and are preferred by the community of Western nations. This way the OSCE managed to observe, monitor and shape the post-socialist governments, their civil societies and even individuals; hence it managed to *conduct the conduct* of other countries, to use the famous Foucauldian words again. This obviously also included the normalization and professionalization of the armed forces, in which process NATO, and not OSCE, had the lead.

To achieve this, the OSCE used various mechanisms: training and mentoring, seminars and workshops, intermediation in a partnership among equals, social influence stressing the benefit of gaining legitimacy by adhering to international norms and standards, and material inducement by promising the input of UN or individual states' assistance. Like we saw before when discussing the ranking of universities (or schools or hospitals), the OSCE used country statistics to observe the developments in those nations and 'examinations' to judge them (Merlingen, 2003: 369–370). When the former communist nations themselves, particularly former Yugoslavia, became unstable and rife with violence, the OSCE stepped up its activities by initiating so-called Long-Term Missions; these consisted of fact-finding and rapporteur missions, peacekeeping activities and ad hoc steering groups.

These efforts were not in vain. However, the moderate results at the time and the current deficits in the democratic character of some of those nations' governments again show that the 'power-knowledge' mechanisms that were revealed by Foucault are not all-encompassing. A similar Foucauldian analysis can be conducted with respect to the UN peacekeeping missions we discussed in Chapter 5. Peacekeeping missions can be interpreted as attempts by the international world to reinforce surveillance and disciplinary mechanisms in order to tame the chaos in conflictual parts of the world (Zanotti, 2006). Sometimes this works, as we saw before, but sometimes much less so, and, if successful, the blessing is nearly always mixed. This conclusion will also apply to current governmental practices in relation to what delineates one state from another: frontiers.

Border management

Michel Foucault never showed particular interest in borders; in the 1970s borders were not contested and politically discussed as they are now (Walters, 2011). Nonetheless, the Foucauldian way of thinking gains particular relevance in relation to policies and practices that deal with the increasing numbers of immigrants and asylum seekers, in Europe and the USA but also elsewhere, for instance in Africa. These rising numbers create political tensions and impel policy makers to augment capabilities to provide responses and solutions. The problems are numerous. The main and most problematic task relates to distinguishing between those who suffer from war, oppressive governments and other crises, and so-called 'economic migrants' (e.g., van Houtum and van Naerssen, 2002). As to the latter, a difference is made between those who can contribute to the economic productivity of the host nation because of their skills and competences, and others who are much less likely to do so. Connected to this task are at least three challenges, i.e. (a) providing rescue and support to the migrants and asylum-seekers during their passage, (b) determining the legality of the immigration attempts, and (c) coping with security threats, as terrorists may be among the migrants.

The Foucauldian perspective is relevant here. It makes clear, for example, how remote, delocalized controls away from the borders, checks of documents and people's stories, as well as biometric examinations – finger prints, iris scans – infuse the 'gazing' system (Walters, 2006; Epstein, 2007). New technologies contribute to these developments. As such, the 'disciplinary society' that Foucault emphasized seems to have changed into an almost inescapable 'control society'. Not really.

At the US–Mexican frontier border enforcement has led to what may be called a 'militarization' of border control. Using massive data bases concerning border transfers, three American sociologists have analysed how the increased budgets and capabilities for US border control and enforcement had significant unintended consequences (Massey et al., 2016). As expected, rising enforcement efforts – a fivefold increase in border patrol officers, a fourfold increase in hours spent patrolling the border, and a twentyfold increase in nominal funding – led to more apprehensions at the border. However, migrants adjusted their border-crossing strategies, shifting to new, less patrolled, more remote and riskier crossing sites, bypassing the Sonora Desert and Arizona. They also made more frequent use of so-called 'coyotes', who guide them across the border (Massey et al., 2016: 1564). More important is that the character of migration changed from a circular flow of male workers going to three states in the USA to an 11-million population of settled families living in fifty states. The reason is clear, as the rise in border enforcement

> had no effect on the likelihood of taking a first undocumented trip northwards or the odds of gaining entry to the United States on such a trip but […] it did have a strong effect in decreasing the likelihood of returning to Mexico once an entry had been achieved.
>
> (Massey et al., 2016: 1588)

Stepping up border enforcement backfired, as it cut off a long-standing tradition of migratory circulation and promoted the large-scale settlement of undocumented migrants.

A more or less comparable situation, but so far approached differently, is occuring along the southern coasts of Europe in Greece, Italy and Spain. There are three types of response to the immigration coming from Africa and Asia as far as the European Union is concerned. The first consists of military/navy units who try to control the borders and immigration through patrolling at sea; the second entails police and border guards who try to filter out those who are entitled to cross the border from those who come with fake stories and criminal intentions; and the third response involves data analysts who use computer systems to distinguish patterns and traces and to check for irregularities (Bigo, 2014). The problems are so complex that supranational institutions need to guide the actions of individual nations, one example being Frontex, the EU border and coastguard agency.

Next to the uniformed agencies (navies, coastguards) a wide variety of humanitarian NGOs play an important role. A difference with the border between Mexico and the United States is that states have no common borders here because the high seas are between them (e.g. Klepp, 2010). This situation makes the passage riskier, and from a legal and political perspective less transparent. In response to the numbers of migrants who – helped by human traffickers – endeavour to make the passage in unsafe boats, coastguards, navies and Frontex work in close cooperation with those NGOs. The main concern is to rescue those in danger at sea, but this refugee protection is likely to be at odds with policies on border control and immigration of the various European nations (Klepp, 2010; Walters, 2011). A dramatic dilemma emerges while 'holding together in an uneasy alliance a politics of alienation with a politics of care, and a tactic of abjection and one of reception' (Walters, 2011: 145).

In this, the uniformed agencies such as national navies and Frontex are sometimes heavily criticized, but such criticism is only a manifestation of the tensions, even the conflict, between the logics of care and control. In fact, border control and policing have a strong humanitarian component and humanitarian support also contains a policing element as it helps to catch 'bad guys' (Pallister-Wilkins, 2015). These tensions are not easy to solve and may in due time even lead to changes in some basic principles of international law (Klepp, 2010). Following Jane Addams, one most of all needs a true understanding of the nature of the migration before solutions will be feasible. For sure, the countries from where the migrants depart need to be involved. Participation of all stakeholders in problem solving is what Addams always advocated. Until now, the recent migration phenomenon has been fairly chaotic and distressful; in fact, it is far from being controlled in a panoptic way. The panopticon is more likely to be seen at today's and future airports.

Airports

Airports are places where border management is particularly relevant. Here security and efficiency concerns need to be aligned and public organizations and private companies must act together in order to run their operations smoothly and safely. They also must make sure that unwanted people are prevented from boarding planes or entering national territories. This is a space where the Foucauldian panopticon becomes reality. Particularly after the gruesome 9/11 terrorist attacks on the USA and at Brussels Airport in 2016, the intensity of border controls at airports has increased considerably. Biometrics, digital risk profiling relying on connected data bases, automatic document checks, closed circuit television and security checks of bodies and goods help to create a system of global surveillance at airports world-wide (e.g. Salter, 2008). These politics of the airport come close to what Foucault had in mind, most likely, however with a different appreciation. Whereas Foucault and others would criticize such a development, many others argue that such developments are inevitable if one is to provide safety and security to passengers boarding a plane.

Conclusion

Michel Foucault achieved star status during his lifetime, an honour that does not often befall social scientists. The implications of his work are far-reaching and are acknowledged by students of organizations and accountants, as well as by scholars in the field of medicine, nursing, geography and border management. However, no matter how valuable his insights may be, his tone is pessimistic, exaggerating the power of the panopticon and neglecting the opportunities for people to control their own lives and escape from the permanent gaze, at least to a certain extent. Besides, the disciplinary character that he at least implicitly criticizes also produced considerable prosperity, wealth, respectable performance, and safety in today's societies. For the military, his insights prove to be valuable too, but the same caveats apply. The military and its soldiers are increasingly put under surveillance themselves, but not completely so, which one can applaud or lament depending on one's perspective and the case at hand.

Bibliography

Bigo, D. (2014) 'The (in)securitization practices of three universes of EU border control: military/navy – border guards/police – database analysts'. *Security Dialogue* 45(3): 209–225.

Boyne, R. (2000) 'Post-panopticism'. *Economy and Society* 29(2): 285–307.

Dandeker, Chr. (1990) *Surveillance, Power and Modernity. Bureaucracy and Discipline from 1700 to the Present Day*. Cambridge: Polity Press.

De Bruijn, H. (2007) *Managing Performance in the Public Sector*. London and New York: Routledge.

Epstein, Ch. (2007) 'Guilty bodies, productive bodies, destructive bodies: crossing the biometric borders'. *International Political Sociology* 1(2): 149–164.

Foucault, M. (1991a [1975]) *Discipline and Punish: The Birth of the Prison*. London: Penguin.

Foucault, M. (1991b [1978]) 'Governmentality'. In G. Burchell, C. Gordon and P. Miller (eds), *The Foucault Effect: Studies in Governmentality*. Chicago: University of Chicago Press, pp. 87–104.

Foucault, M. (2003 [1975/1976]) *Society Must Be Defended* [*Il faut défendre la société*]. Lectures at the Collège de France, 1965–1976). Trans. D. Macey. New York: Picador.

Foucault, M. (2006 [1961]) *Madness and Civilization: A History of Insanity in the Age of Reason*. London and New York: Routledge.

Fox, N.J. (1998) 'Foucault, Foucauldians and sociology'. *British Journal of Sociology* 49(3): 415–433.

Gordon, C. (1991) 'Governmental rationality: an introduction'. In G. Burchell, C. Gordon and P. Miller (eds), *The Foucault Effect: Studies in Governmentality*. Chicago: University of Chicago Press, pp. 1–51.

Heilbron, J. (2015) *French Sociology*. Ithaca NY and London: Cornell University Press.

Hoskin, K.W. and R.H. Macve (1986) 'Accounting and the examination: a genealogy of disciplinary power'. *Accounting, Organizations and Society* 11(2): 105–136.

Hoskin, K.W. and R.H. Macve (1988) 'The genesis of accountability: the West Point connection'. *Accounting, Organizations and Society* 13(1): 37–73.

Jackson, N. and P. Carter (1998) 'Labour as dressage'. In A. McKinlay and K. Starkey (eds), *Foucault, Management and Organization Theory*. London and Thousand Oaks CA: Sage.

Klepp, S. (2010) 'A contested asylum system: the European Union between refugee protection and border control in the Mediterranean Sea'. *European Journal of Migration and Law* 12(1): 1–21.

Koskela, H. (2002) '"Cam-era" – the contemporary urban panopticon'. *Surveillance and Society* 1(3): 292–313.

Massey, D.S., J. Durand and K.A. Pren (2016) 'Why border enforcement backfired'. *American Journal of Sociology* 121(5): 1557–1600.

McCann, L. (2017) '"Killing is our business and business is good": the evolution of "war managerialism" from body counts to counterinsurgency'. *Organization* 24(4): 491–515.

Mennicken, A. and P. Miller (2014) 'Michel Foucault and the administering of lives'. In P. Adler, P. Du Gay, G. Morgan and M. Reed (eds), *The Oxford Handbook of Sociology, Social Theory and Organization Studies: Contemporary Currents*. Oxford: Oxford University Press, pp. 11–38.

Merlingen, M. (2003) 'Governmentality: towards a Foucauldian framework for the study of IGOs'. *Cooperation and Conflict* 38(4): 361–384.

Merlingen, M. (2011) 'From governance to governmentality in CSDP: towards a Foucaldian research agenda'. *Journal of Common Market Studies* 49(1): 149–169.

Mueller, J. (1980) 'The search for the "breaking Point" in Vietnam'. *International Studies Quarterly* 24(4): 497–519.

O'Neill, J. (1986) 'The disciplinary society: from Weber to Foucault'. *British Journal of Sociology* 37(1): 42–60

Pallister-Wilkins, P. (2015) 'The humanitarian politics of European border policing: Frontex and border police in Evros'. *International Political Sociology* 9(1): 53–69.

Rietjens, S., J. Soeters and W. Klumper (2011) 'Measuring the immeasurable? The effects-based approach in comprehensive peace operations'. *International Journal of Public Administration* 34(5): 329–338.

Salter, M.B. (ed.) (2008) *Politics at the Airport*. Minneapolis and London: University of Minnesota Press.

Sauder, M. and W. Nelson Espeland (2009) 'The discipline of ranking: tight coupling and organizational change'. *American Sociological Review* 74(February): 63–82.

Smart, B. (1985) *Michel Foucault*. London and New York: Routledge.

Smart, B. (2002) *Michel Foucault*. Revised edn. London and New York: Routledge.

Sofsky, W. (2008) *Privacy: A Manifesto*. Princeton NJ and Oxford: Princeton University Press.

Szakolczai, A. (1998) *Max Weber and Michel Foucault: Parallel Life-works*. London and New York: Routledge.

van Houtum, H. and van Naerssen, T. (2002) 'Bordering, ordering and othering'. *Tijdschrift voor Economische en Sociale Geografie* 93(2): 125–136.

van Krieken, R. (1990) 'The organization of the soul: Elias and Foucault on discipline and the self'. *Archives Européennes de Sociologie* 31(2): 353–371.

van Thiel, S. and F. Leeuw (2002) 'The performance paradox in the public sector'. *Public Performance and Management Review* 25(3): 267–281.

Walters, W. (2006) 'Border/control'. *European Journal of Social Theory* 9(2): 187–203.

Walters, W. (2011) 'Foucault and frontiers: notes on the birth of the humanitarian border'. In U. Bröckling, S. Krasmann and Th. Lenke (eds), *Governmentality: Current Issues and Future Challenges*. London and New York: Routledge, pp. 138–164.

Zanotti, L. (2006) 'Taming chaos: a Foucauldian view of UN peacekeeping, democracy and normalization'. *International Peacekeeping* 13(2): 150–167.

9 Morris Janowitz

The professional soldier, civil–military relations and the AVF

Although his work certainly also belongs to general and political sociology (Janowitz, 1970; 1975), Morris Janowitz is the only sociologist in this book who can be truly labelled a military sociologist. In fact, Janowitz, who lived from 1919 to 1988, may be called 'the dean of military sociologists' (Cortright, 1975: 3). One can argue that he founded this sociological sub-discipline through his research and many publications as well as through his teaching in graduate and doctorate programmes at the University of Chicago. He stands at the beginning of an American tradition in military sociology that produced prominent names such as Charles Moskos, David and Mady Segal and James Burk. Janowitz has also influenced the international development of military sociology, as he supervised the doctorate work of scholars from all over the world and created networks of social and political scientists in the field (Burk, 1993). His name can moreover be connected with other scholars who began their careers with the end of World War II: Samuel Huntington and Samuel Stouffer, to name but two. Finally, in his lifetime Janowitz provided insights and ideas that helped the US military generate and nurture unit cohesion, something that had previously been so problematic (Segal and Wechsler Segal, 1983: 157).

All this work on the sociology of the military started with his own experience as a military person in the Second World War. Having graduated in economics, he was drafted into the army, where he joined the Research and Analysis branch of the Office of Strategic Services (OSS) in London (Burk, 1991). Like other social science scholars such as Ruth Benedict and Herbert Marcuse who came to fame after the war (Laudani, 2013), Janowitz was asked to contribute to a better understanding of the enemies' societies. More specifically, Janowitz was asked to study aspects of mass communication and propaganda by analysing the content of German radio broadcasts. After D-Day in June 1944 Janowitz left London for the European continent and began to interview German prisoners of war. Together with Edward Shils he collected data for the famous article on cohesion in the German Wehrmacht during World War II that we discussed in the chapter on Emile Durkheim (Shils and Janowitz, 1948).

Before that, Janowitz published an article in the *American Journal of Sociology* – based on data collection from among a hundred German civilians in 1945 – concerning the reactions of the population to Nazi atrocities (Janowitz, 1946).

In this article he revealed that immediately after the war German civilians in general showed themselves to be aware of the existence and function of concentration camps, although they did not know the details or extent. However, they did not show feelings of guilt and they projected the responsibility for the barbarisms onto the Nazi party or the SS. Notwithstanding, all interviewees were conscious about the mistreatment of the German Jewish citizens in the period preceding and during the war. This study is an important early contribution to the history of the German *Vergangenheitsbewältigung*, the long-lasting and deliberate attempts by German politics and society to come to grips with the war.

Janowitz was not involved in the famous *American Soldier* project that turned out to be so influential in the development of empirical sociology and social psychology, including its research methodology (Stouffer et al, 1949a; 1949b; Williams, 1946; Merton and Lazersfeld, 1950; Boëne, 1995; 2011). The unique character of the project was that questionnaires were distributed among several hundred thousand US soldiers deployed to the areas of operations in World War II, i.e. in Europe (including the Mediterranean region) and the Pacific. It produced a goldmine of empirical data on the attitudes, sentiments and behaviour of large numbers of men in the military, before, during and after combat (Merton and Lazarsfeld, 1950: 9). Its size and innovative approaches made the project a classic of survey analysis (Williams, 1989: 159).

These studies were initiated with practical ends in mind. However, they also proved to be valuable in developing scientific theories on primary groups, motivation in combat situations, reference group behaviour including relative deprivation, racial relations, the impact of human resources policies, the statistical analysis of attitudinal data, and more. The practical character of the studies led Janowitz to make a distinction between what he refered to as the 'engineering' model versus the 'enlightenment' model of sociological research (Janowitz, 1969). He associated the names of Paul Lazarsfeld and Robert King Merton, both scholars who were also engaged in the *American Soldier* project, with the engineering model. This type of sociological research, in his interpretation, pertains to applied research using key concepts, postulates, theorems and laws derived from basic sociology. It ascertains the variables relevant to the problem at hand, their values in a given research context, and the relationships between the variables based on generally accepted connections. The enlightenment model, on the contrary, does not stress the distinction between basic and applied sociology (Janowitz, 1969: 89). In the enlightenment model the sociologist recognizes that they interact with their subject and that the output of sociological research influences their subjects and their various audiences. This model emphasizes the importance of the social context and focuses on developing different types of knowledge which can be utilized by policy makers and professions (Janowitz, 1969: 92). In the book that made Janowitz most famous and which continues to create debates until today, he certainly followed the enlightenment model.

The professional soldier

Pursuing interests that had emerged during World War II, Janowitz continued to work on the military institution and organization while he was developing his career as an academic sociologist. Preceded by a number of articles with similar arguments (Janowitz, 1957; 1959), his book *The Professional Soldier*, published in 1960, was immediately seen as an important contribution to military studies and is still relevant today. The book deals with many topics, including the career patterns of military officers, life in the military community, the public service tradition, and pressure group tactics used by the military. As such, the book is the best introduction to military sociology one could possibly imagine. But it is more than that; it holds a number of messages.

In James Burk's succinct summary (1991), it is said that *The Professional Soldier*

> supplied a social and political portrait of the military officer as an emerging profession [...]. Its central argument was that the boundaries separating the military from civilian society had progressively weakened since the turn of the century. It described a military organization in which authoritarian domination gave way to greater reliance on persuasion and manipulation; skill requirements more nearly reflected civilian skill structures; the social base for recruiting officers broadened, creating a more socially representative officer corps; innovative career patterns were increasingly rewarded; and a pragmatic outlook toward war supplanted an absolutist outlook, making military officers [...] more considerate of the political consequences of military actions on foreign affairs.
>
> (Burk, 1991: 13–14)

In line with this analysis, Janowitz diverged from C. Wright Mills' formulations about an almost terrifying unified military power elite dominating the political arena, which view we discussed in the chapter on Karl Marx. Janowitz emphasized that the progressive division of labour in the military led to a dispersion (and not concentration) of power and control among the military elites (Burk, 1991: 14–15).

In his book Janowitz (1960: 283–344) distinguished two types of attitudes among military officers, in the USA and most likely also elsewhere (Shields and Soeters, 2013). These are the 'absolutist' and the 'pragmatist' attitude. The 'absolutist' mentality is based on the belief that warfare, actual or threatened, is the core of international relations and that only victories count. The 'pragmatist' vision, on the contrary, aligns military action with political and economic tools to prevent, contain and solve large-scale violent conflict. The idea that only victories count presupposes fixed ends; the 'pragmatist' vision, on the contrary, would accept that ends and means are flexible and interrelated, leaving room for consideration of the 'indigenous other' who populates the area of operations. This implies that the attainment of some ends may not be possible, because there are limits to military force. In addition, the 'absolutist' thinking in terms of victories implies punishing the adversary who lost, whereas in the other view punitive measurements should not compromise wider political objectives. Finally, the 'absolutist' view stresses geopolitical interests, while the 'pragmatist' view stresses the importance of the state's use of force for a system of international alliances (Shields and Soeters, 2013: 90–91).

A number of remarks can be added to this. In the first place, the distinction between the 'absolutist' and the 'pragmatist' view clearly reminds us of the source of inspiration that Jane Addams found, i.e. the pragmatist philosophy articulated by John Dewey and followers. For sure, Janowitz was inspired by Dewey as much as Jane Addams was. Second, this discrepancy resembles the sociological distinction between functional and substantive rationality, coined by Karl Mannheim. We first encountered this difference in the introductory chapter. The distinction is highly relevant to the military, as it yields completely different views of which type of military action is needed in a certain situation and context. The 'absolutist' view is an expression of functional rationality with clear and close means-to ends-relations ('target and destroy the bridge'), while the 'pragmatist' view raises broader questions pertaining to the wider context in terms of interests, space and time (what will be the situation once the bridge has been destroyed?). Janowitz argues that 'boots on the ground' are more inclined towards the 'pragmatist' outlook than the air force with their 'god's-eye-perspective' (Shields and Soeters, 2013: 90). In addition, Janowitz (1960: 470ff) points to the importance of developing a so-called *constabulary force* with skills and capabilities that are geared to a minimal use of force and practical problem solving, often in the context of peacekeeping operations. It is not difficult to see the differences between the two views emerging in today's discussions and political-military assessments. *The Professional Soldier* has not lost its relevance.

Civil–military relations, in the West and in developing nations

In line with his ideas about the development of the military profession and organization, Janowitz contributed to the debate on civil–military relations and the civilian and political control of the military. The question 'Who guards the guardians?' summarizes the essence of this debate. We have examined the topic of the control of the military in the chapter on Karl Marx, when we discussed military coups and revolutions. Such rebellious events are rare in today's world, but they are certainly not done with, particularly in nations where democracy has yet to come to full maturity (Janowitz, 1988 [1964]). The notorious military coup in Chile in 1973 and the military rebellion in the summer of 2016 in Turkey may serve as illuminating examples here.

Yet, even if military protests, resistance and coups are uncommon, the military's influence on strategic decision making in matters of security and conflict is quite noticeable and needs therefore to be studied (e.g. Feaver, 1999). The question is how great the impact of the military is and should be. For one thing, the military should not escape political control. Military people are servants of the state, not the other way around. Elected civilians are, and are supposed to remain, the political masters (Feaver, 1996). There are two contrasting views in this connection, one of which is formulated by Janowitz. He responded to a book on this theme authored by another famous scholar that had been published some years prior to *The Professional Soldier*.

In 1957, during the heyday of the Cold War, Samuel Huntington published *The Soldier and the State*, in which he developed a clear stance with respect to the civilian control of the military. He coined the concept of 'objective civilian control' that commences with the recognition that the military sphere of action ideally is independent, autonomous and separated from politics (Feaver, 1996: 160; Burk, 2002). Meddling in the conduct of military affairs by politicians should be avoided, according to this view. In Huntington's analysis, military autonomy leads to military professionalization, which leads to political neutrality and voluntary subordination, which in turn will lead to secure civilian control (Feaver, 1996: 160). This reasoning – popular among the military themselves – is questionable in the eyes of others, including Janowitz. For instance, one cannot say that the Turkish armed forces are unprofessional; yet in the summer of 2016 there was a coup d'état initiated and staged by at least parts of those forces. And it was not the first one in the country.

Janowitz rejects the ideal-type division of labour between politics and the military that Huntington suggests; instead, he sees a blurring and interpenetration of the political and military spheres (Burk, 2002). Janowitz follows a more descriptive way of analysing the relations between politics (civilians) and the military. As such, he sees both spheres converging in the sense that politicians and civil servants impact on military decision making through the budget process, the allocation of roles and missions, and advice regarding foreign policy (Feaver, 1996: 165). On the other hand, the military influences political decision making via politicking in the preparation of major decisions (e.g. purchase of weapons systems), work-arounds in the political-bureaucratic arena, inter-service rivalry and extensive lobbying by actors closely connected to the military. Janowitz argues in favour of measures to reduce the military's weight in decision making. He also trusts the officers' professional ethics to control the military, with which argument he comes close again to Huntington's emphasis on military professionalism.

Therefore, the debate on the civilian control of the military has not ended yet and is in need of further refinement and elaboration, also because it is likely to impact on the military's effectiveness in operations (Bland, 1999; Nielsen, 2005). Following economic theories of organizations analysing the relation between owners and corporate managers (e.g. Douma and Schreuder, 1991), Peter Feaver (2003) has applied principal–agent thinking to civil–military relations. While this approach is connected to economic organization theory, it is also close to Weberian thinking about the relation between *die Herren* and the servants in the bureaucracy. Quite logically, Feaver sees the politicians as the principal and the military as the agent, the 'armed servant', conducting tasks on behalf of the principal.

From there on, it is possible to develop an analytical framework in which the principal can decide to monitor the agent's behaviour (yes/no) and the agent can correspondingly decide to work in accordance with what the principal wants or in line with what the agent him or herself wants (work/ shrink). Finally, the principal can decide to punish the agent's inappropriate behaviour when this is observed (yes/no). Combining these alternatives, it is possible to distinguish eight different outcomes. Feaver (2003: 132–152) has used this analytical scheme to study American decisions as to whether or not to use force and the decision regarding how to use force, in the Cold War period between 1945 and 1989. He demonstrated that most of the times the US military worked in accordance with what the civilian politicians wanted. Only in a very limited number of scenarios (e.g. Korea in the 1950s, Grenada 1983, Lebanon 1983) did the military shirk, which is doing something differently from what the elected politicians had in mind and demanded. Sometimes the military were more aggressive, sometimes they were less so. Feaver's work is a very nice specimen of analytical sociology, an approach that deserves to be elaborated in military sociology (e.g. Hedström and Bearman, 2009). However, no matter how fruitful this analytical approach may be, it does not exclude the researcher's personal view from the examination.

Next to Peter Feaver, Rebecca Schiff (2009; 2012) recently contributed to the field of civil–military relations. Schiff (2012) argues that the Huntingtonian 'separation' approach to civil–military relations – civilian politicians decide and let the military run the war – is still influential in American politics and its military operations. In fact, such institutional separation was the ideal that was to be implemented in Iraq after the operations would have ended. This intention failed conspicuously, however, because the model of separating the democratic state from the indigenous Iraqi tribal authorities, which includes the impact on the military, proved not to be the ideal solution for the country (Schiff, 2012: 322).

Therefore, Schiff contends that a new theory, the so-called 'concordance theory', may be helpful to provide a framework for the analysis of civil–military relations, not only in the West but also elsewhere on the globe. She distinguishes four key indicators to study the level of agreement between the military, the politicians and the citizenry. These are: (1) the social composition of the officer corps, (2) the political decision making process, (3) the method of recruiting, and (4) military style. If there is agreement on these indicators among the military, the politicians and the citizenry, military intervention in domestic affairs through coups or shirking is less likely to occur. She applied this framework successfully to a variety of nations, among them India, Pakistan, Argentina, Israel and the United States. The coup in the summer of 2016 in Turkey clearly indicated disagreement between leading politicians, parts of the citizenry and parts of the armed forces, which is fully in line with this framework. However, there are other, economic factors in play too.

'Khaki capitalism' and civil–military relations

Paul Chambers and Napisa Waitoolkiat (2017) have revealed how much armed forces in Southeast Asia, in particular Thailand but also elsewhere on the continent, have gained control over economic resources. They attained such dominance by building an economic empire, sometimes 'by living off the land' (timbering, mining, selling wild animals) or by providing coercive services to private 'clients'. Through maximizing their sources of income, the military have acquired such power that it is difficult for even the best-intentioned civilian governments to control them. This 'khaki capitalism' is certainly not a phenomenon limited to the Far East. In the Middle East and in Africa, for instance in DR Congo, one can find similar dynamics, as we saw before. And we saw that even in the West the armed forces have gradually become an economic factor in itself as a number of industries and military interests have become interwoven to a large degree. In developing nations this interpenetration seems more striking and less in control, however.

This brings us back to Janowitz, in particular to his work on military institutions and coercion in the developing nations, previously called the 'new nations' (Janowitz, 1988 [1964]). In this short book (*Military Institutions and Coercion in the Developing Nations*) he demonstrates with statistical data the increasingly important role of paramilitary forces in developing nations, in Latin America and elsewhere. The role of coercion in such nations requires a perspective that does more than study the regular armed forces. It also requires an examination of the role of the police and paramilitary forces such as the gendarmerie, local defence units and workers' militia, as well as their interconnected roles in internal policing. Janowitz also presented and analysed statistical data on military coups in developing countries in relation to the date of their independence. Using meticulous statistical data on the military in developing nations, he provided an example for current military sociologists to engage in comparative analysis, preferably on the basis of case-by-case assessments, and to work on sociologies of the military that 'connect' the continents of the planet. In this, he revived a lesson that had been taught by Emile Durkheim several decades earlier.

The all-volunteer force

As mentioned in previous chapters, the military in Western nations has experienced a remarkable change over the last couple of decades. Since the times of Napoleon, military organizations had consisted of large numbers of conscripted soldiers. However, soon after the Second World War Canada abolished the draft system, followed by the UK and Australia and the USA in the 1960s and 1970s (Van Doorn, 1975; Burk, 1992). Later, starting in the 1990s, nations on the European continent, such as the Netherlands, Belgium,

France, Germany, Italy and Sweden followed suit (e.g. van der Meulen and Manigart, 1997). After the turn of the century, Central European countries such as Poland, Hungary and Bulgaria did the same. In Russia the conscript system is still alive, even though it is hotly debated. Together with a number of other scholars, including Dutch sociologist Jacques van Doorn, Janowitz analysed this development in an early stage (Janowitz, 1972). During the Vietnam War criticism of compulsory military service swelled because of rising levels of education among the young population, the relative deprivations of military service compared to the 'easy' civilian life, and the declining appeal of nationalism (Burk, 1992: 48). Also, the course of the Vietnam War – broadcasted nation-wide on TV – turned out to be so unfortunate and severe for the Americans especially that it contributed to the waning of enthusiasm for performing military service. For sure, the media added a lot to the critical way the war was perceived at home (Carruthers, 2011), and they may be an element in the theory of the long-term decline of violence that we will encounter in the chapter on Norbert Elias. Similar developments in public and political opinion had emerged in continental Europe. In those countries the probabilities of territorial crises had always been much higher than on the Anglo-Saxon 'islands', but that changed once the Cold War ended in 1989. The combination of these developments and changing technological requirements made the introduction of professional armies conceivable. This happened faster than many analysts had thought possible.

The consequences were applauded. Professional soldiers, volunteers, could be dispatched to operations overseas much more easily than conscripts, one advantage being that the required and available numbers of personnel were considerably smaller. This was a major advantage given the crises in the former Yugoslavia in the 1990s, the later operations in Afghanistan and Iraq and the anti-piracy missions in the Arabian Sea. Furthermore, professional soldiers are self-selected and more likely to be willing and able to use violence. In addition, they can be trained more intensely, leading to better skills, drills and general combat competences than the conscript soldier – the citizen soldier – ever had (e.g. King, 2013). The AVF proved to be beneficial for the job and career opportunities of racial minorities in the USA (e.g. Janowitz and Moskos, 1974). The AVF introduced civilian standards of organizing into the military, including women's access (Dandeker, 1994). The latter was a major breakthrough seen from a civil rights and feminist perspective. Besides, the AVF was understood to be more in line with the increasing occupational, i.e. more calculative, rational, utilitarian and individualistic, orientation of the working population – instead of the institutional orientation that makes men serve their country in the military no matter what (Moskos, 1977; Segal and Wechsler Segal, 1983; Moskos and Wood, 1988). Finally, the AVF proved to be smaller and more flexible, which again was conducive to making swift deployment decisions (Dandeker, 1994). However, there were, and there are, worries too.

Most important, is the concern that the military drifts apart from society at large. In an assessment of the first five years of the all-volunteer force in the

USA Janowitz and Moskos (1979) discussed the various implications. They particularly examined the AVF's consequences with respect to the required size of manpower, the fiscal costs, the educational background and social composition of the force and the political orientation of the professional soldiers including its impact on civil–military relations. The two sociologists were fairly relaxed about the latter because the personnel turnover of professional soldiers is high as their stay in the military usually is only a part of their whole career. Because of this extensive turnover, more than enough men and women from the general population take part in the military, as they claimed (Janowitz and Moskos, 1979: 211).

Yet, the proportion of professional soldiers and sailors compared to the whole working population has not stopped declining over the years (Liebert and Golby, 2017). The political orientation of the senior officer corps in the USA is another worry, as large numbers of professional military officers affiliate with the Republican party (Liebert and Golby, 2017: 119). The number of military officers who call themselves politically independent has decreased in the most recent decades, while on the contrary in the population at large affiliation with any political party has decreased. It renders the professional military in the USA more divergent from mainstream society than it used to be, which may have consequences. One of the possible consequences is that politicians – influenced by the military top brass commanding a 'tribe of warriors' – may more easily decide to engage in operations overseas and prefer combat action over peacekeeping and reconstruction missions. Sometimes this may work out positively, sometimes much less so.

The dilemmas and occurrences in the USA are comparable to, and have an impact on, what is happening in other parts of the globe. However, there may be different policy considerations and doubts in those other countries.

The return of the draft system?

Even though quite a number of Western nations have decided to abolish the conscript system, others have not, and some are on the brink of revising the AVF system. This fluctuation relates to a number of developments. First, threat perceptions differ among nations. The Baltic states perceive Russia to be threatening their borders, particularly in view of their history, the recent events in eastern Ukraine, and the particular situation of the Russian-speaking minorities in their countries. For these reasons, Estonia has never abolished the conscript system and Lithuania is reconsidering its decision to install a professional army. Referring to similar motives (except for the Russian-speaking minorities), Sweden has reintroduced the conscript system, in which conscripts are mixed with volunteers. In Finland, Norway, Israel, Greece and Turkey, threat perceptions have always been so high that the conscript system was never abolished. There are other reasons to question the idea of abandoning the draft. First, it is often difficult to recruit and retain enough personnel, particularly personnel with highly specialized skills and competences. Paying higher wages, hiring more civilian personnel, also for higher positions, and outsourcing work to private military companies are solutions to these problems. Yet, the worries of not having good enough personnel remain. Second, the loss of the citizen soldier, the conscript soldier, may be detrimental to civil–military relations because the military and society may no longer understand and trust each other the way they did, when all men were inserted into the armed forces during a period of their lifetime (Burk, 2002). For one thing, politicians today rarely have any military experience, whereas almost all used to be military men themselves in earlier times.

Conclusion

During his career, Morris Janowitz showed himself to be a believer in and supporter of John Dewey's ideas on pragmatism. As we saw before, Jane Addams was also influenced by these thoughts, leading her to develop a life characterized by political activism. This was not the path Janowitz pursued, but he was convinced that sociology should not be 'self-indulgent'; sociological research should have a clear relation to pressing societal issues (Burk, 1991: 27). His work involved a commitment to social reconstruction and development, based on critical studies of how people organize their common life. In his eyes, sociological research should help to do away with societal strains, define realistic alternative courses of action and clarify their consequences (Burk, 1991: 27). In this Morris Janowitz shared his basic motivation to do scholarly work with other founding sociologists.

Bibliography

Bland, D.L. (1999) 'A unified theory of civil–military relations'. *Armed Forces and Society* 26(1): 7–26.

Boëne, B. (1995) 'Conditions d'emergence et de développement d'une sociologie specialisée: le cas de la sociologie militaire aux Etats-Unis'. Thesis, University of Paris V René Descartes.

Boëne, B. (2011) 'Classiques des sciences sociales dans le champ militaire'. *Res Militaris* 1(3): 1–42.

Burk, J. (1991) 'Introduction: a pragmatic sociology'. In M. Janowitz, *On Social Organization and Social Control* (ed. J. Burk). Chicago and London: University of Chicago Press.

Burk, J. (1992) 'The decline of mass armed forces and compulsory military service'. *Defense Analysis* 8(1): 45–59.

Burk, J. (1993) 'Morris Janowitz and the origins of sociological research on armed forces and society'. *Armed Forces and Society* 19(2): 167–185.

Burk, J. (2002) 'Theories of democratic civil–military relations'. *Armed Forces and Society* 29(1): 7–29.

Carruthers, S.L. (2011) *The Media at War.* 2nd edn. Basingstoke and New York: Palgrave Macmillan.

Chambers, P. and N. Waitoolkiat (2017) *Khaki Capital: The Political Economy of the Military in Southeast Asia.* Copenhagen: NIAS Press.

Cortright, D. (1975) *Soldiers in Revolt: GI Resistance during the Vietnam War.* Chicago: Haymarket Books.

Dandeker, Chr. (1994) 'New times for the military: some sociological remarks on the changing role and structure of the armed forces of the advanced societies'. *British Journal of Sociology* 45(4): 637–654.

Douma, S. and H. Schreuder (1991) *Economic Approaches to Organizations.* New York: Prentice-Hall.

Feaver, P. (1996) 'The civil-military problematique: Huntingon, Janowitz, and the questions of civilian control'. *Armed Forces and Society* 23(2): 149–178.

Feaver, P. (1999) 'Civil–military relations'. *Annual Review of Political Science* 2: 211–241.

Feaver, P. (2003) *Armed Servants.* Cambridge, MA: Harvard University Press.

Hedström, P. and P. Bearman (eds) (2009) *The Oxford Handbook of Analytical Sociology.* Oxford: Oxford University Press.

Huntington, S.P. (1957) *The Soldier and the State: The Theory and Politics of Civil–Military Relations.* Cambridge, MA: Harvard University Press.

Janowitz, M. (1946) 'German reactions to Nazi atrocities'. *American Journal of Sociology* 52(2): 141–146.

Janowitz, M. (1957) 'Military elites and the study of war'. *Journal of Conflict Resolution,* March: 9–18.

Janowitz, M. (1959) 'Changing patterns of organizational authority: the military establishment'. *Administrative Science Quarterly* 3(4): 473–493.

Janowitz, M. (1960) *The Professional Soldier and Political Power: A Theoretical Orientation and Selected Hypotheses.* Ann Arbor: University of Michigan Press.

Janowitz, M. (1988 [1964]) *Military Institutions and Coercion in the Developing Nations.* Chicago and London: University of Chicago Press.

Janowitz, M. (1969) 'Sociological models and social policy'. *Archives for Philosophy of Law and Social Philosophy* 55(3): 307–319.

Janowitz, M. (1970) *Political Conflict: Essays in Political Sociology.* Chicago: Quadrangle Books.

Janowitz, M. (1972) 'Decline of the mass army'. *Military Review* (February): 10–16.

Janowitz, M. (1975) 'Sociological theory and social control'. *American Journal of Sociology* 81(1): 82–108.

Janowitz, M. and Ch.C. Moskos (1974) 'Racial composition in the all-volunteer force'. *Armed Forces and Society* 1(1): 109–123.

Janowitz, M. and Ch.C. Moskos (1979) 'Five years of the all-volunteer force, 1973–1978'. *Armed Forces and Society* 5(2): 171–218.

King, A. (2013) *The Combat Soldier: Infantry Tactics and Cohesion in the Twentieth and Twentieth-First Centuries.* Oxford: Oxford University Press.

Laudani, R. (2013) *Secret Reports on Nazi Germany: The Frankfurt School Contribution to the War Effort.* Princeton NJ and Oxford: Princeton University Press.

Liebert, H. and J. Golby (2017) 'Midlife crisis? The all-volunteer force at 40'. *Armed Forces and Society* 43(1): 115–138.

Merton, R.K. and P.F. Lazersfeld (1950) *Continuities in Social Research: Studies in the Scope and Method of the American Soldier.* Glencoe, IL: Free Press.

Moskos, C. (1977) 'From institutions to occupations: trends in military organizations'. *Armed Forces and Society* 4(1): 41–50.

Moskos, Ch.C. and F.R. Wood (eds) (1988) *The Military: More Than Just a Job?* Washington, DC: Pergamon-Brassey's.

Nielsen, S.C. (2005) 'Civil–military relations theory and military effectiveness'. *Public Administration and Management* 10(2): 5–28.

Schiff, R. (2009) *The Military and Domestic Politics: A Concordance Theory of Civil–Military Relations*. London and New York: Routledge.

Schiff, R.L. (2012) 'Concordance theory, targeted partnership, and counterinsurgency strategy'. *Armed Forces and Society* 38(2): 318–339.

Segal, D. and M. Wechsler Segal (1983) 'Change in military organization'. *Annual Review of Sociology* 9: 151–170.

Shields, P. and J. Soeters (2013) 'Pragmatism, peacekeeping and the constabulary force'. In S.J. Ralston (ed.), *Philosophical Pragmatism and International Relations: Essays for a Bold World*. Lanham, MD: Lexington Books, pp. 87–110.

Shils, E. and M. Janowitz (1948) 'Cohesion and disintegration in the Wehrmacht in World War II'. *Public Opinion Quarterly* 12: 280–315.

Stouffer, S.A., E.A. Suchman, L.C. DeVinney, S.A. Star and R.M. Williams (1949a) *The American Soldier: Adjustment during Army Life*. Princeton, NJ: Princeton University Press.

Stouffer, S.A., A.A. Lumsdaine, M.H. Lumsdaine, R.M. Williams, M.B. Smith, L. Janis, S.A. Star and L.S. Cottrell (1949b) *The American Soldier: Combat and Its Aftermath*. Princeton, NJ: Princeton University Press.

Van Doorn, J.A.A. (1975) *The Soldier and Social Change: Comparative Studies in the History and Sociology of the Military*. Beverly Hills CA and London: Sage.

Van der Meulen, J. and Ph. Manigart (1997) 'Zero draft in the low countries: the final shift to the all-volunteer force'. *Armed Forces and Society* 24(2): 315–332.

Williams, R.M. (1946) 'Some observations on sociological research in government during World War II'. *American Sociological Review* 11(5): 573–577.

Williams, R.M. (1989) 'The American soldier: an assessment several wars later'. *Public Opinion Quarterly* 53(2): 155–174.

10 Norbert Elias

Decline of violence, habitus in combat, international relations

Even though Norbert Elias (1897–1990) published his work not that long ago, its influence on sociological thinking can hardly be overestimated. The theories of this sociologist, who fled the Nazi regime in Germany in the 1930s, have become classical sociology even during his lifetime and they are immensely important in the context of the study of the military institution and large-scale violence (Mennell, 1992; Moelker, 2003; Soeters, 2005; Kilminster, 2007; Dunning and Hughes, 2013). Like Durkheim did at the outbreak of the First World War, Elias (2013) wondered later about the specific role of the Germans in the emergence of so much war and violence in Europe during the nineteenth and particularly the twentieth century. Elias' main sociological message has been constant and pertains to domains that range from behaviour that was displayed in historical court societies to hooligan behaviour in current sports events. Hence, not only military students but also historians and sports officials can profit from his findings and analyses.

Here, we discuss three elements of Elias' work, some of which continue to raise many eyebrows, particularly the first element we are going to discuss. Some people even get angry about it because it clashes with common sense; it seems to contradict what everyone can read in the newspapers.

Civilization and the decline of violence

In 1939, one year before the beginning of World War II, Elias published his magnum opus, *Das Prozess der Zivilisation*, in the English translation *The Civilizing Process* (2000 [1939]). The date of publication, by a Swiss publishing house, was most unfortunate as its main message was at odds with what was about to happen (Van Iterson, 2009).

In this two-volume work Elias showed how people have gradually become more dependent on one another, economically, socially and mentally. In the Middle Ages – Elias' work is truly a specimen of historical sociology – people lived in small-scale local or regional communities, such as counties and duchies. Local wars between knights and their part-time peasant soldiers were rife and frequent; the building of castles – which still stand all over Europe – was not only a matter of luxury and wealth of the local rulers, but it was also an indication of the necessity to protect oneself. As time progressed, the autonomy of counties and duchies gradually disappeared because of the rise of centralized nation-states who were able to enjoy a monopoly on taxation, and more importantly, on violence. The foundation of central police forces and armed forces financed by national taxes and – somewhat later – based on conscription is closely connected with the rise of nation-states (e.g. Tilly, 1992).

This macro-development (*sociogenesis*) went hand in hand with considerable changes in people's behaviour at the micro-level (*psychogenesis*). This first occurred at the courts of the new royals and later among others in the population who started to internalize the changing standards of manners and morality (Van Iterson, 2009: 330). In Elias' words, people's behaviour over the centuries became more *civilized*. Gradually social refinement, in earlier times enforced by external constraints from teachers, clergymen and other authorities, developed into self-restrained and even-tempered behaviour among people. This process is still continuing. The changes in manners referred to eating habits, conversation styles, hygienic norms, standards of informality and sexuality, and opinions about the *lesser* others such as slaves, or today the poor, the powerless and the needy in developing countries. All these changing norms and manners pointed – and continue to point – in the direction of more inhibition and self-restraint, even with respect to the treatment of animals, for instance. And, more important for this book, these changing norms indicated a less prominent place for violence, aggression and cruelty in everyday life and society at large. The use of violence became an exception, no longer an everyday practice.

The military was very much part of these developments. First, as the centralization of nation-states progressed, fighting and warring as an everyday experience, the way it often was in the Middle Ages, gradually disappeared. Instead, fewer people got involved in military action as at first only merchant-soldiers and later only the conscripted draftees – young men – were the ones who experienced war and combat from inside. Other people were excluded from practical military affairs, even though not always from its consequences, such as the citizens of the Syrian city of Aleppo and elsewhere in that country have experienced in recent years. The development of having fewer people involved in military affairs has progressed continuously, most recently by the introduction of the all-volunteer force that once again requires fewer people to join the armed forces and engage in combat. It led British sociologist Martin Shaw to speak about the coming of a *Post-Military Society*, in which 'society has developed beyond the military and militarism as they have been understood in most of the twentieth century' (Shaw, 1991: viii).

Second, as opposition to violence gradually intensified, the use of military violence itself became more restrained, and this trend continues today. Under societal, political and legal pressure, the military felt and feels the urge to avoid collateral damage as much as possible. It also wants to incur much fewer casualties, particularly among its own troops, but also among hostile forces and adversaries in general. The concerns about the latter, however, are much less internalized. As a consequence, casualties among opponents and host national populations are much less well monitored.

Going back in history, one can see that the number of casualties among the soldiers in both world wars has been incomparably larger than the number of soldiers killed in action in the many colonial wars that ensued, including the 'policing actions' of the Dutch in Indonesia (1946–1949), the British counter-insurgency in Malaya (1946–1960), the French operations in Algeria (1950s) and the Vietnam War in the 1960s and 1970s. People are less inclined to find large numbers of casualties acceptable, a trend that began in the second half of the twentieth century continues today.

The number of casualties among American soldiers in the Vietnam War has been much larger than in the more recent operations in Iraq and Afghanistan (if we control for the numbers actually deployed in those wars). The commanders in Vietnam were satisfied if the death count among enemy forces was larger than the number of casualties among their own troops. This led officers in the Vietnam War to engage in reckless, careless and meaningless ways of planning and ordering operations that now, half a century later, is completely unthink-able, let alone acceptable (Caputo, 1999 [1977]). The operations in Iraq and Afghanistan – even though quite violent at some points in time – have led to considerably less bloodshed, at least among Western troops.

The Eliasian analysis of these developments has attracted worldwide attention through the work of Steven Pinker (2011; 2015), a psychologist and linguist from Harvard University who has also written many best-selling works of popular science. His work on 'the decline of violence in history' is fully in line with Elias' thinking and in fact it is even broader. It is based on numerous (historical) statistics, which is something Elias did not work with. And Pinker pays attention to developments Elias did not pay a lot of attention to, such as the humanitarian revolution leading to the abolition of slavery and capital punishment, and the worldwide rights movements focusing on women's, chil-dren's, minorities', gays' and even animal rights. Also, the end of the dictatorial regimes in Southern and Eastern Europe – Portugal, Spain, Greece, Rumania, Bulgaria, etc. – which occurred in a timespan of about twenty years, may be seen as an indicator in this regard. At the beginning of the 1970s those military-backed regimes were still very much alive; in the 1990s none of them existed. Latin American nations, such as Argentina, saw similar developments. Pinker does not stand alone with his analysis of the decline of violence. He is sup-ported by the work of Joshua Goldstein (2011), who also contends that war occurs less frequently and has become less dangerous, his arguments being based on different case-material. There is among others also support from his-torical studies on the development of (violent) crime throughout the centuries (Dunning and Hughes, 2013: 42–43).

Yet, these analyses – no matter how substantiated by academic literature and worldwide comparative, continuously updated statistics – tend to be con-troversial because they are contrary to popular beliefs. Some people react to the message regarding the decline of violence with disbelief, irritation and even anger. With so much violence occurring every day in Syria, Libya and Iraq, with Russia taking over the Crimea from the Ukraine, and with the ceaseless terrorist attacks in Europe and its neighbouring countries such as Turkey, Pinker's message simply cannot be true. It must be incorrect because, after the heavy bombardments, Aleppo in 2016 did not look any different from Berlin in 1945 and Grozny in 2000. Some even tend to think that this analysis belittles the value of lives that are still being lost every day due to violence. Some – particularly military people – tend to think that this analysis is a plea to cut the budgets of armed and other security forces. And some tend to dislike the pacifist odour that seems to accompany the analysis. British journalist John Gray (2015) among others echoes this controversy and displays opinions on Pinker's work in which he can hardly hide his annoyance and condescending stance.

Malešević and Ryan (2012) have criticized Elias' analysis in an academic manner. They argue that his theory of civilizing fails to account for the persistence and proliferation of warfare in the modern age. Matching the whole climate that surrounds this discussion, they make the accusation that Elias' work is 'shaped by a yearning for a fully pacified world' (Malešević and Ryan, 2012: 178; see also Malešević, 2014; 2017). Their rebuttals pertain to the interpretation of the historical documents that Elias used and the mass murders in the twentieth century which are indeed not easy to understand using Elias' reasoning. Remarkably enough, they do not pay much attention to historical developments that may or may not occur or have occurred – the way Elias and Pinker do. Instead, they make a sort of essentialist claim that war has not disappeared, which is something that no one ever denied, let alone Elias or Pinker. Nor would Elias, if he were still alive, and Pinker disagree with Taleb's point (2015) that violence, and dramatic violence too, can break out any time in the near future. That is not the point, though.

Elias' work is too important to disappear in a whirlpool of fact-free controversy. Abraham De Swaan (2015; also 2001) – an Eliasian sociologist from the Netherlands – has also struggled with the Holocaust, like all of us including Elias himself. How could such a pervasive act of immense cruelty and destruction have happened in civilized societies such as Western Europe? How could the Khmer Rouge's actions in Cambodia lead to the death of 2 million inhabitants in the 1970s (Bizot, 2004)? And how could the killing of hundreds of thousands of Tutsis and so-called moderate Hutus have occurred as recently as 1994? Are these developments the ultimate proof that Elias was wrong after all?

De Swaan points at the importance of combining various levels of analysis to understand the occurrence of such gruesome acts of what he coined 'dys-civilization'. First, macro-sociological conditions such as economic depression, military defeat and/or political upheaval leading to the rise of authoritarian regimes create the basic conditions. If this connects with a long term mentality among the general population that incriminates and puts some population groups in a bad light, for instance Jews or Tutsis, the situation worsens. If, at the meso-sociological level, the regime's institutions are capable of mobilizing and recruiting especially those who have an individual disposition to commit violence (also: Collins, 2008), the fire flares up, leading at the micro-sociological level to the actual killing. These are the geographical and time-bound 'killing compartments' that most unfortunately sometimes occur in otherwise peaceful times (De Swaan, 2015).

Apparently, the process of civilization and the decline of violence – as discovered by Elias and elaborated by Pinker and Goldstein – is in constant movement. It goes back and forth, sometimes erratically, with a general tendency towards the controlling of, and hence, the decline of violence (see Figure 10.1).

The movements that can occur in the processes of civilization and de- and dys-civilization may be summarized as follows (Soeters, 2005: 48–51; also: de Swaan, 2001; Tilly, 2003: 55–80). Peaceful times occur in today's civilized societies with a stable, democratic government system and with rationally acting bureaucratic police and military forces; in Tilly's words (2003: 75), *high-capacity democratic regimes*. In these societies the control of violence has progressed over time, implying that violence has declined. Unlike previous – for instance colonial – times, these societies' militaries no longer engage in the careless use of force while on operation. Even if they had the tendency to do so, close observation by news and social media and sensitivities among the general population would prevent this from happening. However, even these civilized societies may encounter serious setbacks, such as the rise of violent subcultures, murderous crimes, terrorist attacks and the consequential upheavals. One could argue that the current wave of terrorist attacks spreading throughout the Western hemisphere is such a setback. It may lead these societies to strike back, most often – not always, though (!) – in controlled, restrained ways. If these societies are capable of intensifying the prevention and control of these internal threats in a restrained, calm, unbiased and legally binding manner, they are likely to bring back peaceful times.

Societies are less advanced in dealing with violence when the political system is less firmly based on democratic and lawful habits and practices, and when the police and armed forces are more patrimonial or pre-bureaucratic; in Tilly's words (2003: 75), *low-capacity undemocratic regimes*, such as those in Somalia, Yemen or Libya today. We have seen before what this may imply. The forces may be weak and ineffective, and, more importantly, they may be biased in composition and attitude while responding to the roots of the troubles that occur. Particularly if the rule of law is weak and corrupted, violence may flare up and may only cease once the perpetrators' blood thirst has been satisfied. Possible external factors, such as interventions by the United Nations, may prevent this from happening, but sometimes they are too weak or too late to respond effectively, as the Rwanda genocide or the civil wars in Congo showed (e.g. Dallaire, 2004). It is not difficult to see such situations evolving in current times; the rise of ISIS in the Middle East has been a topical example. Elias and his followers are right. These are increasingly peaceful times indeed, but not always and everywhere. Unfortunately, civilization comes with erratic instances of de- or dys-civilization. And no one can foretell the future, for sure.

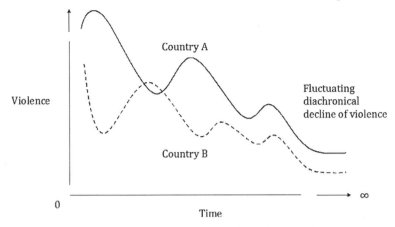

Figure 10.1 Fluctuating diachronic decline of violence in two different countries
Source: Developed in cooperation with Esmeralda Kleinreesink and Jacqueline Heeren-Bogers.

Figure 10.1 shows the tendency for violence to decline, but it does so in an almost erratic manner, with differences between countries. The figure also indicates that a zero level of violence will not be reached in the foreseeable future. In the next chapter we will deal more specifically with national differences in the (military) use of violence.

Habitus in combat

If police and military forces – next to the general political and legal climate – are so important in controlling violence, the question arises of how they do this. Here the concept of *habitus*, made famous by French sociologist Pierre Bourdieu (e.g. Grenfell, 2014), is important. Habitus is about our ways of acting, feeling, thinking, being and making choices that are at least partly dependent on the paths we have followed so far. It is a key sociological concept that aligns the classical sociologists with Elias, Bourdieu and so many others.

Following up on the previous discussion about cohesion at the primary group level, Anthony King (2013) has worked on the issue of 'habitus in combat', and he starts by applauding the combat skills of today's armed forces. He aligns with previous analyses, particularly from World War II, on the relatively poor performance and low cohesion of conscript armies, the 'citizen armies' of the twentieth century. He refers to studies which showed that many American conscripts in their engagements with Japanese troops lost their composure and were not capable of adequate reactions when under attack. Next to World War II, the often-failing performance of US soldiers in the Vietnam War has been another example in this connection (Moskos, 1974). The all-volunteer force was introduced because of the unpopularity of the draft system and because it was deemed cheaper, but it certainly was also a response to the fiascoes in Vietnam (e.g. Janowitz and Moskos, 1979). Since then, armies have become more effective as 'all soldiers in a professional army are trained to a high level to perform a common set of drills'. This is important because 'intense training [...] fundamentally changes the collective performance of which combat soldiers are capable especially in the confusing environment of battle' (King, 2013: 273). Of course, being able to select the 'violent few' (Collins, 2008) for the combat units and specialized forces, which is what all-volunteer forces do, helps to increase the fighting capabilities of today's militaries.

King stresses the invaluable contribution of formal rituals as manifested in training, competences and drills, and the communication and instructions of plans, all leading to the internalization of rules and discipline. Not surprisingly, his emphasis is on combat- or combat support units. A British citizen, he observes much to his satisfaction that other, for a long time more mild-mannered, national armed forces such as those from postwar Germany are taking the same road as the British forces did over the past decades (King, 2013: 278–280). In King's analysis, these formal training rituals prevail over personal bonding or even antagonistic relations between soldiers. It also allows for the inclusion of soldiers who were previously excluded, or set apart, on the basis of ethnicity, skin colour, sexuality or gender: all can be professional soldiers once they have properly internalized the procedures, drills and skills. We will turn to this latter point in Chapter 13 on Cynthia Enloe's work.

For sure, these elements contribute to rendering the modern soldier more self-disciplined, self-controlled and self-confident. External discipline and internal discipline thus coincide. Following the drills and procedures exactly – also because of legal considerations as the ultimate manifestation of external discipline – there is a high degree of self-restraint among today's military men and women. One could even say that the gestures and movements of a platoon in action tend to resemble the choreography of a ballet company, which is another example of what Elias refers to in this connection. Hence, all of this is perfectly in conformance with Elias' idea of increasing self-restraint and self-constraint within and among people in general. This does not always work perfectly, though, as the following text box shows.

Savage restraint

James Ron (2000) studied the way Israeli security forces responded to the Palestinian uprising in the West Bank and Gaza Strip in the late 1980s. Under the influence of civil society, international human rights activists and state functionaries, clear and legally binding instructions were issued by the Israeli Defence Force aimed at the limited use of (lethal) violence. Nonetheless, officers and soldiers were apt to circumvent and work around these rules and instructions. They 'decoupled' rule-conformity for public consumption from practical rule-deviation to get the work done. Ron describes 'operating codes' that did not occur in spite of military regulations but because of them. These included distorted incarceration procedures, extra-judicial beatings, torture and the 'shortened procedure' for apprehending suspects (Ron, 2000: 454ff). This analysis shows that restrained military behaviour is a formal prerequisite in today's democratic societies. However, in everyday military practice this restraint may manifest itself to be fairly rude and savage, in Ron's words.

There is another aspect that requires attention with respect to the process of increasing self-restraint among people in general and the military in particular. Wouters (2007) has analysed how the idea of self-restraint has been going hand in hand with developments towards behavioural *informalization*. Office workers used to be 'decently' dressed, but recently a more casual style has entered the work environment – ties and high heels are no longer obligatory and tattoos are generally accepted. Sexual relations have become more loose and casual, and manners of speech with one another and superiors have become less formal. Even working during traditional working hours ('nine to five') has become less of an official prerequisite. Wouters aligns this development with the general process Elias has revealed, and he referred to this tendency as 'the controlled de-controlling of emotions' in the workplace and elsewhere (see also Van Iterson, 2009). If behaviour becomes less self-restrained, this can only be in a very controlled manner; if not, the social costs of such deviation are likely to be too high.

It is not difficult to ascertain similar tendencies among military personnel, even during operations. As we just saw, today's military displays a high degree of self-restraint, as expressed in legal considerations with respect to the use of violence and bans on alcohol and sexual affairs during operations (even though the latter do not exist in all armed forces in the same manner). Nonetheless, a certain informalization can be observed that pertains to outward appearance and relaxation of hierarchical relations (the increasing use of first names when addressing junior commanders, for instance). Interestingly, this informalization may find its legitimation in safety reasons: growing beards and using first names have a functional background. These practices make the distance from the potentially dangerous host-population at the same time less substantial if host nationals grow beards themselves, and less transparent because first names are generally less specific than family names. Such informal practices are conducive to the actual performance of the operations. Of course, military personnel who are not on duty take part in the general informalization that has occurred in Western societies.

This leaves us with a final point in this connection. In a co-authored study on sport and violence Elias has pointed to the 'quest for excitement in unexciting societies' (Mennell, 1992: 141–143). In today's societies people need to lead a stable life, without emotional outbursts or extravert – crying, singing, dancing, clapping, shouting – spontaneous conduct. Comparable to what we have seen with respect to informalization, this type of behaviour is usually suppressed and only accepted in special situations, or enclaves, during leisure or spare time: music festivals, dance parties, games and sports events. Occasionally, these outbursts are accompanied by violence; hence, the problem of soccer hooliganism. This phenomenon, suppression and restraint of behaviour vis-à-vis incidental outbursts may be seen in the military as well. Morten Braender (2016) found in a survey of Danish soldiers deployed to Afghanistan that those who had been exposed to combat displayed a higher degree of excitement motivation than those who had experienced only a low degree of combat exposure. They are the ones who return from war wanting more. The author compares this with addicts who push up their need for narcotics; here the soldiers' tolerance of excitement gets higher because they have been exposed to danger. For sure, since the introduction of the all-volunteer force the military is an interesting place for those who think everyday life in ordinary society is not exciting enough.

International relations

Linklater (2010; 2011) has pointed to the implications of Elias' general theoretical work on social configurations and processes for the study of international relations, which is obviously one of the key disciplines for the study of the military. Linklater starts with the observation that Elias was unusual in placing international relations at the centre of sociological analysis. He devoted more attention to the relations between societies than did many prominent works in social theory and sociology that have been influential in the IR domain (Linklater, 2011: 48). Elias' work is all about connecting processes and interdependencies, be it among states or among individuals.

As far as the study of international relations is concerned, Elias criticized the tendency to disregard long-term historical processes and see the field of international politics as a domain apart from other spheres of political, economic and social existence. He often blamed today's academics and politicians for retreating into the present. Elias always stressed the growing interconnectedness between people in different hemispheres, between regions, between nations, and between nations and post- or supranational communities. The small world of men and women in the Middle Ages gradually developed into their awareness of the 'world at large', which is essentially a cosmopolitan point of view. This led to the abolition of slavery, then, and today, to a growing awareness of the dangers of environmental pollution which threaten the survival of the planet. This human interconnectness comes with ambiguities, ambivalence and tensions, however (Linklater, 2010).

States are good at self-restrained behaviour, yet the danger of the outbreak of large-scale violence, including nuclear violence, is always there. Today's tensions in international affairs can, according to Elias, be better understood by the notion of the 'double-bind process' (Linklater, 2011: 52; Elias, 1987). Decision makers in the states that are caught up in these processes often exaggerate, and even fantasize about, threats. When perceiving danger, they respond in such a manner that they reinforce feelings of distrust and fear in others, which traps all stakeholders in vicious processes that are hard to stop or turn back. 'The resulting circularity invariably binds people more intensely to their "survival units" and lock them into insider–outsider dualisms [...]. Those problems are magnified by forms of "group love" that celebrate using force against others and towering over them' (Linklater, 2011: 52). For sure, emotions play a large role in crucial decisions concerning war and peace, much more than is often acknowledged in the study of international relations (e.g. Bleiker and Hutchison, 2008).

This analysis, based on Elias' interpretation of previous historical events and written down in 2011, has astonishing relevance when one takes a look at the interaction between the West (NATO) and Russia these days. Russia's take-over of the Crimea in 2014, making use of the participation of Russian minorities in eastern Ukraine, has led to anxious responses. Many people in the Baltic States and Poland fear being taken over by Russia in a similar way, and the West feels the responsibility to protect those states because they are part of the NATO alliance (based on the so-called Article V of the NATO treaty). Russia, however, sees NATO troops being deployed next to its borders, first by air patrols above the Baltic States, then by naval vessels sailing close to its coastal waters, and more recently by land forces on neighbouring ground. Given the fact that their domain of influence has already shrunk in recent decades, it is not difficult to imagine that Russian politicians can and want to make their citizens believe their country's safety is at risk, and hence act accordingly, i.e. in a conflict-prone manner. This in turn is something that NATO perceives as a renewed threat, etc., etc. A similar process is taking place in and in the vicinity of the Korean peninsula. One can only hope that the leaders of all nations involved will display a fair amount of Eliasian self-restraint in dealing with these tensions.

There are other tensions in international relations too, though. These may be understood by reference to some of Elias' other work.

The Established and the Outsiders: human interconnectness in the refugee crisis

Norbert Elias and John Scotson (1965) authored a relatively small study of power relations in two English neighbourhoods in the 1960s. This little book is far more important than the empirical context it is based on. Its relevance can be seen in today's refugee crisis, in which hundreds of thousands of refugees from war-torn Syria, but also from Afghanistan and Iraq and many poor African countries, are seeking asylum in the prosperous and safe Europe. This almost inevitably leads to tensions between the 'established' citizens of European countries and the 'outsiders' who want to come in as asylum-seekers and immigrant workers.

These dynamics are all about power relations, as Elias would never cease to emphasize, which is the struggle over the – so far monopolized – access to scarce resources such as jobs, housing and social benefits, as well as group charisma or superiority and group norms.

In this power game the 'established' seek to stigmatize the others by stressing the bad features of the worst of the 'outsiders' – the 'minority of the worst' – comparing this to the characteristics of the best of the 'established' – the 'minority of the best'. This way they are capable of convincing themselves and others that their arguments are right. Applied to the refugee crisis these arguments boil down to pointing at the danger that potential terrorists and criminals are hiding among the refugees and that women's rights will be threatened by the young male asylum seekers who are said to have no idea of how to behave in an appropriate manner. For sure, all of this has emerged because earlier transnational policies to help the poor countries develop themselves and refrain from exhausting violent conflicts have failed or have not been adequate (de Swaan, 1997).

Conclusion

Norbert Elias is certainly a 'classical sociologist', albeit a relatively recent one. As such, his work is far reaching in space and time, and he has paved the way for more recent theories, particularly with respect to the study of emotions among people in organized settings. His work on the decline of violence has met with severe criticism, but remains an important perspective to balance all too hasty generalizations concerning the occurrence of violence in today's societies. Such hasty generalizations may lead to all too hasty decisions about the use of force.

Bibliography

Bizot, F. (2004 [2000]) *The Gate*. London: Vintage Books.
Bleiker, R. and Hutchison, E. (2008) 'Fear no more: emotions and world politics'. *Review of International Studies* 34(S1): 115–135.
Braender, M. (2016) 'Adrenalin junkies: why soldiers return from war wanting more'. *Armed Forces and Society* 42(1): 3–25.
Caputo, Ph. (1999 [1977]) *A Rumor of War*. London: Pimlico.
Collins, R. (2008) *Violence: A Micro-Sociological Approach*. Princeton NJ and Oxford: Princeton University Press.
Dallaire, R. (2004). *Shake Hands with the Devil: The Failure of Humanity in Rwanda*. London: Arrow Books.
De Swaan, A. (1997) 'The receding prospects for transnational social policy'. *Theory and Society* 26(4): 561–575.
De Swaan, A. (2001) 'Dyscivilization, mass extermination and the state'. *Theory, Culture and Society* 18(2–3): 265–276.
De Swaan, A. (2015 [2014]) *The Killing Compartments: The Mentality of Mass Murder*. New Haven CT and London: Yale University Press.

Dunning, E. and J. Hughes (2013) *Norbert Elias and Modern Sociology: Knowledge, Interdependence, Power, Process*. London: Bloomsbury.

Elias, N. (1978 [1970]) *What Is Sociology?* London: Hutchinson.

Elias, N. (1987) *Involvement and Detachment: Contributions to the Sociology of Knowledge*. Oxford: Blackwell.

Elias, N. (2000 [1939]) *The Civilizing Process: Sociogenetic and Psychogenetic Investigations*. Oxford: Blackwell.

Elias, N. (2007) *The Genesis of the Naval Profession*. Dublin: University College Dublin Press.

Elias, N. (2013 [1989]) *Studies on the Germans: Power Struggles and the Development of Habitus in the Nineteenth and Twentieth Centuries*. Dublin: University College Dublin Press.

Elias, N. and J.L. Scotson (2008 [1965]) *The Established and the Outsiders*. Dublin: University College Dublin Press.

Goldstein, J.S. (2011) *Winning the War on War: The Decline of Armed Conflict Worldwide*. New York: Dutton.

Gray, J. (2015) 'Steven Pinker is wrong about violence and war'. *Guardian*, 13 March.

Grenfell, M. (2014) *Pierre Bourdieu*. London: Bloomsbury Academic.

Janowitz, M. and Ch.C. Moskos (1979) 'Five years of the all-volunteer force, 1973–1978'. *Armed Forces and Society* 5(2): 171–218.

Kilminster, R. (2007) *Norbert Elias: Post-philosophical Sociology*. London and New York: Routledge.

King, A. (2006) 'The word of command: communication and cohesion in the military'. *Armed Forces and Society* 32(4): 493–512.

King, A. (2013) *The Combat Soldier: Infantry Tactics and Cohesion in the Twentieth and Twenty-first Centuries*. Oxford: Oxford University Press.

Linklater, A. (2010) 'Global civilizing process and the ambiguities of human interconnectness'. *European Journal of International Relations* 16(2): 155–178.

Linklater, A. (2011) 'Process sociology and international relations'. *The Sociological Review* 59(1): 48–64.

Lipsky, M. (2010 [1980]) *Street-level Bureaucracy: Dilemmas of the Individual in Public Services*. New York: Russell Sage Foundation.

Malešević, S. (2014) 'Is war becoming obsolete? A sociological analysis'. *Sociological Review* 62(S2): 65–86.

Malešević, S. (2017) 'The organization of military violence in the 21st century'. *Organization* 24(4): 456–474.

Malešević, S. and K. Ryan (2012) 'The disfigured ontology of figurational sociology: Norbert Elias and the question of violence'. *Critical Sociology* 39(2): 165–181.

Mennell, S. (1992) *Norbert Elias: An Introduction*. Oxford: Blackwell.

Moelker, R. (2003) 'Norbert Elias, maritime supremacy and the naval profession: on Elias' unpublished studies in the genesis of the naval profession'. *British Journal of Sociology* 54(3): 373–390.

Moskos, Ch. (1974) 'The American combat soldier in Vietnam'. *Journal of Social Issues* 31(4): 25–37.

Pinker, S. (2011) *The Better Angels of Our Nature: The Decline of Violence in History and Its Causes*. London: Allen Lane.

Pinker, S. (2015) 'Response to the Book Review Symposium: Steven Pinker, *The Better Angels of Our Nature*'. *Sociology* 49(4).

Ron, J. (2000) 'Savage restraint: Israel, Palestine and the dialectics of legal repression'. *Social Problems* 47(4): 445–472.

Shaw, M. (1991) *Post-Military Society: Militarism, Demilitarization and War at the End of the Twentieth Century*. Philadelphia, PA: Temple University Press.

Soeters, J. (2005) *Ethnic Conflict and Terrorism: The Origins and Dynamics of Civil Wars*. London and New York: Routledge.

Taleb, N.N. (2015) 'The "long peace" is a statistical illusion'. www.fooledbyrandom ness.com/pinker.pdf (accessed 28 August 2017).

Tilly, Ch. (1992) *Coercion, Capital and European States, AD 990–1990*. Cambridge: Blackwell.

Tilly, Ch. (2003) *The Politics of Collective Violence*. Cambridge: Cambridge University Press.

van Iterson, A. (2009) 'Norbert Elias's impact on organization studies'. In P.S. Adler (ed.), *The Oxford Handbook of Sociology and Organization Studies*. Oxford: Oxford University Press, pp. 327–348.

Wouters, C. (2007) *Informalization: Manners and Emotions since 1890*. Thousand Oaks CA and London: Sage.

11 Cornelis Lammers

Strikes and mutinies, occupational styles, and cooperation

The Dutch sociologist Cornelis Lammers (1928–2009) has become famous as one of the founding fathers of the sociology of organizations in the Netherlands and Europe (e.g. Lammers, 1967; 1990). He started and ended his career, however, studying the military. His doctoral thesis was about the military, in particular about the recruitment and socialization of officer cadets in the Dutch Navy. But he abandoned the topic during his career as a professor of organizational sociology, studying a variety of organizations including hospitals, and comparing characteristics of organizations in different countries. After his retirement he returned to the military again, connecting his work on the international comparison of organizations with the international comparison of military administrations and occupations. This led to meaningful insights and results, as we are about to see.

Cornelis Lammers was a close colleague of another Dutch sociologist who famously contributed to military sociology: Jacques van Doorn. Van Doorn (1975) analysed the rationalization of military operations and the introduction of military discipline in history, pursuing the line Max Weber had developed. He also predicted the end of the mass army. Together with fellow sociologist Wim Hendrix he published an important study on the use of violence by the Dutch armed forces in the decolonization war in today's Indonesia, which he had witnessed as a draftee. Like Lammers, van Doorn spent most of his academic life studying policy and organization topics outside the military. Unlike Lammers, Van Doorn never returned to the military.

Lammers' return to military sociology is important because his comparative work turns out to be relevant for the assessment of military operations and their consequences today. In connection with other scholars' work it shows that there are different national operational and military-administrative styles, with possibly varying degrees of effectiveness and outcomes. In addition, his work is relevant if we want to understand the dynamics of the ongoing internationalization of the military and their operations. First we start with another comparison, though; this pertains to the comparison of inside-politics in industrial and military organizations.

Strikes and mutinies

We briefly touched upon the issue of mutinies in the chapter on Karl Marx when we discussed the phenomenon of military coups. Here we return to this topic as we discuss Lammers' comparative analysis of strikes in industrial organizations and mutinies in the armed forces (Lammers, 1969). As we will soon discover, Lammers' work matches Durkheim's approach in stressing the importance of comparative studies and emphasizing the institutional and cultural aspects of social and organizational life. Yet, the connection with Marx is clear as well. From the beginning of his career Lammers (e.g. 1967) has been interested in the concept and practice of power, participation in decision making, and relations between the rulers and the ruled. He matured as a scholar in the 1960s and 1970s when critical thinking permeated social life and sociological theorizing. He never lost touch, however, with mainstream views more common in other professional spheres. He certainly never claimed to be a Marxist. The influence of Weber on his thinking (power and legitimacy!) is at least as strong as Marx's.

His study of twenty mutinies – mostly on navy vessels – and twenty strikes is a first example of his interest in relations between rulers and ruled. The study makes use of historical cases ranging from the seventeenth century to the mid-twentieth century. Lammers regards both strikes and mutinies as protest movements that are inspired by interests as regards income or other working conditions. This is the most frequent logic of action leading to the emergence of strikes and mutinies. Other goals may be secession motives, i.e. the striving for autonomy, and/or the seizure of power, i.e. collective action by subordinates to replace a superior or a group of superiors (Lammers, 1969: 558ff). Those goals are not mutually exclusive as there may be multiple goals in a strike or mutiny. Besides, goals can be perceived differently by actors at the various hierarchical levels, and they may change and be redefined over time. For the rank and file a conflict may only be about payments or working conditions, whereas the higher levels in the organization may see the same act of insubordination as a seizure of power.

According to Lammers, both strikes and mutinies can be viewed as conflicts that become overt when opposition to the rules is met with counter-movement by the rulers. Violence may occur in both types of protest movement. However, violence is more likely to surface and be more serious in mutinies and strikes that are about secession or seizure of power; violence by strikers or mutineers displaying such motives is usually met with counter-violence (Lammers, 1969: 563). Most often, strikes and mutinies about the promotion of direct, work-related interests result in work stoppages only.

Making use of simple coding and statistical procedures, Lammers was able to show that the outcomes of strikes and mutinies were determined by similar factors, such as the relative strength of the protesters in comparison to that of the rulers. He found a differentiated impact of interventions by third actors, indicating that these are more significant in mutinies. In strikes the conflicting parties can relatively freely settle the dispute among themselves. In mutinies, on the contrary, higher-level decision makers are more likely to enter the arena given the significant political and legal aspects surrounding military organizations.

Lammers (1969: 569) concluded that similar forces have similar effects on both strikes and mutinies so that comparisons between industrial and military organizations are a relevant research approach. However, the manner in which variables operate is conditioned by the institutional context of either the industrial or military organization. In military organizations conflicts are likely to rapidly transform into political conflicts that concern the society at large. Applying these conclusions to a later collection of historical studies of mutinies, Lammers (2003b) was able to validate his previous distinctions, concepts and findings.

Bringing this work to bear on more recent military practice, one is inclined to think of the (quasi-) mutinies by American GIs in the Vietnam War (Cortright, 1975: 29ff). These reflected and influenced both the course of events in the operations and in the political climate at home. This resistance, open or less visible, was the gravest manifestation of the critical climate during the war in Vietnam, as evidenced by the large numbers of applications for conscientious objection, the many cases of administrative discharges, drug abuse and frequently occurring desertions. The resistance in operations consisted of minor combat refusals and the evasion of enemy engagements while on patrol, but the latter stages of the Vietnam War produced at least ten major incidents of mutiny (Cortright, 1975: 35). This in connection with the numerous fragging incidents – superiors being attacked by their own men – shows that the American military was also involved in an 'other war', a battle with insurgents in its own ranks (Cortright, 1975: 43).

As Lammers demonstrated, it is important to study mutinies: they affect politics and are likely to be indicators of failing military leadership and policies. Even though this phenomenon seems to be something from times past, it still constitutes the core of persistent and wicked problems related to the military and large-scale violence in many parts of the world. In the more recent operations in Afghanistan for instance, the so-called 'green on blue' attacks, insider attacks by members of the Afghan National Security Forces on members of US and coalition forces, were a reason for growing concern (e.g. Long, 2013). If one wants to understand the nature of many conflicts in the world, one needs to study how dissatisfaction, relative deprivation, dissent, rebellion and mutinies in the armed forces play a role in those conflicts.

Rebellion in DR Congo

Compared to Western militaries – particularly after conscription was abolished – armed forces in developing countries seem to suffer more often from mutinies and rebellion from within. This seems to be the fate of the under-bureaucratized armed forces that we met in the discussion about Weber's bureaucracy theory. A case in point is the Democratic Republic of Congo (DRC). This nation has been plagued by decades of internal fighting and civil war. One important feature of the attempt to end the conflict was the integration of the fighting forces into a new national army (Erikson et al., 2013). The intention of mixing individual soldiers from different backgrounds into new units – the 'brassage' – failed, however, because several factions withheld their troops and sabotaged the process. The reasons often related to feelings of unpredictability and unfairness. These emerged for instance if the positions allocated in the new army were considered too low compared to the previous ranks one had in one's own armed group (a major for instance instead of a 'commander'). Dissent also occurred if proper benefits (salaries, housing, food) were not available. As a result, the integration process did not really succeed, as indicated by large numbers of army deserters and the proliferation of small-scale dissident militias. Disintegration, rebellion and looting increased because it seemed profitable to do so as rewards were promised to those who threatened with desertion and violent resistance. Inside the new army, parallel command and control structures developed, undermining centralized orders and witnessing low degrees of unit cohesion (Also: Thakur, 2008; Neethling, 2014).

It is important to realize that protest within the military does not always pursue the path of violence. Soldiers, particularly conscript soldiers, sometimes try to influence operations in a direction that is different or opposite to what commanders tell them to do. Whistle blowing, 'grey' refusals, foot dragging and collective bargaining about deployments provide soldiers with a certain degree of 'control from within', as experiences in the Israeli military have shown (Levy, 2017).

Occupational and administrative styles

At the end of his career, Lammers pursued his interest in relations between the rulers and the ruled. He again delved into historical sources, but this time he focused on the occupation of European nations and colonies by German and Japanese forces during World War II (Lammers, 1988; 1991; 1995). Later, after retirement he practised this type of work studying colonial occupations and administrations that had existed in the twentieth century and earlier. He again developed an international comparative approach. As a professor of the sociology of organizations, he pursued a similar approach comparing the study of work organizations in the USA, the UK, Germany, France and the Netherlands (Lammers, 1990). In this comparison he found that next to a relatively strong tendency to international convergence, there was also a certain degree of international variation in studying organizations. In his own words: organizations are both alike and unlike. He was soon to reveal that occupation regimes are alike and unlike as well (Lammers, 2003a; 2005).

As noted, Lammers had a penchant for international comparisons as regards military studies. He had read an interesting example of a comparative military study, Gerke Teitler's (1977) book on the genesis of the professional officer corps based on a analysis of developments in Great Britain, France, the Netherlands and then Prussia. A first result of Lammers' curiosity with regard to the military was a study of the inter-organizational control of three European nations that were occupied by Nazi Germany between 1940 and 1944/1945, i.e. Belgium, the Netherlands and Norway (Lammers, 1988; 1991; 1995).

In his conceptualization he again used the perspective of the rulers and the ruled, who have their own ways of influencing each other. The new rulers install so-called *control organizations*, whereas the ruled rely on *representative intermediaries*. In the case of the three occupied nations there was a rapid change from a more or less loosely structured network of representative institutions (political parties, labour unions, churches, welfare organizations, professional associations, broadcasting channels) to a rather tightly controlled hierarchical network of organizations. This happened through the establishment of Nazi top-control and other new control agencies, the elimination or conversion of 'unsuitable' representative organizations and the centralization, strenghtening and rationalization of overall inter-organizational administrative networks (Lammers, 1988: 446ff). Over time it turned out that the control approach needed to become more repressive in order to be more effective. However, as repression increased effectiveness did not. Repressive control became counter-productive, as there were certain thresholds beyond which top-down repression and coercion gradually created fruitful soil for the growth of societal and in fact violent resistance. This is a phenomenon that will return again and again. In Weberian terms, it is important to realize that – except in real wartime-conditions – 'naked power' based on negative, punitive sanctions is only rarely effective in the long run. Occupational power needs to be accompanied by a certain degree of authority and legitimization stemming from positive sanctions and rewards in order to appease the populace.

From studying the occupations in Europe during World War II, it is not a giant step to examine the way European nations and the USA organized their (colonial) administrations in distant regions. In a number of publications Lammers (2003a; 2005; 2014) analysed the 'occupational regimes' of France, the UK and the Netherlands in colonial times, and later US military missions abroad. Again, Lammers used the perspective of the rulers and the ruled, but now he distinguished *loyal elites* – legitimized from above – from *native elites* – legitimized and trusted from below – as major intermediary actors. Both elites play different roles, and this variation is dependent on what the 'occupational regimes' wish and allow to happen. Loyal elites are limited in effect when their legitimacy is weakened and they come to be seen by the population as traitors. 'Too much force undermines the capability of the occupier to preserve or maintain a certain minimum of quasi-authority' (Lammers, 2003a: 1384).

Using these notions and concepts and examining historical sources and studies, Lammers (2003a) came to the conclusion that French colonial rule – in Northern Africa and Indochina in the nineteenth and twentieth centuries – had been relatively direct. It had transformed the pre-existing system of governance into a centralized and bureaucratic, top-down system with the aid of French or Frenchified, assimilated loyal elites. The British and the Dutch colonial occupations (in India and Indonesia respectively), on the other hand, favoured some sort of decentralized system of rule, leaving pre-colonial structures intact and allowing native elites a certain amount of autonomy. There was at least one other difference between those two colonial powers, though. Compared to the British, the Dutch seemed to more closely supervise the native elite (Lammers, 2003a: 1395).

These are all relative, not absolute differences, as for instance French colonial occupation sometimes also ventured into indirect rule and the British approach in India gradually came to exhibit features of direct rule. Nonetheless, the differences in occupational and administrative styles as summarized in the box below are considered real and they are certainly relevant for today's military operations in regions abroad.

Different occupational and administrative styles

- German style during the Nazi regime in World War II

Centralization, loyal elites, close coercive and lethal supervision

- French colonial style

Centralization, loyal elites, close supervision

- British colonial style

Restoring old order, native elites, distant supervision

- Dutch colonial style

Restoring old order, native elites, close supervision

- American administrative style

Regime change, native elites, laissez-faire.

(Derived from Moelker, 2014: 101)

At the very end of his life, Lammers transferred these ideas to more topical situations, beginning with the administration of post-Nazi Germany from 1945 on. It appeared (Lammers, 2014: 55) that the French employed 18 functionaries per 10,000 German inhabitants in their zone, the British 10 per 10,000 inhabitants and the Americans managed their zone in occupied Germany with an even smaller staff of 3 per 10,000. The first two numbers support the findings we just saw, which were based on a more distant past. The last number, administration the American way, provided the incentive to study more

American cases. The American occupation of Iraq starting in March 2003 is such a case.

Lammers (2014: 57) kicks off by pointing to the military interventions that the USA has undertaken in many parts of the world, near and far. He further reveals a characteristic pattern: American interventions are mostly of short duration, are often called 'liberations', and are aimed at protecting American interests. Furthermore, the Americans tend to impose their will via native or quasi-native elites, without undue qualms about the fate of the citizens. In general, American interventions are perceived as being first and foremost military actions, not administrative or occupational endeavours. The period of Ambassador Bremer as the Coalition Provisional Authority in Iraq was different, consisting of direct rule and dismantling host-national security structures, i.e. the military, the police and the general state bureaucracy. That, however, did not turn out to work well, as resistance and attacks on American troops during this period fiercely increased; many previous powerholders had lost their positions, which created feelings of relative deprivation, frustration and anger (Lammers, 2014: 60). After about a year of Bremer's direct rule, sovereignty was transferred to an Iraqi Interim Government, which was more in line with usual American practice: short interventions of a military nature to do away with influences that are deemed harmful to the country.

The operations in Iraq and in Afghanistan, the other large-scale operation at the onset of the twenty-first century, offer opportunities to compare different national approaches. Many Western nations participated in both missions; next to the English-speaking countries almost all European NATO partners provided troops, in particular to the Afghanistan operations since 2001, i.e. after 9/11.

In the Netherlands, for instance, participation in the Iraq mission and the relatively large contribution to the Afghanistan mission could only be 'sold' to the Dutch public as 'reconstruction missions'. 'Reconstruction missions' were said to help the regions develop their administrative and security organizations (police, military), to rebuild the roads, and to build up their health care and educational organizations again (Moelker, 2014). Memories of the failed mission in Indonesia from 1945 to 1949 (Groen, 2003) and the tragedy in Bosnia in the 1990s had made the Dutch electorate suspicious about new military adventures abroad, hence these new emphases. Now the stress was not on the military only, but on the military combined with civilian workers or military personnel with more or less civilian tasks. More than other national contributions in Afghanistan, the Dutch contingent consisted of a mixture of military and civilian elements, at the end leading to full double leadership: a brigadier-general working at the same level as the highest ranked civil servant from the Ministry of Foreign Affairs. The logic of such double leadership was not easy to understand for American commanders, let alone be considered as a serious alternative to their own way of conducting operations which was more battle-oriented.

The so-called 'Dutch approach' (Gooren, 2006) was praised by America's top politicians of the time, President Obama and Secretary of State Clinton (Lammers, 2014; Moelker, 2014). This approach was clearly different from a 'naked power'-approach as it stressed the legitimacy aspect of the Dutch military's presence and the need to cooperate with local powerholders in the region (Al Muthanna in Iraq and Uruzgan in Afghanistan). It emphasized the need to pay attention to not only what the (new) rulers do, but to what the ruled (the subjugated) feel about the rulers' conduct. Such a sociological approach with operational impact – counterinsurgency! – is what Lammers had identified as an important factor all along.

Eventually, other scholars contended that this analysis was too rosy. The Dutch may have conducted their operations in a relatively unproblematic region of Iraq, and like the Americans and British they had fought a number – albeit a relatively small number – of war-type battles in Afghanistan as well. Moreover, the British and Americans had also eventually adopted the idea of collaborating with local power holders as a strategy of counter-insurgency (e.g. King, 2010). Nonetheless, the main conclusion still holds that the 'Dutch approach' stressing legitimacy and cooperation with host-national power holders may have been something different, although not perhaps completely unique (e.g. Soeters, 2013a; also: Kitzen, 2016).

More important, however, is the more general notion stemming from Lammers' work, namely that there are different operational, occupation and administrative styles among nations' armed forces. Apparently, there is no such thing as 'one best way of doing military things', just as there is no 'one best way of organizing', which has been received wisdom in organization theory for decades. This notion is easily illustrated by a relatively large number of studies that, like the Dutch, focus on the national – Danish, British, French, Norwegian, Canadian, Portuguese – approach of operating militarily (e.g. Jakobsen, 1998; King, 2008; Jauffret, 2002; Laugen Haaland, 2010; Jardine and Palamar, 2013; Carreiras, 2014). This 'bias' towards one's own military and the corresponding tendency to cherish the national approach is not so surprising. Military scholars often only have access to their own national forces, preventing a comparative approach to studying multinational military operations and the conditions under which they become effective. Apparently, Durkheim's recommendations concerning the importance of comparison are still difficult to apply.

Nonetheless, there are a couple of studies that connect operational outcomes with national styles of military conduct in wartime. It has been demonstrated that before and during World War II, culture-related differences in doctrines and operational styles existed between the warring nations – Germany, the USA, the UK and France – with remarkable operational consequences (Legro, 1994; Kier, 1995; Visser, 2010). Even an inadvertent escalation of hostilities in World War II could be related to military beliefs and customs, i.e. national military cultures in Germany and Britain (Legro, 1994). International comparisons are not just fun to do, as Lammers never got tired pointing out, they enhance our understanding of military operations because of the co-variation of their nature on the one hand and the general outcomes and effectiveness on the other; it is only a matter of studying this co-variation (Soeters, 2013b). A recent illustration of this approach is provided by Chiara Ruffa (2017) who published a comparison of French and Italian contributions to the operations in Lebanon and Afghanistan, revealing systematic variations in behaviour between both national contingents – even though the operational conditions were very similar. However, she did not go as far as making the connection with the general effectiveness of the varying operational styles.

Next to these comparative operational studies, a discourse has evolved over the years as to so-called national strategic cultures (e.g. Gray, 1999; Biehl et al., 2013). Strategic cultures comprise the whole of national history, traditions, customs and beliefs concerning the need and value of expenditures on the military and the actual use and deployment of military means. Even in the Western hemisphere there are considerable differences in this regard that can even lead to political tensions. A number of American presidents have stressed the need for European members of NATO to spend more money on the military, as most of them – except for the UK, Poland, Estonia, Greece and Turkey – have not even reached the 2 per cent level that was agreed upon when the Treaty was signed. When president Trump increased the pressure, European nations, headed by large and wealthy Germany, were quick to make promises to pay their dues. However, doubt remained as to the effectiveness of increased funds for the military. European leaders such as Angela Merkel deemed funds for development assistance, diplomacy and crisis management at least as important. It seems that different views held by politicians from different national strategic cultures are quite persistent (also: Soeters, 2013a). Other domains that are impacted by national strategic cultures are the space that is granted to military unions (Bartle and Heinecken, 2006) or military role conceptions that are related to decisions concerning the outsourcing of military activities (Cusumano, 2014). These are only a few examples of a more general phenomenon.

Isomorphism and cooperation

All of this is the consequence of armed forces still being organized and administered by nation-states. From this perspective, it is not surprising to see that nations, their politicians and their citizens tend to attach national characteristics (and virtues) to their armed forces, as if they were national soccer teams. After all, in times of conscription – the citizen army – the people constitute the military and the military constitute the nation-state. As said earlier, the military has often been the dominant factor in creating the nation-state. Therefore, it comes as no surprise that ideas about founding a 'European army' meet with large resistance from national politicians and citizens alike. If ever, a true 'European army' is not likely to come about in the foreseeable future. That is not the end of the story, though. Increasing international collaboration is inevitable, because financial, manpower and material resources of (small) nations are too short in supply to cope with all possible demands. Hence, one can observe the internationalization – or trans-nationalization – of national armed forces in many ways, particularly in Europe.

One can see increasing international exercises and common training, international participation in each other's staff courses, and internationalization of manpower at previously national headquarters (e.g. King, 2005; Bagayoko-Penone, 2006). For many years now it has been possible for a British major-general to be the second-in-command in an Italian HQ. In the bi-national German–Dutch HQ at least 15 per cent of the positions are filled by officers from other NATO nations, and the same applies to other previously strict national NATO HQs. There may also be true mergers: Dutch tank units, due to persistent budget cuts, no longer exist as independent elements and their remains are now inserted into German cavalry units. In 2016 the Dutch 11th Mobile Brigade officially joined the German army. The Belgian and Dutch navies are almost fully integrated. The Euro-corps contains contingents from a number of European nations, but its core consists of the bi-national Franco-German brigade, i.e. troops from two nations that have been hostile for long periods in history (Leonhard and Gareis, 2008). Comparable arrangements have been made between Germany and Poland, and elsewhere. Military air transport has been internationalized to a large degree at the European level. And as we have seen before (Chapter 2), overseas operations and missions are nearly always international in composition (Soeters and Szvircsev Tresch, 2010). The challenges are simply too large, too far away and too demanding for separate one-nation actions. Given their enormous manpower and financial resources, this would not pose such a problem to the Americans, but the USA attaches great importance to increasing the legitimacy of their actions through cooperation with others.

All of this is made possible by, and in fact also reinforces, a phenomenon that has been noted by organizational sociologists Paul Dimaggio and Walter Powell (1991: 63–82). We have already referred to this phenomenon briefly. It is known as *isomorphism* and it refers to the tendency among organizations within one sector or organizational field – for instance health care, museums, banking – to converge, to become alike in terms of strategies, structures, technologies and practices. This tendency occurs under the impact of *coercive, mimetic* and *normative* pressures.

Coercive pressures are the result of the influence of a higher authority, such as NATO in the context of the Western militaries. For one thing, NATO develops doctrines that guide the development of national doctrines. It also enforces maintenance and quality control systems on its member states' forces, and certifies them only when all requirements have been met. Also, national and international politicians requiring more international cooperation because of budget restraints exert such impact. In another security-related domain, the EU recently imposed upon its member states a shared management system in the field of border management. Uncertainty about how to do things is a powerful force encouraging imitation; hence the importance of *mimetic* pressures. Organizations, armed forces included, tend to model themselves after similar organizations that they perceive to be more legitimate or successful (Dimaggio and Powell, 1991: 70). *Normative* impact emerges from increasing international professionalization, formal education and standard career development. Only military officers who have spent some time in an international context (through formal international education or temporary positions in an international HQ or mission), may aspire to climb higher in the national hierarchy. Also, the impact of technological innovations that national armed forces adopting the same weapon-systems will experience, leads to normative, profession-related isomorphism.

The question, however, remains in which direction this isomorphism will go: towards the more resourceful and technologically advanced armed forces stressing military solutions, or towards the more peacekeeping-and-development oriented militaries? Perhaps there will be no convergence of those two worlds; perhaps isomorphism will only occur inside one of them. Only time will tell.

Cooperation in UN missions

As cooperation within NATO becomes gradually stricter and more successful, cooperation within UN missions is still far from perfect. The cultural heterogeneity between troop-contributing countries is significant, the differences in resources is sizable, and exchanges of experiences are still limited, superficial and very much based on the national background of the participants (Ben-Ari and Elron, 2001). It gets even more complicated when cooperation between UN troops and host national forces is at stake. Verweijen (2017) studied cooperation between the UN's blue helmets and the Congolese army in the DRC and found that there was a considerable degree of distrust and not-so-joint operations; the degree of general cooperation between the two forces as a result was weak because of a 'paternalistic' attitude among the UN forces towards the host nationals and an 'opportunistic' attitude among the Congolese military vis-à-vis the UN troops. Cooperation between UN troops and host national troops may not be that bad elsewhere, or may not be that negative in the eyes of other researchers, though.

Conclusion

Lammers' contribution to the study of the military and military operations is substantial. As well as studying internal conflicts within the military, he has provided insights with respect to national differences in occupations and administrations that have been conveyed by many other scholars as well, but not in such a sociologically systematic manner. Through comparisons he was also able to point at differing degrees of effectiveness of those operational, occupational and administrative differences. As such, he paved the way for future studies that may be leading the discovery as to which features of military operations in which conditions are most effective.

Bibliography

Bagayoko-Penone, N. (2006) 'L'Européanisation des militaires Français: socialisation institutionelle et culture stratégique'. *Revue Française de Science Politique* 56(1): 49–77.

Bartle, R. and L. Heinecken (eds) (2006) *Military Unionism in the Post-Cold War Era: A Future Reality?* London/New York: Routledge.

Ben-Ari, E. and E. Elron (2001) 'Blue helmets and white armor: multi-nationalism and multi-culturalism among UN peacekeeping forces'. *City and Society* 13(2): 271–302.

Biehl, H., B. Giegerich and A. Jonas (eds) (2013) *Strategic Cultures in Europe: Security and Defence Policies Across the Continent.* Wiesbaden: Springer.

Carreiras, H. (2014) 'The sociological dimension of external military interventions: the Portuguese military abroad'. *Portuguese Journal of Social Science* 13(2): 129–149.

Cortright, D. (1975) *Soldiers in Revolt: GI Resistance during the Vietnam War.* Chicago: Haymarket Books.

Cusumano, E. (2014) 'The scope of military privatisation: military role conceptions and contractor support in the United States and the United Kingdom'. *International Relations* 29(2): 219–241.

Dimaggio, P.J. and W.W. Powell (1991) 'The Iron Cage revisited: institutional isomorphism and collective rationality in organizational fields'. In W.W. Powell and P.J. Dimaggio (eds), *The New Institutionalism in Organizational Analysis.* Chicago and London: University of Chicago Press.

Erikson Baaz, M. and J. Verweijen (2013) 'The volatility of a half-cooked bouillabaisse: rebel–military integration and conflict dynamics in Eastern DRC'. *African Affairs* 112(449): 563–582.

Gooren, R.H.E. (2006) 'Soldiering in unfamiliar places: the Dutch approach'. *Military Review,* March/April: 54–60.

Gray, C.S. (1999) 'Strategic culture as context: the first generation strikes back'. *Review of International Studies* 25(1): 49–69.

Groen, P. (2003) 'Militant response: the Dutch use of military force and the decolonization of the Dutch East Indies, 1945–1950'. *Journal of Imperial and Commonwealth History* 21(3): 30–44.

Jakobsen, P.V. (1998) 'The Danish approach to UN peace operations after the Cold War: a new model in the making?' *International Peacekeeping* 5(3): 106–123.

Jardine, E. and S. Palamar (2013) 'From Medusa past Kantolo: testing the effectiveness of Canada's enemy-centric and population-centric counterinsurgency operational strategies'. *Studies in Conflict and Terrorism* 36(7): 588–608.

Jauffret, J.-Ch. (2002) 'The war culture of French combatants in the Algerian conflict'. In M.S. Alexander, M. Evans and J.F.V. Keiger (eds), *The Algerian War and the French Army, 1954–62: Experiences, Images, Testimonies.* Basingstoke and New York: Palgrave.

Kier, E. (1995) *Imagining War: French and British Military Doctrine between the Wars.* Princeton, NJ: Princeton University Press.

King, A. (2005) 'Towards a transnational Europe: the case of the armed forces'. *European Journal of Social Theory* 8(3): 321–340.

King, A. (2008) 'The British way in war: the UK approach to multinational operations'. In J. Soeters and Ph. Manigart (eds), *Military Cooperation in Multinational Peace Operations: Managing Cultural Diversity and Crisis Response.* London and New York: Routledge.

King, A. (2010) 'Understanding the Helmand campaign: British military operations in Afghanistan'. *International Affairs* 86(2): 311–332.

Kitzen, M. (2016) *The course of co-option: co-option of local power-holders as a tool for obtaining control over the population in counterinsurgency campaigns in weblike societies*. Ph.D. dissertation, University of Amsterdam.

Lammers, C.J. (1967) 'Power and participation in decision-making in formal organizations'. *American Journal of Sociology* 73(2): 201–216.

Lammers, C.J. (1969) 'Strikes and mutinies: a comparative study of organizational conflicts between rulers and ruled'. *Administrative Science Quarterly* 14(4): 558–572.

Lammers, C.J. (1988) 'The interorganizational control of an occupied country'. *Administrative Science Quarterly* 33(3): 438–457.

Lammers, C.J. (1990) 'Sociology of organizations around the globe: similarities and differences between American, British, French, German and Dutch brands'. *Organization Studies* 11(2): 179–205.

Lammers, C.J. (1991) 'Macht und Autorität des Deutschen Besetzers in den Niederlanden während des zweiten Weltkrieges. Ansätze zu einer Soziologie der Besatzung'. *Journal für Sozialforschung* 31(4): 401–415.

Lammers, C.J. (1995) 'Levels of collaboration: a comparative study of German occupation regimes during the Second World War'. *Netherlands Journal of Social Sciences* 31(1): 3–31.

Lammers, C.J. (2003a) 'Occupation regimes alike and unlike: British, Dutch and French patterns of interorganizational control of foreign territories'. *Organization Studies* 24(9): 1379–1403.

Lammers, C.J. (2003b) 'Mutiny in comparative perspective'. *International Review of Social History* 48(3): 473–482.

Lammers, C.J. (2005) *Vreemde Overheersing: Bezetten en Bezetting in Sociologisch Perspectief*. Amsterdam: Bert Bakker.

Lammers, C.J. (2014) 'The American occupation regime in comparative perspective: the case of Iraq'. *Armed Forces and Society* 40(1): 49–70.

Laugen Haaland, T. (2010) 'Still homeland defenders at heart? Norwegian military culture in international deployments'. *International Peacekeeping* 17(4): 539–553.

Legro, J.W. (1994) 'Military culture and inadvertent escalation in World War II'. *International Security* 4(Spring): 108–142.

Leonhard, N. and S.B. Gareis (eds) (2008) *Vereint Marschieren – Marcher uni: Die deutsch-französische Streitkräftekooperation als Paradigma europäische Streitkräfte?* Wiesbaden: VS Verlag für Sozialwissenschaften.

Levy, Y. (2017) 'Control from within: how soldiers control the military'. *European Journal of International Relations* 23(1): 192–216.

Long, A. (2013) '"Green on blue": insider attacks in Afghanistan'. *Survival* 55(3): 167–182.

Moelker, R. (2014) 'The genesis of the "Dutch approach" to asymmetric conflicts: operations in Uruzgan and the "softly, softly" manner of approaching the Taleban'. *Armed Forces and Society* 40(1): 96–117.

Neethling, Th. (2014) 'Rebel movements in the DRC: the phenomenon of sub-national terrorism and ungoverned spaces'. *African Security Review* 23(4): 339–351.

Ruffa, Ch. (2017) 'Military cultures and force employment in peace operations'. *Security Studies* 26(3): 391–422.

Soeters, J. (2013a) 'Odysseus prevails over Achilles: a warrior model suited to post-9/11 conflicts'. In J. Burk (ed.), *How 9/11 Changed Our Ways of War*. Stanford, CA: Stanford University Press.

Soeters, J. (2013b) 'Do distinct (national) styles of conflict resolution exist?' *Journal of Strategic Studies* 36(6): 898–906.

Soeters, J. and T. Szvircsev Tresch (2010) 'Towards cultural integration in multinational peace operations'. *Defence Studies* 10(1/2): 272–287.

Teitler, G. (1977) *The Genesis of the Professional Officer's Corps.* Thousand Oaks, CA: Sage.

Thakur, M. (2008) 'Demilitarising militias in the Kivus (eastern Democratic Republic of Congo)'. *African Security Review* 17(1): 52–67.

Van Doorn, J.A.A. (1975) *The Soldier and Social Change: Comparative Studies in the History and Sociology of the Military.* Beverly Hills CA and London: Sage.

Verweijen, J. (2017) 'Strange battlefield fellows: the diagonal interoperability between blue helmets and the Congolese army'. *International Peacekeeping* (online).

Visser, M. (2010) 'Configurations of human resource practices and battlefield performance: a comparison of two armies'. *Human Resource Management Review* 20: 340–349.

12 Arlie Russell Hochschild

Emotions in organizations and in the military

While studying emotions and feeling rules in organizations, Arlie Russell Hochschild (b. 1940) followed the path trodden by Erving Goffman before her. There is also a clear connection with the work of Norbert Elias, who stressed society's influence on the way people learn to restrain and discipline themselves and essentially control their emotions. The grand old men of sociology certainly also paid attention to the emotional aspects of social life. W. E. B. Du Bois had an ear for the emotions associated with music. Of note is Georg Simmel's work on respect, friendship, gratitude, love and jealousy; and notable too are Karl Marx's thoughts about alienation in labour. Arlie Hochschild is part of a long tradition of critical sociology, as she has always been wary of the 'commodification of emotion' (Smith, 2014). And Durkheim's influence cannot be discounted either.

The list of emotions that people may feel is long: joy, love and liking, gratitude, compassion, hope and pride, empathy, sadness and grief, nostalgia, depression, frustration, anger, fear, indignation, disgust, contempt, guilt, anguish, envy, jealousy, pity, embarrassment, shame and humiliation – all belong to the field of biology and psychology, but they are certainly also part of the sociologist's domain (e.g. Greco and Stenner, 2008). Emotions and feelings are – at least to a certain degree – social.

Arlie Hochschild's work on emotions in organizations became well known through her study of flight attendants and debt collectors. While examining the behaviour of employees in these occupations, she coined a concept that became instantly famous and inspired a lot of new research: the *managed heart* (Hochschild, 1983). Comparable to the impact of Goffman's work, Hochschild's work became not only important in academic sociology, but also among the public at large. During the 2016 presidential elections in the USA, she published a study on the 'strangers in their own land', about the anger and the mourning of the people who feel lost in the globalizing economy and whose views are on the conservative end of the political spectrum (Hochschild, 2016).

The relevance of her work for the military can hardly be overestimated. If anything, using and undergoing violence is an emotional experience. Acts of violence come with feelings because violence affects oneself as well as others, be they close colleagues, people who are targeted or accidental bystanders. The display of violence in itself may create feelings of fascination, enjoyment and celebration (Ben-Ari and Frühstück, 2003). Surviving violent situations such as combat or life-threatening attacks without loss of limb is likely to create feelings of happiness, invincibility or at least satisfaction. However, even if such an action has taken place according to plan, the experience is likely to leave an emotional scar long after the event has passed, particularly when one has observed the direct consequences of fighting power on others. If the action did not go as planned, emotions are likely to be more intense, and more negative.

This may even result in health-related problems that might last for the rest of one's life. It may lead soldiers to kill themselves, as we saw before. Not surprisingly, today's professional armed forces go out of their way to control the negative impact of soldiers using and experiencing violence, during but also after an operation. But soldiers are not the only people involved. Fierce emotions of course also occur among the population in the midst of violence. War and severe conflicts may create joy and happiness among the general public and the soldiers, particularly when there are victories to celebrate. More often, however, the sorrow of war prevails, as for instance a retired combatant of the Viet Cong has written about with much depth and understanding (Ninh, 1998 [1991]). One of his opponents from the US Marine Corps in the same war has done the same (Caputo, 1999 [1977]), as have Russian soldiers deployed to Afghanistan a decade later (Alexievich, 2017 [1989]). And they are clearly not the only ones who have reported such feelings.

Emotional work and management

As mentioned above, Hochschild (1979; 1983) studied the way flight attendants and debt collectors do their job and are trained and managed to do so. The concept of 'emotional work (labour)' refers to actions that affect the feelings of others – such as a parent consoling a child. It is considered *work* if this is done for payment; a nanny taking care of the child, to stay with the same example (Smith, 2014: 397–398). Emotional labour is different from manual or mental work, where unfeeling objects are transformed for others to use later. The object of emotional work is another person or persons. This work may take place in a profit- or a non-profit context. Examples of emotional work of the latter kind are the jobs of teachers, nurses, diplomats and police officers. Examples of emotional work in a for-profit context are the cabin crew Hochschild studied as well as entertainers and sales personnel.

The basic feature of emotional work is that it relates the worker's personal feelings and their expression to the impact this is intended to have on the other(s). Emotional work is very much about interaction, encounters and performances, which brings this concept very close to what was central to Erving Goffman's work. In the sociologist's view, an emotion or a feeling is 'something we *do* by attending to inner sensation in a given way, by defining situations in a given way, by managing in given ways. [...] The very act of managing emotion can be seen as part of what the emotion becomes' (Hochschild, 1983: 27). Emotional workers' behaviour, then, is learned and *scripted behaviour*, which aligns with the requirements of working inside a bureaucracy, in accordance with the expectations of the organization. The script is a set of feeling rules, concerning not only what to do, but more specifically what to feel, if necessary suppressing one's own feelings (Hochschild, 1983: 56–75).

There is a script for employees that tells them what to do if passengers in an aircraft or customers in a shop start behaving stressfully or aggressively. And those scripts have been rehearsed many times, in such a way that *acting the role* has become the most important element of workers' behaviour. It is for this reason that Hochschild speaks of the *managed heart*. The flight attendants in Hochschild's study (1983: 8) often spoke of their smiles being *on* them instead of being *of* them. Some found it difficult to switch off at the end of a shift, smiling at strangers in the train or the bus on the way home (Smith, 2014: 401). The problem for the workers – and even for the people who are affected by them – is to distinguish between feeling and feigning. To the extent that a worker is feigning emotions through actions such as such as smiling, telling jokes or being spontaneous, alienation and anomie – to use two famous and notorious concepts from classical sociology – are nearby.

Hochschild's work has been criticized for being too pessimistic and deterministic, as if workers do not have a choice as to how specifically act in their role. Instead, it has been argued that there is always discretionary space to interpret, manipulate and implement the managerially prescribed rules of engagement (e.g. Bolton and Boyd, 2003: 303). Furthermore, Hochschild is said to have exaggerated how alienated emotional workers really feel while doing their job (Smith, 2014: 405). Finally, there have been rebuttals that she focused too much on the interests of the workers and their employers while neglecting to some extent the interests of the customers or bystanders (Wouters, 1989). Despite these comments, her insights have been applied and further developed in numerous settings (Steinberg and Figart, 1999; Wharton, 2009), for instance in hospitals and in highly successful retail chains (Martin et al., 1998). Of particular interest here are studies of the emotional work of firefighters in Quebec (St-Denis, 2013), of leaders in sites of school shootings (Fein and Isaacson, 2009) and of flight attendants post-9/11 (Santin and Kelly, 2017).

In the study of the firefighters in Quebec, the aspect of black humour emerged as a major factor for the operators in dealing with the dramas they faced. However, this caused tensions with people who were close to them but outside the profession – family members for instance. 'Black humour' gave the impression that the firefighters were insensitive, that they were much less than the heroes they were supposed to be (St-Denis, 2013: 150–152).

The study on flight attendants post-9/11 is especially important as it coins additional concepts regarding emotional work in security-related situations. Santin and Kelly (2017) revealed that since 9/11 a new emphasis on safety over courtesy provided cabin crew with a normative resource to be more independent and assertive in interactions with passengers. Particularly when safety is under threat, flight attendants are allowed to go beyond the role of displaying mere courtesy. They can switch to acting according to the 'firefighter' role and then even to the soldier's 'frontline' role of protecting all passengers on board against potential security threats. However, passengers' ability to record flight attendants' behaviour and upload these recordings to social media – creating the panopticon that Michel Foucault was so fearful of – put a new strain on their jobs. Enter the military.

The military and the family as 'greedy institutions'

Next to her analysis of emotional work, Arlie Hochschild paid attention to what she called 'the second shift', being the efforts of parents to combine two full time jobs and raise young children (Hochschild and Machung, 1989). This seemed more of a problem for the mothers than it was for the fathers. In the military these problems are also very well known.

Following up on the idea of the total institution, American sociologist Lewis Coser (1974) coined the concept of the 'greedy institution'. These are social arrangements that make great demands on the individual's time, loyalty and energy, as they require nothing less than 'undivided commitment'. Coser referred to the social position of priests and housewives as examples of what he had in mind.

Mady Segal (1986) pointed to the fact that being a military person and a member of a family are also examples of such institutions and that military families live at the intersection of both. Separately the military and the family impose substantial demands on their members; the intersection of both in military families creates the tension of spillover, stress and conflict. In today's world military personnel, including reservists, are frequently deployed on missions abroad, making it impossible for them to take care of their children during that period. Relocation to distant places is still a common practice in the military. All of this is likely to create extra problems for dual-military couples, and dual-earner or dual-career couples in general. With the increasing participation of women in the labour market, dual-earner families are on the rise. Clearly, problems at the military/family interface have not shown the tendency to disappear since Segal's work; on the contrary, both institutions look likely to become even greedier (De Angelis and Wechsler-Segal, 2015).

Dealing with emotional labour in the military

The military primarily deals with violence-related emotional work by keeping the action away from direct experience and by keeping it brief, as much as possible. As we saw before, the professional soldier likes his or her wars 'clean, short and decisive', and one may add today 'at a long distance'.

Modern technologies render the latter increasingly feasible, as we will see in Chapter 14. Removing the direct encounter with violence from the equation is one way of dealing with the consequences of emotional labour in the military.

But even in air forces – used to applying violence from a distance – emotions play a role, particularly when errors are made. Errors may impact on the safety of the pilots and the aircraft themselves, but they may also produce unjustified, collateral damage on the ground. How do pilots deal with risks and errors that lurk in the air, and once an error has occurred how do they acknowledge and learn from it? The answers to such questions are closely connected to emotions such as pride, over-confidence, shame, uneasiness and doubt. In fact, such emotion-related behaviour is part of the more general (safety) culture of the organization (Catino and Patriotta, 2013). Cultures that are more open and less prone to an air of superiority and invulnerability tend to make acknowledging errors relatively easier. Even among pilots with *sangfroid* the role of emotions cannot be neglected.

Another way for the military to deal with the impact of personnel being engaged in the use and experience of violence, is to select the right people from the population at large. Following Randall Collins (2008), the 'violent few' tend to be most apt at performing high-intensity, forceful action in the military. They are likely to stay cool and insensitive, at least to some extent. The transformation from conscript armies to all-volunteer forces has made the selection of those people easier. Not surprisingly, since the introduction of the AVFs the motivation among soldiers to become engaged in combat has increased (Van den Aker et al., 2016). In conscript forces similar selection processes are in place and those processes are geared towards allocating the 'violent few' to combat and combat-support units, i.e. to the units where the action is. Proportionally, however, the number of the 'violent few' is lower in the draft system.

Snipers at work

One particular category of military people who must remain relatively untouched by emotions is the small group of snipers. Snipers have the task of 'eliminating' special targets, hostile individuals who are considered to be particularly dangerous to one's own troops and operations. Snipers are military soloists engaged in lethal action.

A study by Israeli scholars Neta Bar and Eyal Ben-Ari (2005) revealed how Israeli Defence Force snipers deal with the emotional pressures, dilemmas and moral aspects of their work. First, the snipers are very much guided by the formal rules of engagement that apply in the specific operational context. As Hochschild indicated, emotional work is rule-led, scripted behaviour. Furthermore, they rely on their previous training, craftsmanship, the instructions of commanders and the legitimation provided by politicians. Snipers also resort to a kind of dehumanization of the targeted person when looking through their telescope or binoculars. Here, the distance and technical procedures play their mitigating role. In the words of a specialist from the US Marine Corps: 'Sight alignment, trigger control, breath control. Focus on the iron sights, not the target. The target should be blurry' (Klay, 2014: 15).

Despite all this, the snipers in the Israeli study showed feelings of doubt and hesitance, as well as moving and contradictory emotions: guilt about killing a human being. But they were also proud of a good professional job done. The snipers did not feel any anger or hate but they depersonalized the other and objectified the killing by talking about 'neutralizing the threats'. The snipers also felt that fellow soldiers treated them with a certain unease because their work is mostly done while concealed and unseen.

The other mechanisms through which armed forces try to contain the negative impact of violence relate to what Elias, Goffman and subsequently Hochschild have revealed. It is all about preparing, training and guiding soldiers to balance their actions between the justified and controlled use of violence on the one hand and violence getting out of control on the other. This, in fact, is the control of emotions.

There is where Hochschild comes in: 'Erving Goffman once wrote: "When they issue uniforms, they issue skins." And we can add, two inches of flesh' (Hochschild, 2008: 47). Here resonates Durkheim's notion that society penetrates the individual mind; in the case of the military, it is the military society and culture that penetrate the military person … and the military body, in Hochschild's words.

This does not always happen without hesitation and doubt, though. A former captain in the Israeli forces, Eyal Ben-Ari (1989; 1998) was among the first to study emotions and emotion management among military people in action. Surprisingly, without explicitly referring to Hochschild's or Elias' seminal work, Ben-Ari was in a perfect position to study actual experiences and feelings of soldiers in action, particularly at the time of the intifada in the city of Hebron, one of the major urban centres of the West Bank. He was a reserve captain in the IDF for eight years, and being a professional anthropologist he was perfectly suited to conduct fieldwork in operational conditions. As a reservist and 'a deeply troubled participant', Ben-Ari (1989: 373) wanted to find an answer to the question of how people perform acts that are totally different from the way in which they behave while civilians. His account stresses the strangeness the reservists feel when they enter the military again to be deployed to the area of operations. Putting their uniforms on again is like the wearing of a mask. This comparison is not without significance. The use of masks and disguises involves a special potential for different conduct. Even though the reservists' battalion was said to do policing work, they quickly turned to acting militarily again. This included the focus on neutral, operational effectiveness and role performance without caring much about the legitimacy of what they were doing (Ben-Ari, 1989: 383). After deployment, returning to civilian life, the author noticed a long period of experiencing uneasiness, irritation and internal turmoil (Ben-Ari, 1989: 384).

In a short book published nearly ten years later, Ben-Ari (1998) returned to the emotional aspects of military work among IDF reservist battalions deployed to Hebron. Not unlike what we have seen in other analyses, he described the need for soldiers to be cool during the action, keeping the balance between not acting and action getting out of control. The 'cold spirit' of the military person is what counts. The military organization objects to soldiers pushing, beating and firing among civilians – even if it is in the air – as they see this as a loss of emotional control and 'undue force'. Soldiers who lose control should be replaced as if they were spare parts of a machine.

Nonetheless, the military tends to reapply conventional military attitudes to the protesting civilians in Hebron and surrounding areas, who are clearly not trained soldiers. Apparently, the military way of thinking – the military culture – is so pervasive that it returns almost immediately once the operations have started. This may explain Ron's analysis of the IDF's rule-deviation practices in order to get the work done, which we discussed earlier. Strikingly, Ben-Ari (1998: 82–88) characterizes the emotional appraisal of the 'military other' – the adversary, the foe or the enemy – in terms of depersonalization instead of demonization; demonization implies that the other is simply evil and not even a human being, and is more likely to occur in fierce combat situations, such as those in which American forces find themselves engaged from time to time.

Following in Hochschild's and Ben-Ari's footsteps, the Swedish sociologist Louise Weibull (2011; 2012) published a doctoral thesis in which she also focused on emotion matters, this time during peace support operations, to which Swedish forces contributed. Primarily basing herself on data collected during fieldwork in Liberia and Kosovo, she revealed (2011; 2012) that a relatively high degree of depersonalization characterizes the soldier's job during deployment. Uniforms make everyone seem alike; everyone is visible all the time; there is not a lot of free time after work; and one always needs to adapt to the rules of the group one works with and the comrades that sleep in the same tent or cabin. Furthermore, she noticed the importance of being able to switch between different emotional displays at short notice, a phenomenon that Goffman had already pointed to as 'juggling and synthesizing'. Checking cars at roadblocks and then having a coffee with village authorities require different roles, but these occasions may be separated by only a brief interval. De-escalation of emotions after violence has emerged is challenging as well. In general, soldiers are asked to behave firmly and show 'stony-faced' demeanour while on the streets of Liberia or Kosovo, no matter what they really think and feel and despite the Swedish tendency to want to 'do good'. In general, the operational environment is full of conflicting and contradictory characteristics and demands. Like other authors before her, Weibull noticed the role humour played in security workers' dealing with emotions. However, the emotions dealt with in this study – though challenging in themselves – are less extreme compared to what military men have experienced in other situations.

> **Dutch soldiers' emotions in Indonesia, 1945–1950**
>
> Former US president Barack Obama describes in his memoirs how Dutch soldiers who were deployed to the so-called 'policing actions' in Indonesia set his stepfather's family's house aflame and killed his family members (Obama, 2007: 42). The operations between 1945 and 1950 are not something the Dutch are particularly proud of, mainly because of the damage done to the Indonesian people, their homes and possessions. The goals the Dutch aimed at – to bring peace and quiet under a sort of colonial rule – seem nowadays morally abject and only caused anger and sadness among 'the wretched of the earth' in the Indonesian archipelago (Fanon, 2004). On the other side, the veterans recalled that they felt misunderstood and were never listened to with any great interest or appreciation. Only recently did they receive more attention from historians, who tried to uncover the emotions that had been suppressed for such a long time. Fear, anger, frustration, feelings of revenge and shame, are some of the emotions of the soldiers who are now said to have been engaged in operations on the 'wrong side of history' (Oostindie, 2015).

A final aspect of emotional work in the military relates to the experience of death and how the military organization deals with it once it befalls. Death is inherent to the military profession and organization, and is routinely understood to have a meaning: the good cause being the father- or motherland or the freedom of all. Nonetheless, in some cases soldiers die in car accidents or comparable mishaps, which makes acceptance much more difficult (Ben-Ari, 2005). In general, though, acceptance of death is arduous; today's casualty aversion and the military's efforts to avoid casualties of their own go hand in hand with the apparent decline in violence we observed in the chapter on Norbert Elias.

When death occurs, the military organization needs to step in. In a number of publications Morten Ender and colleagues have looked at the role of Casualty Assistance Officers (CAOs) in the US forces, whose occupation is to provide administrative and caregiving support to surviving families (Bartone and Ender, 1994). They stressed that the role prescriptions in the *Casualty Assistance Handbook* provide applicable guidelines with respect to the administrative part, but do not offer guidelines for providing emotional support and dealing with extreme grief (Ender et al., 1999). This is where emotional complexities among the CAOs themselves arise, particularly when they have to deal with 'post-modern' families, in which family members are separated, divorced, remarried or 'secondary next-of-kin' and all have their own feelings and demands (Ender and Hermsen, 1996).

After work: from 'being cool' to Post-Deployment Disorientation and PTSD

Following other scholars, Ben-Ari (1998) pointed at the emotional footprint military service is likely to leave on adults' private lives after work. Military service and the military occupation tend to inculcate in men certain emotional attitudes to the world: being 'cool', having certain views with respect to 'manly' or otherwise proper behaviour, and displaying certain (political) values. These are emotions that are not likely to disappear after work and in fact are likely to remain in the minds of many retired soldiers for the rest of their lives. The military mindset and culture persist long after the military organization has been left behind.

Almost immediately after deployment, another phenomenon develops. In her thesis which we discussed before, Louise Weibull (2012) described the development of what she coined as Post-Deployment Disorientation, a feeling that develops among servicemen and servicewomen after the mission has ended. She drew attention to the reality check of being confronted with the poverty abroad – in Kosovo and Liberia – compared to the standard of living at home, which was seen as a sound wake-up call but which was quite disorienting as well. Another source of disorientation referred to the specific personal growth that many soldiers and officers had undergone during their deployment but which met with ignorance and lack of understanding at home.

Military memoirs

One way to look at how soldiers experience being involved in military action is to study military memoirs. Esmeralda Kleinreesink (2016) did a Ph.D study on fifty-three autobiographies published by soldiers and veterans from the USA, the UK, Canada, the Netherlands and Germany; all of them had been deployed to Afghanistan in the period up to 2010. From her comparative content analysis it appeared that military men and women had produced narratives that described the whole gamut of emotional experiences: from maturing and education to disillusion. Descriptions of disillusionment, and negative stories in general, occurred much more often in the writings of combat soldiers than in those of support staff such as medical doctors and agricultural specialists. However, almost always, signs of Post-Deployment Disorientation could be noticed. Almost all the authors had experienced problems of adapting after returning home from deployment.

Often – or rather, very often – emotional problems after work become more intense, more complicated and more persistent. These may affect the well-being of the whole family (e.g. Kramer, 2007), especially when the problems the military person faces get out of control and turn into trauma. Post-Traumatic Stress Disorder (PTSD) has become a notorious syndrome associated with the military (even though it also occurs among those who have undergone stressful

events in general, hence also outside the military realm). PTSD is often associated with people who have transgressed deeply held moral values and beliefs,
resulting in what is known as moral injury, which may manifest itself in feelings
of guilt, shame, anger, disgust and contempt (Farnsworth et al., 2014). In cases
of PTSD domestic violence may occur and some soldiers seek refuge in suicide,
something we saw in the chapter on Emile Durkheim. PTSD is recognized as a
serious concern that requires the careful attention of the military organization
and its health care facilities.

This phenomenon is, of course, not limited to soldiers from the Western
hemisphere, and the consequences elsewhere may even be harsher. Studies
have demonstrated that former Ugandan and Congolese child soldiers suffering
from extreme PTSD are less open to reconciliation and more subject to feelings
of revenge (Bayer et al., 2007). If not recognized and treated properly, rehabi-
litation and reintegration of those children into civilian society will be trying; it
is not unlikely that they will take up violent action once more, perpetuating
the hostilities again and again.

Conclusion

Arlie Russell Hochschild has contributed to the sociology of emotions in ways
that have been helpful to studying important phenomena in organizations. She
has published critical analyses of the way work is managed and organized, and
how this affects emotional work and the emotions employees experience while
at work. As such, her analyses have proven to be of vast relevance to the
military, to the way soldiers are trained, what they feel during and – no less
important – after the job, and how this impacts on their performance, health
and well-being throughout their lives. Her insights have gone further, however.
In a passionate manner, she once analysed how military action and war have
been used by politicians to channel the frustration of those who feel lost and
neglected in today's societies and globalized economies, often white blue-collar
workers. Those people will never be rich, and they will even be poorer and less
important than they or their parents were in earlier times. But there is a 'solution'
to this, as Hochschild contends. Those people can be proud of their nation
when their military engages in operations overseas. 'Let them eat war', instead
of the steaks that one usually finds in the refrigerator, as she critically combines
politics and military action (Hochschild, 2003: 182).

Bibliography

Aker, P. van den, J. Duel and J. Soeters (2016) 'Combat motivation and combat action:
    Dutch soldiers in operations since the Second World War: a research note'. *Armed
    Forces and Society* 42(1): 211–225.
Alexievich, S. (2017 [1989]) *Boys in Zinc*. London: Penguin Books.
Bar, N. and E. Ben-Ari (2005) 'Israeli snipers in the Al-Aqsa intifada: killing, humanity
    and lived experience'. *Third World Quarterly* 26(1): 133–152.

Bartone, P. and M. Ender (1994) 'Organizational responses to death in the military'. *Death Studies* 18(1): 25–39.

Bayer, Chr.P., F. Klasen and H. Adam (2007) 'Association of trauma and PTSD symptoms with openness to reconciliation and feelings of revenge among former Ugandan and Congolese child soldiers'. *Journal of the American Medical Association* 298(5): 555–559.

Ben-Ari, E. (1989) 'Masks and soldiering: the Israeli army and the Palestinian uprising'. *Current Anthropology* 4(4): 372–389.

Ben-Ari, E. (1998) *Mastering Soldiers: Conflict, Emotions and the Enemy in an Israeli Military Unit*. New York and Oxford: Berghahn Books.

Ben-Ari, E. (2005) 'Epilogue: a "good" military death'. *Armed Forces and Society* 31(4): 651–664.

Ben-Ari, E. and S. Frühstück (2003) 'The celebration of violence: a live-fire demonstration carried out by Japan's contemporary military'. *American Ethnologist* 30(4): 540–555.

Bolton, S. and C. Boyd (2003) 'Trolley dolly or skilled emotion manager? Moving on from Hochschild's Managed Heart'. *Work, Employment and Society* 17(2): 289–308.

Caputo, Ph. (1999 [1977]) *A Rumor of War*. London: Pimlico.

Catino, M. and G. Patriotta (2013) 'Learning from errors: cognition, emotions and safety culture in the Italian Air Force'. *Organization Studies* 34(4): 437–467.

Collins, R. (2008) *Violence: A Micro-Sociological Approach*. Princeton NJ and Oxford: Princeton University Press.

Coser, L. (1974) *Greedy Institutions: Patterns of Undivided Commitment*. New York: Free Press.

De Angelis, K. and M. Wechsler-Segal (2015) 'Transitions in the military and the family as greedy institutions: original concept and current applicability'. In R. Moelker, M. Andres, G. Bowen and Ph. Manigart (eds), *Military Families and War in the 21st Century: Comparative Perspectives*. London and New York: Routledge.

Ender, M. and J.M. Hermsen (1996) 'Working with the bereaved: U.S. Army experiences with nontraditional families'. *Death Studies* 20(6): 557–575.

Ender, M., M. Wechsler-Segal and S. Carson-Stanley (1999) 'Role conformity and creativity: soldiers as administrators and caregivers after loss'. *Journal of Personal and Interpersonal Loss* 4(X): 1–23.

Fanon, F. (2004 [1963]) *The Wretched of the Earth*. New York: Grove Press.

Farnsworth, J., K.D. Drescher, J.A. Nieuwsma, R.B. Walser and J.M. Currier (2014) 'The role of moral emotions in military trauma: implications for the study and treatment of moral injury'. *Review of General Psychology* 18(4): 249–262.

Fein, A.H. and N.S. Isaacson (2009) 'Echoes of Columbine: the emotion work of leaders in school shooting sites'. *American Behavioral Scientist* 52(9): 1327–1346.

Greco, M. and P. Stenner (eds) (2008) *Emotions: A Social Science Reader*. London and New York: Routledge.

Hochschild, A. Russell (1979) 'Emotion work, feeling rules, and social structure'. *American Journal of Sociology* 85(3): 551–575.

Hochschild, A. Russell (1983) *The Managed Heart: Commercialization of Human Feeling*. Berkeley: University of California Press.

Hochschild, A. Russell (2003) 'Let them eat war'. *European Journal of Psychotherapy, Counselling and Health* 6(3): 175–185.

Hochschild, A. Russell (2008) 'Feeling in sociology and the world'. *Sociologisk Forskning* 45(2): 46–50.

Hochschild, A. Russell (2016) *Strangers in Their Own Land: Anger and Mourning on the American Right*. New York and London: The New Press.

Hochschild, A. Russell and A. Machung (1989) *The Second Shift: Working Parents and the Revolution at Home*. New York: Viking.

Klay, Ph. (2014) *Redeployment*. New York: Penguin Books.

Kleinreesink, E. (2016) *On Military Memoirs: A Quantitative Comparison of International Afghanistan War Autobiographies, 2001–2010*. Leiden and Boston: Brill.

Kramer, Z.A. (2007) 'After work'. *California Law Review* 95(2): 627–667.

Martin, J., K. Knopoff and C. Beckman (1998) 'An alternative to bureaucratic impersonality and emotional labor: bounded rationality at the Body Shop'. *Administrative Science Quarterly* 43(2): 429–469.

Messinger, S.D. (2013) 'Vigilance and attention among U.S. service members and veterans after combat'. *Anthropology of Consciousness* 24(2): 191–207.

Ninh, B. (1998 [1991]) *The Sorrow of War*. London: Vintage Books.

Obama, B. (2007) *Dreams from my Father: A Story of Race and Inheritance*. Edinburgh: Canongate.

Oostindie, G. (2015) *Soldaat in Indonesië 1945–1950: Getuigenissen van een oorlog aan de verkeerde kant van de geschiedenis*. Amsterdam: Prometheus Bert Bakker.

Ron, J. (2000) 'Savage restraint: Israel, Palestine and the dialectics of legal repression'. *Social Problems* 47(4): 445–472.

Santin, M. and B. Kelly (2017 [2015]) 'The managed heart revisited: exploring the effect of institutional norms on the emotional labor of flight attendants post 9/11'. *Journal of Contemporary Ethnography* 46(5). doi: doi:0891241615619991

Segal, M.W. (1986) 'The military and the family as greedy institutions'. *Armed Forces and Society* 13(1): 9–38.

Smith, St. (2014) 'Arlie Russell Hochschild: spacious sociologies of emotion'. In P. Adler, P. Du Gay, G. Morgan and M. Reed (eds), *The Oxford Handbook of Sociology, Social Theory and Organization Studies: Contemporary Currents*. Oxford: Oxford University Press, pp. 393–413.

St-Denis, K. (2013) 'Entre reconnaissance sociale et cohérence personelle: management des émotions chez les pompiers de Québec'. *Reflets* 19(2): 142–161.

Steinberg, R.J. and D.M. Figart (1999) 'Emotional labor since The Managed Heart'. *American Academy of Political and Social Science* 561: 8–26.

Weibull, L. (2011) 'La gestion des émotions dans les operations en faveur de la paix'. *L'Année Sociologique* 61(2): 407–430.

Weibull, L. (2012) *Emotion Matters: Emotion Management in Swedish Peace Support Operations*. Karlstad: Karlstad University Studies.

Wharton, A.S. (2009) 'The sociology of emotional labor'. *Annual Review of Sociology* 35: 147–165.

Wouters, C. (1989) 'Flight attendants and the sociology of emotions: Hochschild's *Managed Heart*'. *Theory, Culture and Society* 6(1): 95–123.

13 Cynthia Enloe

Feminist views of the military and its surroundings

Stressing the position and role of women in and around the military, Cynthia Enloe, born in 1938, followed in Jane Addams' footsteps. Like Addams and others she linked the feminist perspective to the search for peace (e.g. Goldstein, 2006: 34–58). Developing a feminist view on military affairs, however, was not Enloe's first scholarly activity. In the first part of her career she studied the relation between the police and the military, as well as aspects of ethnicity in the military (e.g. Enloe, 1977; 1978; 1980). Her work on ethnicity in the military is related to the research that was discussed in the chapter on W. E. B. Du Bois. In the current chapter, however, emphasis will be on her feminist perspective on the military, which will turn out to be quite radical in the eyes of many.

She has published this work in a number of best-selling and often quoted books (Enloe, 1983; 2000; 2004b; 2014; 2016). Next to her connection to Jane Addams, her work reminds us of the tone and strictness of reasoning that Charles Wright Mills exhibited; we saw his work in the chapter referring to Karl Marx. Current scholars who take up a similar, radical way of reasoning are Noam Chomsky (e.g. 2017) and Naomi Klein (1999). Even though – or perhaps because – this type of reasoning does not follow the beaten path, it is worth getting to know it.

In her analysis of the position of women in relation to men and other gender-related themes, Cynthia Enloe is in good sociological company, for instance of Pierre Bourdieu (2001) who has published a book on *Masculine Domination*. The strength of her analyses is that they are based on information collected from all over the world, and therefore demonstrate how to conduct 'connected sociology'. If anything, her work is a demonstration of practising substantive rationality, which is asking the broader questions that are often seen as less directly relevant. We first encountered this concept in the introductory chapter of the book.

As a start, Enloe (2016) argues that all military-related analyses should begin with *feminist curiosity*, which is based on the questions *Where are the women?*, *Which women are specifically there?* and *Why is this natural?* The same questions need to be asked with respect to men. These questions constitute the foundation for a gendered analysis. From there on, she defines a number of concepts that are helpful in her work.

Feminization refers to ideas that any particular thing is 'naturally' or 'especially' aligned with women, girls and femininity, whereas *masculinization* promotes anything that is 'naturally' or 'especially' aligned with men, boys and manliness. Commonly feminized roles are nursing, elementary school teaching and taking care of children. Soldiering and crafting the state's national security strategies belong to the typically masculinized roles (Enloe, 2016: 5). *Militarism* refers to the package of ideas that foster military values and beliefs in both military and civilian affairs – for instance, the idea that hierarchies of command are a natural part of society, the belief that in human affairs it is natural to have enemies (Enloe, 2016: 11–13), or that combat and warriors are inevitable, natural phenomena of life.

Militarization is the process by which people gradually absorb the ideas and resultant practices of militarism. In more formal terms, one can say that militarization is the step-by-step process by which something becomes controlled by, dependent on or derives its value from the military or military criteria (Enloe, 2000: 291). Enloe points at border policing and intelligence agencies as the most likely engines of militarization today (Enloe, 2016: 19). As to border policing, we saw this point being made earlier in the chapter on Michel Foucault. It also applies to disaster management, as shown in the corresponding text box. The process of militarization often evolves without people noticing they are actually contributing to it, which may even apply to people with a favourable inclination towards female soldiers. Authors who are enthusiastic about women taking up combat roles often do not seem to question the usefulness of combat in general.

Demilitarization is also a step-by-step process, but it results from activists – and novelists such as Virginia Woolf (2006 [1938]) – who deliberately want to create policies that lead to less military involvement in and solutions to conflicts. Enloe mentions the Women's International League for Peace and Freedom (WILPF), founded by Jane Addams and colleagues in 1915, and the ICBL – the present day International Campaign to Ban Landmines (Enloe, 2016: 123–143). Both Jane Addams and the ICBL were awarded the Nobel Peace Prize. But there are more, many more, feminist peace movements all over the world. Finally, Enloe explicitly pays attention to the impact of *globalization* on military affairs, such as can be seen in international weapons sales or the activities of private military companies. Globalization is not something new as it dates back to historical developments, particularly with respect to the military in colonial times.

Disaster as war

Kathleen Tierney and Christine Bevc (2007) authored a chapter in a volume on *The Sociology of Katrina* about the way the military assisted in response and recovery efforts after the hurricane struck New Orleans. More than 63,000 National Guard and active military personnel were deployed to conduct search and rescue operations, to deliver relief supplies, to transport and provide shelter to evacuees, but also to deal with 'urban insurgents' to restore order. To do the latter task, military personnel were armed with loaded weapons and combat gear. The ammunition, however, was provided in smaller quantities than is typical during combat operations.

The deployment of such large numbers of military personnel was not a coincidence. There is a traditional connection in the USA between disaster management and war-related concerns, particularly as regards the preparation and protection of the population in a nuclear war. This connection has become stronger. The authors claim that the 'war metaphor', which is often used by American politicians ('war on drugs', 'war on terrorism'), has led to increasing support for military involvement in a variety of activities that would normally be carried out by other entities.

In the aftermath of the hurricane, media reports started to depict the evolving situation as social breakdown and lawlessness, resulting from what they claimed to be rampant looting and violence. The consequence was a huge deployment of military personnel to 'fight a war on two fronts' – the consequences of the disaster itself, and the urban riots that were said to be taking place all over the area. As large portions of the military personnel that were dispatched to New Orleans had previous deployment experience in Iraq, the comparison was easily made. According to the authors, the intensifying interrelations between disaster management and military affairs are the result of 'a climate of militarism that places ultimate confidence in institutions based on the use of force' (Tierney and Bevc, 2007: 46; also: Tierney et al. 2006).

The militarization of women's lives

Before discussing the role of women in today's militaries, it is important to pay attention to women who are formally not in the military but experience its influence nonetheless. Their lives are being militarized, as Cynthia Enloe (1983; 2000; 2014) argues. She and others distinguish a number of roles in this connection:

- Women who do formal work for the military, as civilians inside the garrison, base or camp;
- Women who do formal or informal work for the military outside the garrison, base or camp;
- Women in the host national population who experience the consequences of military activities;
- Women who are married or have an intimate relation with a military man – the so-called military wives;
- Soldiers' mothers.

Non-military women in garrisons, bases or camps mostly perform non-core jobs such as laundry, cleaning, catering and administrative work. These women leave the base after working hours; they and their families are dependent on these jobs. The relevance of this phenomenon particularly pertains to women who work at military bases of Western nations in developing nations, such as the many US or French bases that are spread all over the world. Working for the French military in Gabon or Senegal, for instance, is a profitable endeavour for local women. The same applies to working for the US military on the Pacific island of Guam. But it creates inequality in the wider society as not everybody in the region or country can work on base for the military.

Civilian women who do formal work outside of the camp or base can be anyone, including fellow compatriots who perform specialist work on-line from their homes. Most often these women are employed in defence industries of whatever kind, particularly in wartime when the male workers are deployed in operations (Enloe, 1983). Throughout history defence industries could not have existed without female workers. Women who live close to a base and gain their wages from servicing the military usually work in shops and small business. Often they belong to the entertainment industry, being employed by pubs, bars, restaurants and even brothels. Well known are the stories about American male soldiers on leave from combat in the jungles of Vietnam who tried to find solace in the arms of Thai and other Asian women. To this day the pattern of male soldiers seeking paid or unpaid sex with local women has been a reason for concern in UN operations, as it may have an impact on the social and economic fabric of the region.

The presence of military troops in one's immediate surroundings does not always lead to *paid* work. A notorious example of the opposite is the destiny of the so-called 'comfort women' from Korea, the Philippines, Indonesia and China who were forced to work as prostitutes to service Japanese soldiers during World War II (Enloe, 2000: 79–89). This is a specific example of an appalling general phenomenon, i.e. women in the direct surroundings of troops often becoming the victims of war crimes, such as kidnapping, rape, human trafficking and sexual exploitation (e.g. McKay, 1998; Goldstein, 2006). Sometimes, girls are even compelled or seduced to participate in terrorist attacks within the context of a war (McKay, 2005). Of quite a different note is the willing interaction of local women with foreign soldiers, which should not be a problem but may cause upheaval nonetheless. For instance, the presence of African-American soldiers stationed in the UK in World War II caused controversy among the local population and national politicians as local British women started to date, marry and have children by the American soldiers. This was not in line with the common values at the time and it led to informal pressures inside and outside the military environment to suppress such bi-racial and bi-national interaction (Enloe, 2014: 135–141).

This brings us to the military wives, the women who are married or have an intimate relation with military males (or females in same-sex relations). Their lives are certainly militarized, as Enloe (2016: 71) argues, because they have to move frequently with their families, often sacrifice their own career aspirations, endure the loneliness of being a single mother when their husbands are on deployment, stay publicly cheerful while at home husbands are stressing out, and remain quiet in their grief when their husbands have died in action. Military wives play the pivotal role in managing the family, 'keeping the home fires burning' (Enloe, 1983: 46ff). This is not easy because the military and the family are both 'greedy institutions' as we saw before.

Most of the time, military wives manage to keep their marital relations stable despite the many kinds of stress they experience while their partner is on deployment (Aducci et al., 2011). Of course, negative aspects of military family life are outweighed by advantages related to community life, proper income and social benefits, and, for a number of their husbands, good career prospects from which the women profit as well. If the balance between benefits and sacrifices gets out of proportion, however, the voice or the exit-option can be used: protest or divorce. Women's dissatisfaction with military life is a reason of particular concern to commanders and recruiters, as it may lead to manpower shortages when lovers or wives discourage their partners from starting or continuing to work for the armed forces (Enloe, 2015).

For the last category of militarized women – the mothers and the mothers' mothers – there is only the 'voice'-option if the problems get out of hand. Complaints from soldiers' mothers have often had an important influence in terminating military abuse and even in bringing wars to an end. Well-known are the mothers and the grandmothers of the Plaza de Mayo in Buenos Aires, Argentina, who continued their protests against the military government for years, even after that government had been replaced by a democratically elected one. It seems likely that Russian mothers' complaints about losing their sons in the war in Afghanistan contributed to the end of that war (e.g. Alexievich, 2017 [1989]). Not surprisingly, militaries worldwide go out of their way to prevent mothers from objecting to their son's enlistment, for instance by mobilizing the mothers' feelings of patriotism and by trying to increase their commitment to their sons' military work (Enloe, 2000: 244–260).

For sure, all of these women's lives are militarized; but women who are inside the military – the female soldiers, sailors, NCOs and officers – are likely to experience the military's consequences most.

Women inside the military

Throughout history, in times of war women have always played their part in the military, even though only in incidental cases did they play a major role in those armies and wars (Goldstein, 2006: 1–58). The phenomenon of female combatants has been a rare one but can be seen in all times and all over the world (e.g. Goldstein, 2006: 59–127). More prevalent has been their work in supporting roles. Nursing the military – as Florence Nightingale did – was one of the original and highly appreciated tasks of women in the armed forces (Enloe, 1983: 92ff). The events during World War II on all sides of the arena may serve as telling examples. White, African-American and Japanese-American women did military service in the US forces, though mostly in support units and positions. In this capacity they helped obtain the victory and end the war (Moore, 1996). Women's experiences in the Soviet Red Army were as horrifying as they were exceptional. Over 1 million women participated in the battles against the Nazis in all kinds of positions, simply because so many men fell in combat. The women experienced great losses too (Alexijewitsch, 2015). But with the war's end, the women of the Soviet Union and elsewhere returned to their homes again. In peacetime, the military was not a woman's place. That changed once the *male* conscript system approached its end in many nations.

Since the abandonment of the conscript system in many nations, women inside the military, i.e. female soldiers, have become a focus of debates, policies and academic interest worldwide (e.g. Weber, 2015; Woodward and Duncanson, 2017). Through the introduction of the all-volunteer force, formal barriers for women to access the military have been lifted. There still were and are societal and institutional barriers, however. In the first place, young women, it seems, are not interested in pursuing a military career as much as young men are. The military still does not seem to fully align with widely shared ideas about femininity. Second, military organizations themselves may not always be that interested in having many young women on board, because the military culture still seems stubbornly masculine and, hence, is still ambivalent about full gender mainstreaming. An example refers to the general working and living conditions female sailors experience(d) on navy vessels (e.g. van Wijk and Finchilescu, 2008). Both reasons may account for the fact that numbers of female military personnel have not increased considerably over recent decades, a phenomenon that can be observed in almost all national forces (e.g. Soeters and van der Meulen, 2007; Enloe, 2016).

At the moment, the proportions of women in active military duty vary from 5.5 per cent (Japan), 7.5 per cent (China), via 8.5 per cent (Germany), 10 per cent (Russia, UK), 12.5 per cent (Australia), 14–16.5 per cent (Canada, USA, France, New Zealand) to 26 per cent (South Africa) and 30 per cent (Israel, Eritrea) (Enloe, 2016: 84). Not a single national force comes close to a 50–50 per cent distribution. The abolishment of conscription has helped gender integration, but the record in the Western hemisphere is held by the Israeli Defence Forces with their enlistment system that has been compulsory for men and women since 1948 when the state of Israel was founded.

It makes sense to refine such statistical averages to illustrate, for instance, patterns of racial under- or overrepresentation among female soldiers. In the USA, for instance, the number of African-American female soldiers has been relatively large since women entered the military (Enloe, 2000: 280–281). This may be related to the economically and socially less advantageous conditions for this population group in American society at large. For women, good pay is an important, even though not overridingly important, component of a military job (Shields, 1988: 105).

The reasons for encouraging the entry of women to the military since the end of the conscript system are not feminist per se, as Enloe argues (2000: 280). She points to the need for the military to recruit and retain a workforce that is large and skilful enough. If the number of young people in general declines and young men's interest in joining the military falls behind, women are the first way to compensate for the deficiencies. This compensation may be a matter of quantity and/or quality – women having the required skills that men who want to enlist do not have. Also, the wish to look 'modern' or 'democratic', as well as the need to comply with women's demands for 'first-class citizenship', has more to do with reputational and legal concerns than with a feminist orientation, as Enloe argues. But frankly, the 'true' motivation behind the decision to open up the military for women is perhaps not that important.

Given these relatively strong reasons to increase the number of women in the military, there is still a remarkably persistent debate about whether or not women are actually capable of doing the military job. This discussion focuses especially on the so-called combat or 'warrior' roles that can be found in specialized infantry units, special operations forces and marine corps. It is predominantly an Anglo-Saxon, more precisely an American and British debate (Enloe, 2014: 152–153), possibly related to those militaries' preoccupation with combat and 'warrior' identity (e.g. Woodward, 2000; Burke, 2004). In the 1990s US scholars (Shields et al., 1990) revealed that other NATO members were the first to employ female pilots in combat cockpits. Among other NATO members such as Belgium, Norway stands out, as it together with Israel was the first country to completely abolish gender barriers in the armed forces, opening combat positions to women in 1988 (Braw, 2017). Currently, Norway has introduced a system of gender-neutral conscription, and it successfully completed a two-year experiment with a 50 per cent male and 50 per cent female air and missile defence battalion, surveyed by social anthropologist Nina Hellum. The outcome was that in performance evaluations gender differences could not be observed, as 'one is just seeing soldiers' (Braw, 2017). Yet, this battalion is still not where the 'real' fighting, the 'man-to-man' fighting in ground combat, goes on. The access of women to these situations is still a point of discussion for some.

Without questioning the implications and effectiveness of war and combat, British sociologist Anthony King (2016) gets excited about the idea of women taking up combat and warrior roles. He argues that the professionalization of the armed forces after the end of conscription, and particularly due to the increase of operational demands in Iraq and Afghanistan, caused a professional bonding among soldiers in units despite differences in gender, race and general background. Soldiers can work together in units because of their professional, combat competences and not because they are alike in those terms. In fact, a process of assimilation occurs, making women similar to men, particularly in terms of their skills and competences but also in terms of how they look. Hence, the relatively easy access of female soldiers to ground combat units in Iraq and Afghanistan, even when this had not yet been formally allowed by defence policy (King, 2016: 129). Morten Ender produced similar findings with respect to American 'G.I. Janes' in Iraq (Ender, 2009: 87ff). As an earlier study found, gender integration is perceived to have only a relatively small impact on readiness, cohesion and morale in units (Titunik, 2000: 248). These experiences confirm the results of the Norwegian experiment with the air and missile defence battalion.

Other experiences in Israel, however, indicate that even if female soldiers are allowed 'masculine roles', this happens only rarely. Women remain marginal in the Israeli Defence Force as they see no options to change the masculine hegemony, despite their large numbers in comparison with other national forces (Sasson-Levy, 2003). In addition, there are increasing tensions coming from religious male soldiers who want to exclude women from military service (Levy, 2013). Also, the professional bonding between women and men in US and UK combat units could be a temporary affair, that loses importance once operational missions with all their tensions no longer demand large numbers of personnel. The box below relates to such operational high tension situations.

Feminist reflections about Abu Ghraib

In April 2004 shocking pictures of American soldiers abusing Iraqi prisoners – mostly in a sexualized context – began appearing on television news programmes. Both male and female guards at the Abu Ghraib prison could be seen; all of them were smiling broadly. Among the guards one female soldier captured the special attention of editors, viewers and readers: the 20-year-old enlisted army reservist Lynndie England. The commander of the prison was female general Janice Karpinsky. The fact that women were involved contributed to the societal and political upheaval following publication of the pictures.

Enloe (2004a; 2016: 99–122) raises a number of intriguing questions in this connection that seem to have been overlooked by many. Those are the sort of questions that are always relevant in order to conduct a gendered analysis.

Who took the pictures? Why did Lynndie England in particular attract so much attention? Why was her sexual partner Charles Graner, who was also pictured, not the focus of media attention? Enloe and others do not accept the explanation that the abuses were the result of the misbehaviour of a few 'bad apples'. Some authors (e.g. Chwastiak, 2015) relate the abuse to the legitimation and normalization of 'enhanced interrogation techniques' by the authorities, whereas these techniques should in fact be seen as torture. Enloe relates the abuse in the Iraqi prison to an organizational climate in the US military in which sexual harassment, abusive behaviour towards women and even rape are rife, because masculine values and practices still dominate the scene. As long as one does not see and change the bigger picture pertaining to the whole military, Enloe contends, a clear understanding of what happened in Abu Ghraib (and Guantánamo) will not be possible.

Faits divers

Joshua Goldstein (2006) did a large review of the existing literature on war and gender. Specifically, he tested a number of interdisciplinary hypotheses on the consistency of gendered war roles, making use of insights and knowledge belonging to the whole gamut of sciences, from biology to psychology and the social and political sciences. He found out that relatively small numbers of women have participated in combat throughout world history, yet those who did in general fought well; women can make good soldiers. The fact they do not often participate in combat is related to innate, biological differences (size, strength), but more importantly to gender segregation in childhood and formative years. The toughening up of boys is found across cultures, whereas girls are socialized to support the men in their traditional masculine roles. Testerone levels do not play a role, nor do female hormones or male bonding. Proportionally, somewhat more women than men oppose wars, but most women support wars (Goldstein, 2006: 403–407). Hence, peace movements such as the one founded by Jane Addams, and analyses that are critical of the military such as the ones published by Cynthia Enloe, are often feminist in nature. However, this neither means that those movements and critics are exclusively female nor that all women have similar views.

In line with these findings, a study by Sasson-Levy et al. (2011) uncovered statements of Israeli women ex-soldiers who developed anti-war attitudes during their deployment in the occupied Palestinian territories. They gave testimonies about their military experiences during two years of service which were compiled by activists of the Breaking the Silence movement. Hence, these testimonies are not provided by randomly selected witnesses, but they are highly important as not everyone is critical of what is happening or dares to express his or her views. Importantly, those statements did not challenge the occupation directly. In general, the testimonies of those female ex-soldiers reveal the women's ambivalent stance vis-à-vis the military. They were critical about the atmosphere of military masculinity that made them ceaselessly being tested to ascertain if they were capable of exhibiting enough violence towards Palestinians, and being enthusiastic about it. They were critical about the insensitive, robot-style manner that many of their male colleagues displayed when approaching Palestinian citizens and entering Palestinian houses. The women's declarations also showed the capacity to identify with *the other*, being the Palestinian citizens, women, men and children. Via their testimonies these women ex-soldiers used their legitimate position of having served in the military and being a witness and military expert, to engage in political mobilization.

A final point concerns aspects of military performance outside the realm of combat and warrior roles. In UN missions there is not usually a lot of combat involved. It should be kept in mind that in terms of time taken up, combat is actually the exception in military performance, not the rule. The aim of international UN operations is to bring and keep peace, in a stabilizing manner, having the population, the whole population – women, men and children! – involved. Seen from this perspective, a gender-neutral composition is important for realizing such goals because chances are higher that such a balanced workforce will help cope with the many aspects and challenges of the mission. A greater proportion of female military personnel is likely to engender trust and improve the reputation of peacekeepers among the host national populations (Bridges and Horsfall, 2009). UN missions are too important to be left to men only. We have seen this point before in the chapter on Jane Addams.

Conclusion

As said earlier, Cynthia Enloe links the feminist perspective on the military with the ambition to reduce violence, war and combat as ways to solve problems at hand. That is not so surprising as women throughout history have had less to do with military affairs and are in general somewhat more inclined than men to seek peaceful solutions to tensions between adversary groups and nations. By ceaselessly criticizing the size and impact of war and violence, including their consequences for the host population, Enloe seems to contradict the findings of Norbert Elias and Stephen Pinker about the decline of violence. But that may be an illusion. Elias and Pinker sketch, theorize and empirically support their theses, whereas for Cynthia Enloe and others the conduct of military operations – in fact, any military performance – needs to be scrutinized and criticized from a normative, moral point of view. These approaches are not contradictory but refer to different questions in different areas of study.

Bibliography

Aducci, C.J., J.A. Baptist, J. George, P.M. Barros and B.S.N. Goff (2011) 'The recipe for being a good military wife: how military wives managed OIF/OEF deployment'. *Journal of Feminist Family Therapy* 23(4): 231–249.

Alexijewitsch, S. (2015 [2008]) *Der Krieg Hat Kein Weibliches Gesicht.* Berlin: Suhrkamp.

Alexievich, S. (2017 [1989]) *Boys in Zinc.* London: Penguin.

Bourdieu, P. (2001) *Masculine Domination.* Stanford, CA: Stanford University Press.

Braw, E. (2017) 'Norway's radical military experiment: how full gender integration paid off'. *Foreign Affairs*, 19 January.

Bridges, D. and D. Horsfall (2009) 'Increasing operational effectiveness in UN peacekeeping: toward a gender-balanced force'. *Armed Forces and Society* 36(1): 120–130.

Burke, C. (2004) *Camp All-American, Hanoi Jane, and the High-and-Tight.* Boston: Beacon Press.

Chomsky, N. (2017) *Who Rules the World?* London: Penguin Books.

Chwastiak, M. (2015) 'Torture as normal work: the Bush administration, the Central Intelligence Agency, and "enhanced interrogation techniques"'. *Organization* 22(4): 493–511.

Ender, M. (2009) *American Soldiers in Iraq. McSoldiers or Innovative Professionals?* New York and London: Routledge.

Enloe, C. (1977) 'Police and military in the resolution of ethnic conflict'. *Annals of the American Academy of Political and Social Science*, 433(1): 137–149.

Enloe, C. (1978) 'Police and military in Ulster: peacekeeping or peace-subverting forces?' *Journal of Peace Research* 15(3): 243–258.

Enloe, C. (1980) *Ethnic Soldiers: State Security in Divided Societies.* London: Penguin.

Enloe, C. (1983) *Does Khaki Become You? The Militarization of Women's Lives.* London: Pluto Press.

Enloe, C. (2000) *Maneuvers: The International Politics of Militarizing Women's Lives.* Berkeley, Los Angeles and London: University of California Press.

Enloe, C. (2004a) 'Wielding masculinity inside Abu Graib: making feminist sense of an American military scandal'. *Asian Journal of Women's Studies* 10(3): 89–102.

Enloe, C. (2004b) *The Curious Feminist: Searching for Women in a New Age of Empire.* Berkeley, Los Angeles and London: University of California Press.

Enloe, C. (2014) *Bananas, Beaches and Bases: Making Feminist Sense of International Politics.* Berkeley, Los Angeles and London: University of California Press.

Enloe, C. (2015) 'The recruiter and the sceptic: a critical feminist approach to military studies'. *Critical Military Studies* 1(1): 3–10.

Enloe, C. (2016) *Globalization and Militarism: Feminists Make the Link.* 2nd edn. Lanham, MD: Rowman & Littlefield.

Goldstein, J.S. (2006) *War and Gender: How Gender Shapes the War System and Vice Versa.* Cambridge: Cambridge University Press.

King, A.C. (2016) 'The female combat soldier'. *European Journal of International Relations* 22(1): 122–143.

Klein, N. (1999) *No Logo: Money, Marketing, and the Growing Anti-Corporate Movement.* New York: Picador.

Levy, Y. (2013) 'The military as a split labor market: the case of women and religious soldiers in the Israeli Defense Forces'. *International Journal of Politics, Culture, and Society* 26(4): 393–414.

McKay, S. (1998) 'The effects of armed conflict on girls and women'. *Peace and Conflict: Journal of Peace Psychology* 4(4): 381–392.

McKay, S. (2005) 'Girls as "weapons of terror" in Northern Uganda and Sierra Leonean rebel fighting forces'. *Studies in Conflict and Terrorism* 28(5): 385–397.

Moore, B. (1996) *To Serve My Country, To Serve My Race: The Story of the Only African American WACs Stationed Overseas during World War II.* New York: New York University Press.

Moore, B. (ed.) (2017) 'Special issue: women in the military'. *Armed Forces and Society* 43(2).

Sasson-Levy, O. (2003) 'Feminism and military gender practices: Israeli women soldiers in "masculine" roles'. *Sociological Inquiry* 73(3): 440–465.

Sasson-Levy, O., Y. Levy and E. Lomsky-Feder (2011) 'Women breaking the silence: military service, gender, and antiwar protest'. *Gender and Society* 25(6): 740–763.

Shields, P. (1988) 'Sex roles in the military'. In Ch.C. Moskos and F.R. Wood (eds), *The Military: More than Just a Job?* Washington DC: Pergamon-Brassey's.

Shields, P.M., L. Curry and J. Nichols (1990) 'Women pilots in combat: attitudes of male and female pilots'. *Minerva – Quarterly Report on Women and the Military* 8(2): 21–35.

Soeters, J. and J. van der Meulen (2007) *Cultural Diversity in the Armed Forces: An International Comparison.* London and New York: Routledge.

Tierney, K. and Chr. Bevc (2007) 'Disaster as war: militarism and the social construction of disaster in New Orleans'. In D.L. Brunsma, D. Overfelt and J.S. Picou (eds), *The Sociology of Katrina: Perspectives on a Modern Catastrophe.* Lanham, MD: Rowman & Littlefield, pp. 35–49.

Tierney, K., Chr. Bevc and E. Kuligowski (2006) 'Metaphors matter: disaster myths, media frames, and their consequences in hurricane Katrina'. *Annals of the American Academy of Political and Social Science* 604: 57–81.

Titunik, R.F. (2000) 'The first wave: gender integration and military culture'. *Armed Forces and Society* 26(2): 229–257.

van Wijk, Ch.H. and G. Finchilescu (2008) 'Symbols of organizational culture: describing and prescribing gender integration of navy ships'. *Journal of Gender Studies* 17(3): 237–249.

Weber, C. (2015) (ed.), *Les femmes militaires*. Rennes: Presses Universitaires de Rennes.

Woodward, R. (2000) 'Warrior heroes and little green men: soldiers, military training, and the construction of rural masculinities'. *Rural Sociology* 65(4): 640–657.

Woodward, R. and C. Duncanson (eds) (2017) *The Palgrave International Handbook of Gender and the Military*. London: Palgrave.

Woolf, V. (2006 [1938]) *Three Guineas*. Orlando, FL: Harvest, Harcourt.

14 Bruno Latour

Science and technology in society and the military

Technology plays an important role in social and organizational life, and this role is becoming more and more significant. Bruno Latour, born in 1947, is a French sociologist, anthropologist and philosopher, who has studied processes leading to the development, application and impact of science and technology in societies. His work has preceded renewed attention to technical work in organizations and the interplay between the material and the social world, the so-called 'socio-materiality discourse' in organization studies (e.g Barley, 1996; Orlikowski and Scott, 2008). This attention was much needed, as technology and science had been neglected in organization studies for far too long. In fact, this is the main message Latour has dispatched all the time: humans – social agents – should not be separated from non-humans, since 'things', too, belong to the real world. Sociology should not only deal with social but also with physical phenomena, as Latour (2000) rightly claims.

As Bruno Latour's alter ego, Jim Johnson (1988: 304) published a brilliant article in which he analysed how a humble technological artefact such as a door-closer affects the way people solve problems that have always been taken for granted but that are crucial in organizing social life. In order to separate a space in different rooms that can be used for different purposes, one needs walls; in order to go from one room into another, doors have been invented; in order to minimize efforts to close the door, door-closers have been devised. Traditionally, sociologists would not pay attention to all these things, except perhaps in their description of a study's context. But that is wrong: stuff matters (Miodownik, 2013).

Bruno Latour started his scholarly career with an analysis of work processes in a laboratory for neuroendocrinology in California. He hit on the idea of examining the practices in the lab in the same way he had conducted an earlier study during his military service in Ivory Coast in West Africa, one of France's former colonies (Blok and Elgaard Jensen, 2011: 7). Influenced by anthropologists, Latour had examined the French tradition of technical education and training in that country. As happened to that other giant of French social sciences, Pierre Bourdieu (2012 [1960]), military service in one of France's African ex-colonies turned out to be a source of inspiration for his future work. That work would take place soon, when Latour got the opportunity to study the 'construction of scientific facts' in the laboratory in California. Together with a colleague (Latour and Woolgar, 1986), he based his findings on long-term fieldwork, 'slow' descriptions, close observation and careful analysis of events, conversations, technical schemes and photos, made by themselves. Hence, they worked in a most anthropological way to produce admirably detailed descriptions.

Their analysis is bewildering as it demonstrates that scientific facts are not simply 'out there' waiting to be discovered by a genius. Instead, Latour and Woolgar showed how scientists' work consists of 'constantly relating countless different kinds of materials: machines, texts, people, animals, linguistic statements and so on' (Blok and Elgaard Jensen, 2011: 27). 'Inscription devices' are sets of lab technicians, machines such as computers and cameras, and laboratory devices that transform substances, derived for instance from rats, into visual display; these displays are used to present the new scientific results in journal articles and presentations. It should be noticed that Latour and Woolgar (1986) combine humans and non-humans in one analysis and treat them as equally important. This indeed was something new in the social sciences.

Latour (1987) argues that scientists' work is a matter of expanding networks that need to collaborate in order to produce scientific facts. Scientists have to formulate their findings and ideas in such a way that other people become interested. They can do so by 'translating' interests, which comes down to making explicit that the interests of scientists and sponsors are the same, or that interests can be reshuffled in such a way that they become the same. Also, goals can be changed, new goals can be invented, new interest groups can be discovered, and all of this should lead to making oneself indispensable in the 'construction of scientific facts' (Latour, 1987: 108–132).

Given the importance of these translation capabilities, labs are fact-producing factories that depend as much on organizing and politicking capabilities as on genial scientific insights or the inspiration of the main researchers. Latour's account of how Pasteur organized the public proof of the effect of the vaccine he had developed – applying it to an experimental group of sheep at a farm – (Blok and Elgaard Jensen, 2011: 42) demonstrates how important it is to recruit and combine allies and expand one's networks in order to 'construct scientific facts' successfully. Pasteur needed the help of the farmer and co-researchers as well as of politicians, journalists and the general public. Similar stories can be found in Latour (1987: 104–107), about the way the diesel engine was initially developed, from its basic idea to production and marketing. As Latour (1987: 10) put it, both statements are true: 'once the machine works people will be convinced' and 'the machine will work when all the relevant people are convinced'.

Both statements are true, and this fact not only characterizes the success of technological innovations but also the lack thereof. If the creators do not supply sustained commitment, if not enough allies have been recruited who are convinced the machine will work, technological inventions are doomed to fail (Latour, 1996). This is true no matter how sophisticated the innovation may be. In the end a technological innovation, such as an advanced, automated urban transportation system in Paris, may not live because it has been killed, or 'it is just that nobody loved him enough to keep him alive' (Czarniawska, 2014: 92). After all, about technological *projects*, one can only be subjective, as Latour (1996: 75) put it. All of this one can recognize in today's innovations with respect to renewable energy. For decades, not 'all the relevant people' were convinced of its importance, and consequentially not a lot happened in this domain. If one looks at the current advances in the field of renewable energy, however, one can conclude that new technological results are not the consequence of 'science being that far ahead', but of growing networks of 'all the relevant people' being convinced.

All these insights resulted from Latour's painstaking work in the Californian lab and other studies, and they are of great value to both science studies and social sciences. But the interrelation between the two is not without complexities.

Sociological controversies

Latour (2000: 107) opens one of his articles with the joke that all is well with the social sciences except for two tiny words: 'social' and 'sciences'. He has used this joke on different occasions. It displays Latour's somewhat condescending stance towards sociology ever since the time of Durkheim (Blok and Elgaard Jensen, 2011: 125, 160–162; Latour, 2005). Perhaps more than in other sciences, sociology suffers from insider rivalries and competition. 'Wars' have been waged about the superiority of developmental versus universal, stability-oriented theories, or about qualitative versus quantitative research methods. These 'wars' may have various backgrounds. Some social and political scientists are morally motivated to reduce social inequalities between classes, population groups, men and women, and the various regions in the world. Cynthia Enloe's often sharp analyses also have a lot to do with her deeply felt aversion to violent, military solutions to problems. But often the rivalries can be traced back to the self-centred exaggeration of new insights that are claimed to replace older ones, but in fact most often add to the preceding ones. Latour's insights with respect to the connection of humans and non-humans and the construction of scientific facts provide novelty to the discipline but do not render previous results and understandings dispensable.

Despite his personal experience of military service, Latour did not write a lot about the military. However, he is fully aware that the defence sector plays an enormous role in a country's research and development (R&D). In quite a number of countries the budget for science and technology spent by the defence sector is considerably higher than any other budget for R&D (Latour, 1987: 171–173). Furthermore, in a short book Latour (2002) talked about the post-9/11 world. He argued that the West has wrongly believed, particularly since the Cold War, that its way of living, including its buzzwords *progress* and *modernity*, could be expanded to the rest of the world, assuming that there were no wars at all. In fact, one should be aware that 'a war of the worlds has been raging all along, throughout the so-called 'modern age' (Latour, 2002: 3). That is because, '[...] the world of Science, of Technology, of the Market, Democracy, Humanity, Human Rights [...] suffered from being a little ethnocentric, if not a trifle imperialist' (Latour, 2002: 9). Only after one has become aware of this 'war of the worlds' is it possible to bring diplomats to the negotiation table. There they can try to seek compromises between democratic *agoras* [Greek: assembly, market place] and other assemblages of living, discussing, deciding and administering that prevail in so many parts of the globe (Latour, 2002: 49–51). This is a fresh perspective of the kind that that Latour so typically offers.

One can also recognize this freshness in the final aspect of his work we discuss here. This concerns his idea about *Political Ecology* and *Dingpolitiek*, the 'politics of things' (Blok and Elgaard Jensen, 2011: 75ff). This idea is all about making things – environmental issues, Islamic headscarves, genetically modified food, architecture, weapons of mass destruction – the centre of political discussion, conflict and compromise. Nature and the environment, science and non-humans should become the objects of appropriate communal discussion and decision making. The reason is that objects often trigger fierce and passionate disputes. Politics is often more about objects than about opinions. Latour contends that democracy should install procedures to ensure that, in the first place, the representatives are legitimately assembled and, second, that the facts and objects are represented to the public in a legitimate manner. He uses the example of US secretary of state Colin Powell showing pictures of weapons of mass destruction allegedly ready for use by the Iraqi government of that time. Those pictures were blurry and, therefore, hardly sufficient evidence to justify an invasion. In general, Latour asks for more attention to, and discussion about, things. For these discussions to be adequate, the objects, the things, need to be presented and illuminated publicly and as accurately as possible. That is what Latour means by 'object-oriented' democracy (Blok and Elgaard Jensen, 2011: 84–87).

How is all this related to military affairs?

Technology and innovation in the military

Ages ago the capability to defend oneself started with engineering and constructing castles, fortifications, canals and cities that could resist long sieges. Military engineering, architecture and construction preceded civilian engineering (e.g. Mukerji, 2006; Sparavigna, 2015). Military academies delivered the foundational know-how to be used in civilian technical universities for architecture and construction (e.g. van Doorn, 1975: 18).

Next to making use of advances in construction for defence purposes, the military has always profited from technological novelties in battles and attacks in general. From time immemorial, the military has obtained victories over other forces through technological innovation (Moelker and Schenk, 2017). In World War I a number of highly effective technological innovations were introduced, such as the machine gun and the tank, both of which, prior to being used, met with considerable resistance from traditionalist circles in the military, who preferred to believe in the 'admirable' character of man-to-man bayonet fighting. After their introduction, however, the machine gun and the tank would fundamentally change the course of events in battle.

As we saw in the discussion of Simmel's stranger, mostly military men with experience of colonial wars and in 'strange' places such as the navy, provided the networks and alliances of building capabilities – to use Latour's wordings – that made the introduction of these innovations possible (Moelker and Schenk, 2017). The new technologies needed advocates with a broad organizational and operational overview to overcome the resistance that was deeply rooted in established military culture. Sometimes such resistance may even lead to what may be called sabotage from within the military, as the example of the malfunctioning M16 gun in the Vietnam War illustrates (Moelker and Schenk, 2017). All these stories underline that what Latour emphasized holds true: technological and scientific innovations are not simply 'out there'. In order to become successful, they need alliances and expanding networks of things (!) and people. Innovations will only work 'when all the relevant people are convinced' (Latour, 1986: 10).

Of course, technological innovation need to go hand in hand with innovations in the structure and functioning of the military organization. The increase of soldierly discipline organized by the Prince of Orange in the Low Countries' struggle for independence from Spain in the sixteenth and seventeenth centuries is an example that we saw earlier in the discussion of the Weberian bureaucracy. This rise in discipline and mastery of skills and drills was needed to facilitate the efficacious use of technologically advanced firepower, the musket in particular (Van Doorn, 1975). This is only one example in a long, age-old history of military and scientific innovations made possible by accompanying organizational renewals.

In general, it pays to study the ways in which military organizations employ technical people. Like other organizations, military organizations are increasingly dependent on scientists and technicians, in or out of uniform. Not only innovations in hardware technologies, but particularly information- and communication-related inventions constitute significant advances that make the hiring of growing numbers of scientists and technologists by the armed forces foreseeable. Increasing these numbers is likely to come alongside concerns about recruitment and retention and the feasibility of steering the organization vertically from above, the traditional bureaucratic way. Horizontal ways of organizing are likely to be more fruitful in organizations where professionals in technology and science will be progressively more important (Barley, 1996; 2005). Their importance, and the way they act as 'social activists designing societies or social institutions to fit those machines' (Law and Callon, 1988: 284), can be observed once more in the box below.

Validating the virtual

Inspired by Bruno Latour's way of working, Dutch military scholar Maarten van Veen studied the way military training simulators are validated. Latour (1987: 247–248) himself has often pointed at the importance of scale models and simulators in technological innovation, for instance in the space and aviation industry. Other authors have also pointed to the significant impact of digital simulation technologies on work processes (Bailey et al., 2012). In the military, training simulators are widely used to provide soldiers with the experience of operational circumstances and dynamics that come close to real involvement in war and battle. Such simulators are said to be cheaper, provide more effective training, save the environment and are, all in all, more 'realistic' than training by other means (van Veen, 2014: 202). The question is whether these claims about the connection between the reality and the virtual are really true. Van Veen studied the process of validation using the perspective that validity is not something inherent in a military training simulator, but something that is attributed by an expanding network of relevant people and technologies. Something that 'all the relevant people are convinced of'.

He distinguishes validation at four levels:

- practical validation by the trainers,
- industrial validation by the procurement department and the engineers of the military industry,
- military validation by the operational staff supported by the US army, and
- political validation by the minister and parliament.

Each level or type of validation involves different actors and non-humans, i.e. technologies and documents. Validation never was a given element, but had to be obtained via the co-producing and lumping together of different interests. In the end, passing the tests of the training device was the new reality of being a good soldier.

The process of validating the virtual demonstrates that science and technology have penetrated all levels of the military organization. In World War I technological innovations may have been introduced somewhat hesitantly but already in World War II and during the ensuing Cold War, technology and science became dominant factors in military affairs – one only needs to think of the introduction of radar, the computer, nuclear power, satellites, numerical weather prediction and, today, of unmanned vehicles (e.g. Harper, 2003; Rappart et al., 2008). All these innovations have determined the course of events in international relations in recent decades, and they will continue to do so in future. Technology and the military make a good couple.

However, as we saw in the introduction to Latour's work, a scientific innovation may also be 'killed' even before its inception. Or it may die anyway because
of a lack of alliance building capabilities, i.e. because too few of the relevant
people are convinced or because some part of the network has been damaged
(Latour, 1987: 10, 249; Latour, 1996). A spectacular 'miscarriage' in the field of
the social sciences was the so-called Camelot project in the 1960s, that intended
to map the antecedents and dynamics of revolutions, including their theoretical
backgrounds and implications in the various regions of the world. The project
was generously funded by the military and a large number of famous sociologists
and other social scientists were connected to it. However, as the Vietnam War
came to a peak, the suspicion rose that this project had political, ideological and
military objectives, albeit in a covert, secret manner. The turmoil that ensued in
academia and society led to the cancellation of the whole project. Clearly, not
all the relevant people had been convinced (Solovey, 2001).

Military history is rife with other examples, particularly in the R&D trajectory.
John Law and Michel Callon (1988) studied the development of a British
military project, the TSR2, a light bomber and reconnaissance aircraft. They
traced how the project was conceived, designed and developed in the 1950s
until its cancellation in 1965. It was cancelled because the project had caused
overspending and delays, thus increasing the number of sceptics who became so
influential that they started to undermine the project. In connection with a
change in the political climate fewer relevant people had become convinced of
the project's value, making the network decline.

Stagnating or fragile networks of relevant, convinced people occur in particular when international technological projects are attempted. Uiterwijk et al.
(2013) analysed the development of the NH-90, a helicopter to be used in the
context of NATO transport and maritime operations. After the United Kingdom had withdrawn from the programme, it was carried through by four
European countries, i.e. France, Italy, Germany and the Netherlands. Here
ceaseless overspending, continual programme delays, a lack of product standardization and quarrels about the international division of workshare led to a final
product that not many people were really in love with. The love for this
international NH-90-project – to use Czarniawska's words (2014) – was not
brittle and unstable enough to make it die, but the project was less successful
than people had imagined at its inception.

The same seems to apply to the development and introduction of the
nuclear-powered-and-armed Trident submarine commissioned by the British
MoD in the 1980s and 1990s (Mort, 2002). This submarine has been presented
as a great success; however, one could also argue that it has been born out of
controversy. In a Latourian fashion, Maggie Mort reconstructed the development
of the network that enabled the development and construction of the four
Trident submarines. She analysed how the alliance of convinced people came
into being, but also how people and machines were jettisoned from the network (Mort, 2002: 11). In particular, employees who felt increasingly uneasy
about their company's dependence on MoD orders and about the lethal

capabilities of the submarine searched for alternative technologies to produce. This game could not be won, however. The final report these workers and technicians produced in 1987 was entitled *Oceans of Work*. It contained a list of alternative technologies to be developed that look surprisingly fresh today – e.g., oceanic energy production systems and open-sea mari-culture. At the time of its publication, however, the report 'was greeted by a wall of silence' (Mort, 2002: 152–153).

This reconstruction of a Latourian network intended to create this new technological device is not without significance. Nuclear-powered constellations are risky in many ways, and those risks are as real as the sinking of the Russian submarine *Kursk* (Barany, 2004) and the more recent Fukishima disaster have demonstrated. Organizational sociologist Charles Perrow developed a highly influential theory of high-risk technologies that entail so many structural complexities that failures are inevitable and accidents must be considered 'normal' (Perrow, 1999a). Ways to reduce the vulnerabilities of complexity imply the involvement of external stakeholders to keep the risky system honest. However, secret organizations such as intelligence and military organizations are the least likely to adapt to such changes (Perrow, 1999b). As such, Perrow connects a Weberian line of thinking about organizational structures with the secrecy dynamics proposed by Georg Simmel.

A dramatic example of a 'normal accident' waiting to happen was the explosion of the space shuttle *Challenger* on 28 January 1986, with the loss of all seven crew members. NASA is not a military organization, but it is surely connected to the security sector.

The *Challenger* launch decision

Sociologist Diana Vaughan (1996) conducted an in-depth study of the process that led to the decision to launch the space shuttle despite engineers' concerns that the cold weather conditions during the planned time of take-off could create problems. These concerns related to rubberlike, so-called O-rings that were designed to seal a tiny gap created by pressure at ignition close to the external tank containing liquid hydrogen and oxygen. However, the rings' resilience was impaired by low temperature as previous experiences had indicated, possibly leading to a situation in which the tank could explode.

In a teleconference meeting, engineers from the responsible contracting company voiced their concerns but during the process of deliberation they were out-voted by their superiors. As in this case, when available data are insufficiently clear, preferences, views and opinions count, and more so the higher one's rank. At the moment of final decision making, the worried engineers kept silent as they 'had already given their analysis and opinion'. Interestingly, before and after the tragic accident, outsiders – non-engineers, strangers so to speak – provided the data about the rings' performance at varying temperatures; these data most likely would had been sufficient to delay the launch decision until a time when the outside temperature was higher (Vaughan, 1996: 382–383, 417). Surprisingly, these outsiders retrieved the data without encountering any noteworthy difficulties.

The analysis demonstrates that 'the machine will not work when not all the relevant people are convinced'. Vaughan argues that next to having outsiders involved, the empowerment of those who are closest to the technology will help reduce the risks associated with such complex technological systems (Vaughan, 1996: 417–419).

The connection between bureaucratic structure, secrecy dynamics, the potentially profitable role of outsiders and complex technological systems also plays a role in the issue of information sharing between allied forces in multinational operations. This is a problematic issue since there are often complaints that valuable operational information is not shared because of fear of information leakages. This may lead, for example, to situations in which one conducts an operation in a region of Afghanistan while unaware of possible overspill effects coming from the adjacent region due to operations there. The background of this problem becomes apparent when one studies both the human and technical aspects of communication sharing (Van den Heuvel, 2017), much in the way Latour has always advocated. If used properly, such analyses may render multinational military operations more successful and less dangerous.

New stuff: things unmanned and things in cyberspace

Non-humans, i.e. things from the realm of nature, science and technology, are increasingly important in today's military and they are expected to become even more significant in the military of the near future. Two developments stand out: the use of unmanned vehicles, vessels and aircraft, i.e. the introduction of machine-operators in actions, and cyber operations. All these devices are controlled at a safe distance, by *tele-soldiers* so to speak (Royakkers and van Est, 2010). Unarmed machine-operators on the ground, such as devices for surveillance and reconnaissance and for clearing an area of mines and improvised explosive devices, are often used in today's operations. Unmanned aircraft – 'drones' – have been increasingly deployed in recent years and have had a serious lethal, operational impact in areas overseas.

Killer robots on the ground are less often employed but that may be a matter of time. The same applies to the use of fully autonomous weapon systems that function without the steering of tele-soldiers. Worries about such developments are growing because time may come when these devices, once deployed, start 'thinking' for themselves. If in the wrong hands, such devices may have a disastrous impact. A global initiative to prevent the installation of autonomous weapon systems may be needed as much as the world needs the global ban on landmines.

The development of unmanned devices is being pushed ahead by 'all the relevant people who are convinced' (Latour, 1987). They are the result of an increasing reluctance among politicians and the public to put people's lives at stake; that is, the lives of those of their own organization, country or alliance. This is not the only benefit. Such devices provide a risk-free war for one's own people, but they also increase operational effectiveness and they provide organizational prestige because they are a token of modernity (Wiesner, 2017). The use of these devices seems to fit into the general tendency for violence to decline that Norbert Elias and Stephen Pinker have claimed.

However, this concern does not extend to the lives of the people who are consciously targeted, nor to the lives of the people who live in the targeted areas. Apparently, not all people's lives are equally important, as we discovered before. The host nationals in the targeted areas live under constant threat and they experience the feeling of being monitored continuously, which reminds us of Foucault's panopticon (Asaro, 2013). This may render the inhabitants reluctant to help the wounded after a first attack because there may always follow a second attack. Even more, it may influence the social interaction in villages and vicinities because social gatherings of any kind may attract the attention of the tele-soldiers (Wiesner, 2017). In general, inhabitants may be killed because of collateral damage prompted by the drone attacks that, because of their claims of superiority, may be launched more easily and frequently than traditional weapon technologies (Wiesner, 2017). The overall lethal impact of drones, although advocated as an ideal and precise weapon, may be much larger than that of traditional military operations.

The negative consequences for the tele-soldiers themselves are multiple (e.g. Royakkers and van Est, 2010; Asaro, 2013). In general, this type of work comes with increasing stress levels, one of them induced by the psychological complexity of switching, every day again, between remote combat operations overseas and domestic and family life in the suburbs. Additionally, there is the intimate nature of video surveillance before and after an attack; although the distance covers continents, the cameras bring the targeted situation and its participants very close. Next to the emotional distress this causes, there is also a high demand for these operators, requiring overtime working on an almost structural basis (Asaro, 2013: 205). In addition, there are moral or ethical worries. Who is responsible for the consequences of the attacks launched from far away? Here the same sort of dynamics may come to play as we saw when discussing Bauman's analysis of the bureaucratically organized chain of small elements that taken together produce the worst violence imaginable. Flying drones is certainly not the same but the organizational logic of dividing the whole of the operational process into different parts is quite similar, and so are the consequences. Ethical, legal and health-related concerns are on the agenda (Asaro, 2013). Here, questions of substantive rationality are most relevant.

The second impactful technological innovation in the military today concerns cyber operations, i.e. operations related to the internet, digital information and computers in general. Such dangers do not exclusively belong to the domain of the military, as civilian institutions such as power plants, hospitals, firms and banks suffer from cyber attacks as well. The military also suffers from such attacks on an almost daily basis, but differs to the extent that it may be expected to conduct offensive cyber operations, too. The most spectacular example so far has been the notorious Stuxnet-attack, the computer worm that disrupted Iran's nuclear enrichment infrastructure in 2010. It was an example of the new digital warfare causing physical damage across international borders (Lindsay, 2013).

Some people think this new threat will be the most menacing development in the near future. One may doubt, however, whether cyber operations will be more disquieting than ordinary weapon systems, other than being a permanent nuisance requiring a wide span of attention (Lindsay, 2013). A positive aspect of cyber operations is that even though the impact can be fairly disruptive, it will not be as damaging, destructive and bloodstained as traditional military engagements tend to be. Therefore, responses to cyber attacks are usually inconspicuous and restrained. On the basis of empirical research on current practices, it may be expected that in the near future cyber combat will be effectively managed through restrained action (Maness and Valeriano, 2016).

Nature and infrastructure in times of war and after

As we mentioned at the beginning of this chapter, Bruno Latour has formulated conditions to adequately address object-related issues, with a particular focus on nature-related and ecological issues. He talked about the need to 'do political ecology' (Blok and Elgaard, Jensen, 2011: 75). This concern applies to military affairs, too.

Scholars in the field of human geography have put military landscapes on the research and policy agenda. They have done so for a long time, since 'all geography is military geography' (cited in Woodward, 2005: 13). In operational matters, military space is something that must be considered, as for instance the location of military camps in missions may have serious implications for the social and economic fabric in the area of operations (Higate and Henry, 2009). As to peacetime conditions, there are implications regarding how military landscapes affect the general surroundings, how military landscapes may be used for memorial and touristic purposes, how military land use can be promoted by government, and – the opposite – how military spaces may be turned into other destinations once the military need to occupy the area has gone (Woodward, 1999; 2005; 2014). An example of the latter is the conversion of military land to wildlife refuges (Havlick, 2011). The smaller the proportion of military land, the more peaceful a country is likely to be.

Next to the use of space, there is the connection between military operations and war-related cultural heritage, which is not a very happy one. Over the last two decades, buildings, and particularly *architectural totems* – such as the World Trade Center towers, the remains of classical cities in the Middle East, mosques from Iraq to Bosnia, and statues of the Buddha – have been destroyed in terrorist attacks, war events and military operations (Bevan, 2016). In previous times the destruction was even harsher: Rottterdam, Warsaw and Dresden are but a few ominous names in this regard. With the destruction of buildings and cities people's cultural memory tends also to become eradicated. At least that is often the purpose of the destruction. It depends on the networks of 'all the relevant people who are convinced' (Latour, 1987: 10) whether or not that purpose will be realized after the violence has passed. The following box provides an illustration.

Archeologies of the Spanish Civil War

A good example of Latour's observation that objects often trigger fierce and passionate disputes is the way the Spanish population and its politicians deal with the remnants of the Civil War. This war started in 1936 with a military coup initiated by General Franco. It was intended to overthrow the democratically elected left-wing government. The conflict was soon internationalized, as foreign nations such as Nazi Germany intervened. Franco's faction won and remained in power until 1975 when he passed away. During the war and in the years thereafter, tens of thousands of people were killed. When Franco died, the country made a peaceful transition to democracy. After some time, a climate emerged in which the memory of war no longer needed to be suppressed, which made it possible to exhume the victims and to excavate military remains in trenches and graves. Yet, many more victims still wait to be uncovered, in unmarked graves all over the country. The removal of statues reminding one of the Franco era still sparks remarkable upheaval and controversy. This shows that coordinated efforts need to be in place to deal with the troubled objects, the unsettling heritage of a recent past (González-Ruibal, 2007).

Conclusion

Like Michel Foucault, Bruno Latour is one of the world's most often quoted scholars (Heilbron, 2015: 2). French sociologists appear to have something to say to the world. Latour put technology, science and objects back on the agenda of organization studies, and hence on the agenda of military studies, too. The interaction of humans and non-humans is what matters most in studying military progress, because this makes it easier to comprehend future and near revolutions in military affairs. Science fiction would have us believe that non-humans in due time will take over power from humans. That may be an exaggeration, but the very idea of science fiction reveals that Latour was quite right in stressing the need to study humans and non-humans at the same level. Almost no sociologist would have thought of this before.

Bibliography

Asaro, P.M. (2013) 'The labor of surveillance and bureaucratized killing: new subjectivities of military drone operators'. *Social Semiotics* 23(2): 196–224.

Bailey, D.E., P.M. Leonardi and S.R. Barley (2012) 'The lure of the virtual'. *Organization Science* 23(5): 1485–1504.

Barany, Z. (2004) 'The tragedy of the Kursk: crisis management in Putin's Russia'. *Government and Opposition* 39(3): 476–503.

Barley, S.R. (1996) 'Technicians in the workplace: ethnographic evidence for bringing work into organization studies'. *Administrative Science Quarterly* 41(3): 404–441.

Barley, S.R. (2005) 'What we know (and mostly don't know) about technical work'. In S. Ackroyd, R. Batt, P. Thompson and P.S. Tolbert (eds), *The Oxford Handbook of Work and Organization*. Oxford: Oxford University Press, pp. 376–403.

Bevan, R. (2016) *The Destruction of Memory: Architecture at War*. 2nd expanded edition. London: Reaktion Books.

Blok, A. and T. Elgaard Jensen (2011) *Bruno Latour: Hybrid Thoughts in a Hybrid World*. London and New York: Routledge.

Bourdieu, P. (2012 [1960]) 'War and social transformation in Algeria'. In F. Schultheis and Chr. Frisinghelli (eds), *Picturing Algeria*. New York: Columbia University Press.

Clegg, S.R., M. Pina e Cunha, A. Rego and J. Dias (2013) 'Mundane objects and the banality of evil: the sociomateriality of a death camp'. *Journal of Management Inquiry* 22(3): 325–340.

Czarniawska, B. (2014) 'Bruno Latour: an accidental organization theorist'. In P. Adler, P. Du Gay, G. Morgan and M. Reed (eds), *The Oxford Handbook of Sociology, Social Theory and Organization Studies: Contemporary Currents*. Oxford: Oxford University Press, pp. 87–105.

González-Ruibal, A. (2007) 'Making things public: archeologies of the Spanish Civil War'. *Public Archeology* 6(4): 203–226.

Harper, K. (2003) 'Research from the boundary layer: civilian leadership, military funding and the development of numerical weather prediction (1946–1955)'. *Social Studies of Science* 33(5): 667–696.

Havlick, D.G. (2011) 'Disarming nature: converting military lands to wildlife refuges'. *The Geographical Review* 101(2): 183–200.

Heilbron, J. (2015) *French Sociology*. Ithaca NY and London: Cornell University Press.

Higate, P. and M. Henry (2009) *Insecure Spaces: Peacekeeping, Power and Performance in Haiti, Kosovo and Liberia*. London and New York: Zed Books.

Johnson, J., alias B. Latour (1988) 'Mixing humans and non-humans together: the sociology of a door-closer'. *Social Problems* 35(3): 298–310.

Latour, B. (1987) *Science in Action: How to Follow Scientists and Engineers through Society*. Cambridge, MA: Harvard University Press.

Latour, B. (1996) *ARAMIS or the Love of Technology*. Cambridge, MA: Harvard University Press.

Latour, B. (2000) 'When things strike back: a possible contribution of "science studies" to the social sciences'. *British Journal of Sociology* 51(1): 107–123.

Latour, B. (2002) *War of the Worlds: What about Peace?* Chicago: Prickly Paradigm Press.

Latour, B. (2005) *Reassembling the Social: An Introduction to Actor-Network-Theory*. Oxford: Oxford University Press.

Latour, B. and Woolgar, St. (1986) *Laboratory Life: The Construction of Scientific Facts.* Princeton, NJ: Princeton University Press.

Law, J. and M. Callon (1988) 'Engineering and sociology in a military aircraft project: a network analysis of technological change'. *Social Problems* 35(3): 284–297.

Lindsay, J.R. (2013) 'Stuxnet and the limits of cyber warfare'. *Security Studies* 22(3): 365–404.

Maness, R.C. and B. Valeriano (2016) 'The impact of cyber conflict on international interaction'. *Armed Forces and Society* 42(2): 301–323.

Miodownik, M. (2013) *Stuff Matters: The Strange Stories of the Marvellous Materials That Shape Our Man-Made World.* London: Penguin Books.

Moelker, R. and N. Schenk (2018) 'Mixing up humans and military technology'. In: G. Caforio (ed.), *Handbook of the Sociology of the Military.* New York: Kluwer Academic.

Mort, M. (2002) *Building the Trident Network: A Study of the Enrollment of People, Knowledge, and Machines.* Cambridge MA and London: MIT Press.

Mukerji, Ch. (2006) 'Tacit knowledge and classical technique in seventeenth-century France: hydraulic cement as a living practice among masons and military engineers'. *Technology and Culture* 47(4): 713–733.

Orlikowsky, W. and S.V. Scott (2008) 'Sociomateriality: challenging the separation of technology, work and organization'. *Academy of Management Annals* 2(1): 433–474.

Perrow, C. (1999a) *Normal Accidents: Living with High-Risk Technologies. With a New Afterword.* Princeton, NJ: Princeton University Press.

Perrow, Ch. (1999b) 'Organizing to reduce the vulnerabilities of complexity'. *Journal of Contingencies and Crisis Management* 7(3): 150–155.

Rappart, B., B. Balmer and J. Stone (2008) 'Science, technology and the military: priorities, preoccupations and possibilities'. In E.J. Hackett, O. Amsterdamska, M.E. Lynck and J. Wajcman (eds), *The Handbook of Science and Technology Studies.* 3rd edn. London: MIT Press.

Royakkers, L. and R. van Est (2010) 'The cubicle warrior: the marionette of digitalized warfare'. *Ethics and Information Technology* 12(3): 289–296.

Solovey, M. (2001) 'Project Camelot and the 1960s epistemological revolution: rethinking the politics–patronage–social science nexus'. *Social Studies of Science* 31(2): 171–206.

Sparavigna, A.C. (2015) 'An example of military engineering in 16th century: the Star Fort in Turin'. *International Journal of Sciences* 4(12): 62–67.

Uiterwijk, D., J. Soeters and P. van Fenema (2013) 'Aligning national "logics" in a European military helicopter program'. *Defense and Security Analysis* 29(1): 54–67.

Van den Heuvel, G. (2017) 'Information sharing in military organizations: a socio-material perspective'. In I. Goldenberg, J. Soeters and W. Dean (eds), *Information Sharing in Military Operations.* Cham, Switzerland: Springer, pp. 165–182.

Van Doorn, J.A.A. (1975) *The Soldier and Social Change: Comparative Studies in the History and Sociology of the Military.* Beverly Hills CA and London: Sage.

Van Veen, M. (2014) 'Validating the virtual: an extensive case-study of a military training simulator'. Ph.D. thesis, Universiteit voor Humanistiek, Netherlands.

Vaughan, D. (1996) *The Challenger Launch Decision: Risky Technology, Culture, and Deviance at NASA.* Chicago: University of Chicago Press.

Wiesner, I. (2017) 'A sociology of the drone'. *Journal of Military and Strategic Studies* 18(1): 42–59.

Woodward, R. (1999) 'Gunning for rural England: the politics of the promotion of military land use in the Northumberland National Park'. *Journal of Rural Studies* 15(1): 17–33.

Woodward, R. (2005) 'From military geography to militarism's geographies: disciplinary engagements with the geographies of militarism and military acitivities'. *Progress in Human Geography* 29(6): 1–23.

Woodward, R. (2014) 'Military landscapes: agendas and approaches for future research'. *Progress in Human Geography* 38(1): 40–61.

15 From the classics to the future in military studies

Conclusions, themes and prospects

The previous chapters have provided an overview of how sociological theories, insights and findings in one way or another have implications for the military today. The founding scholars discussed in this book have all in their own way contributed to our current knowledge of the armed forces in their societal context. Even if they did not specifically discuss the military, they developed theoretical and empirical insights that can fruitfully be applied to the military environment. The topics and perspectives they discussed are quite diverse and may even produce a fragmented impression. However, it became gradually clear that the various chapters are also 'speaking to one another' as the founding insights, theories and empirical findings presented in those chapters have been influencing each other continuously. There are similarities and differences in topics, overlapping and contradicting perspectives, as well as comparable and distinct emphases. Although the – often seemingly unrelated – variety of topics and insights may look confusing, it is possible to create an overview of the many contributions and to derive a number of lessons from them.

Categorizing the contributions

One way of coming to grips with the founding fathers' and mothers' variety of contributions is to become aware that the authors discuss issues at different levels of sociological analysis (e.g. Turner, 1991). Without wanting to over-simplify matters, the previous review of classical and current sociology and its relevance for military studies may be categorized as follows:

- the *macro-level*, which is the level of the military in the context of the society at large and of national societies interacting with one another in supra-national arrangements;
- the *meso-level*, which is the level of organizations – either governmental, civil society or market agencies – and of institutions, such as laws, rituals and practices;
- the *micro-level*, which is the level where the actual behaviour and interactions between people take place.

It should be kept in mind that such categories are perhaps too crude, and should in no way be seen as static or independent of one another. Social dynamics play out at all levels, influencing each other continuously, and changing all the time. People shape their own lives at the micro-level, whereas they are influenced by the opportunities and limitations that occur at the meso- and macro-levels (Giddens and Sutton, 2013). In fact, people at the micro-level also co-create those influences, opportunities and limitations at the meso- and macro-level. They have a vote in democratic elections, they have a say in their organizations and they are involved in shaping the organization's working practices, at least to a certain extent, and, finally, they can have an influence on civil society as volunteers and active citizens. The space to manoeuvre, however, may be small for some and larger for others. Human behaviour is always behaviour in context. This applies to human behaviour and social life in general, but also to human behaviour and social life in the military domain.

In the table below we have listed the main ideas of the founders of sociology at these three levels. Some names and concepts occur at more than one level as – like we just saw – social phenomena have implications beyond the level at which they are usually defined.

In addition to this listing of topics, it may be important to draw up a number of central tendencies that emerge from the previous discussion of the relevance

Table 15.1 Contributions of founding sociologists at the macro-, meso- and micro-level.

Society and societies interacting	Macro	Violence – content and development; enemies; host population; inequality in economy and society; race and gender; suicide; mediation; conflict resolution and social development; science and technology.	Durkheim, Marx, Addams, Du Bois, Foucault, Elias, Enloe, Latour.
Organization/ institution	Meso	Bureaucracy – content and development; professionalization; 'total institution'; networks and positions; outsourcing (private military companies); commodification; composition work force; surveillance: civil–military relations; comparing (national) militaries; technological innovations and policies.	Weber, Durkheim, Simmel, Marx, Addams, Du Bois, Goffman, Foucault, Janowitz, Lammers, Enloe, Latour.
Interaction between people	Micro	Cohesion in groups; restrained behaviour; talking with adversaries and strangers; secrecy in operations; 'strangers' inside and outside the force; diversity at the behavioural level; emotions at and after work.	Durkheim, Simmel, Addams, Du Bois, Goffman, Janowitz, Elias, Hochschild, Enloe.

of sociology's founding authors for military studies. These central tendencies may be valuable to guide today's sociological study of the military. They may create an appetite for doing research on problems that relate to military sociology but have so far been neglected or forgotten.

Towards a sociology of military operations

It is important to realize that war, violence and military conduct are essentially social phenomena, 'social facts' so to speak. There is nothing 'un-sociological' about firing a gun, bombing a building or launching a drone. Military action always concerns other people, it influences their actions and reactions, their hopes as much as their worries.

This implies that sociologists should not refrain from studying the dynamics of military operations and their immediate and further resonating impact. A number of the classic authors we discussed in this book have specifically expressed their views about violence and war (e.g. Grutzpalk, 2002) and they studied military conduct on the battlefield, albeit mostly from the safe environment of their libraries and offices. Examining military conduct in operations is something that needs to be pursued much more, and perhaps with less distance from the action than the founding sociologists usually had.

Military sociology today mostly studies civil–military relations, political–military relations including the mass media, as well as military management and human resources issues. Among those latter topics of study are leadership, recruitment and retention of personnel, the impact of training and education, the role of deployment conditions, the experience of stress and the well-being of military families. These are all important phenomena. However, they constitute a second layer, not the core of the military organization and soldiers' conduct. They precede or follow upon military action, or if these studies accompany direct military action such as in the study of operational leadership, they take place at a safe distance from the real action.

Military sociology today rarely studies military action from nearby. It most often does not review the conduct in and the dynamics of operations themselves. Social scientists seem not particularly keen on studying military action when the heat is on, when the military is in the process of killing and getting killed. These events are left to military professionals and journalists or retrospectively to historians. There are exceptions, however. Morten Ender (2009), Delphine Resteigne (2012) and Chiara Ruffa (2014) did fieldwork among the military in action, though not during the more heated moments, and they were more focused on the militaries themselves than on their impact on the region of operations. There is a pressing need to study the impact of military action on the host population and how the host population and its various constituents copes and responds. Interestingly, female social and political scientists such as Funmi Olonisakin (2000), Beatrice Pouligny (2006), Fotini Christia (2012) and Séverine Autesserre (2014) – and there are quite a number of others – seem to be taking the lead in this. Basing themselves and their fieldwork among host nationals, something that is often not without its risks, they pave the path towards an empirical sociology and anthropology of military operations, a path that was relatively unexplored until today. Taking the founding authors seriously would imply that sociologists need to bring military action back into the social science arena. Going beyond them means doing this in the operational area itself.

Studying the diffusion of military beliefs

The diffusion of military ideas, ideologies and practices needs further scrutiny. This starts with the notion that there is no such thing as an objective truth in military decision making or conduct. As we know from the sociology of knowledge, 'realities' and what we make of these 'realities' are socially constructed (Berger and Luckman, 1984; Zerubavel, 1997). Hence, it is not easy to define a superior way of conducting military operations, because determining superiority depends on the goals and priorities one wants to attain, the values one endorses, and the beliefs one holds about causes-and-consequences. Most likely there are nationally defined patters of such goals, values and beliefs, as we saw in the chapter on Cornelis Lammers. The Anglo-Saxon pattern of military-related values and beliefs seems to differ from the current continental Western-European configuration, to give just one example. The African way of conducting military operations is certainly different from the Anglo-Saxon and Western-European operational styles, or the Russian and Chinese ways of military operating, which may not be similar either.

From the sociology of organizations we know that organizations within one sector tend to become alike, even across national borders or continents. This process is called isomorphism, which in the literal sense of the word is the tendency to develop similar forms. The question for social scientists to address is how these processes develop and in which direction they will turn. Most likely, during recent decades the Anglo-Saxon, particularly the American, style of conduct in military affairs has tended to have the biggest influence. This has to do with technological, economic and cultural dominance. In fact, we saw this happening when the Soviet Union collapsed and the national armed forces of Central and Eastern Europe such as those of Poland, Hungary and Bulgaria, came under the umbrella of NATO. Such diffusion patterns could also be observed during the operations in Afghanistan. In the chapter on Michel Foucault we have seen how such processes come about.

Nonetheless, this direction of influence need not necessarily be continued in the future. Balances, beliefs and priorities can change fairly rapidly. The dominance of a military style is likely to be judged by its goal attainment, effectiveness and general success, in the short run but certainly also in the long run. These experiences are likely to lead to learning processes and adaptation within national militaries but possibly also to changes in diffusion across national armed forces. As soon as scholars, military practitioners and politicians start seeing and studying different operations as sources of variation and selection, discussion about which way to go will emerge. One could imagine that UN peacekeeping will gradually become more important for Western armed forces than it has been over the past twenty years or so.

Changes in strategic priorities are important as well. A particular case in point may be the intensification of military cooperation among EU forces, which is due to occur in the very near future. America's reluctance to keep on shouldering all responsibilities in this part of the world and the growing threats in Europe's neighbouring regions are accelerating this process, which will be most interesting to study.

In addition, it is important that the scope of the study of the military be extended to the southern and eastern parts of the globe, in order to create 'connected sociologies of the military'. It may well be that militaries that are now seen as less important players in the field may in fact be able to supply interesting input regarding how to prevent, contain and solve violent conflicts in the various parts of the world. In this way, a future military sociology could go beyond the scope of the founding authors, who – it needs to be admitted – were predominantly concerned with Europe and America.

Bringing the others in

In the chapter on Jane Addams it became clear that conflict prevention, containment and solution are largely dependent on interaction with those factions that have a stake in the violent processes. These may be prominent actors, or bystanders who suffer from what is going on, often women. In a way, such interaction is not natural. The obvious idea is that in conflicts one encounters foes that one needs to fight, not discuss with. But the idea of the *polymetis* soldier and, for instance, the analysis of the strength of weak ties in the chapter on Georg Simmel, make it clear that Jane Addams may have been right. It helps to talk to the other, to put oneself in someone else's shoes, to ponder the feelings of the person at the other end of your gun, even if he or she is an adversary, even if the other faction can be considered hostile. 'Above all, we have to be sociological about ideals, our own as well as everyone else's', as Randall Collins (2011: 18) once put it.

This is not an easy thing to do, as it requires the capability to tackle contradictions. As such, this way of operating closely follows the ideas of *pragmatism*, which are foundational to both Jane Addams' and Morris Janowitz' thinking and reasoning, and which, as we saw, relate back to John Dewey's fundamentals (Shields and Travis, 2017).

This way of working, stressing the interaction with and participation of the other(s) and accepting the processual character of missions, is still a weak point in military operations and decision making. Even in UN missions the participation of host nationals in the area of operations is limited to specific responsibilities such as language mediation, broadcasting and communication in indigenous languages, and mundane jobs such as cleaning and laundry. In addition, there is contact with host nationals regarding the provision of general facilities for the military to fulfil their mission, such as transport, power supply and access to airports and harbours. However, no matter how important, those are all merely facilitating jobs and do not engage with the essence of what is going on.

Without question, during the mission's operations there are also negotiations at all levels with authorities and representatives from the host nation about the conflictual dynamics in play. Every interaction is an element of an ongoing, long-term process. Those levels may vary from talking with people on the streets to formal negotiations with authorities from regional and national governments. But generally such negotiations are relatively brief, superficial and limited in number. There may be differences related to military operational styles, however. Military sociologists would do well to study the variance in such interactions between and within missions, and to determine their impact on general mission effectiveness. This aligns with Erving Goffman's and others' ideas about the significance of interaction patterns. From there on, new insights on the importance of interacting with the other(s) could be implemented in military education and training.

Truly blending methods

Pursuing and even going beyond sociology's founding scholars, the need for empirical research in military studies needs to be stressed. In the first place, we should take to heart and follow Durkheim's and others' lessons about the importance of comparison. Only through comparisons one can develop insights as to which dynamics are most conducive to prevent, contain and solve the violence at hand. Studying stand-alone cases enables the researcher to describe the events in detail, possibly leading to the development of a hypothesis, but nevertheless without making or breaking a hypothesis. A number of cases considered together, however, can create an overview that may lead to theory building and empirical substantiation. While researchers' own views should not and cannot be excluded from conclusions, comparative research approaches offer yardsticks and criteria that go beyond these personal factors.

Second, it seems important to bridge the various levels of action and analysis (e.g. Autessere, 2014). Military missions always play out at various levels, and all these levels need to be studied, preferably simultaneously. One cannot understand what is happening on the streets without apprehending the bigger picture of a mission, and vice-versa. For instance, the restrained behaviour of individual soldiers − or the opposite thereof − cannot be understood without comprehending the societal tendencies to violence control or the lack thereof, as Norbert Elias demonstrated. In this connection, it would make sense to form teams of both military academics and practitioners to study military operations, with options for co-authorship with military personnel. The apparent gap between theory and practice needs to be closed as much as possible, in order to enable true research in action, which is research that is useful in everyday practice.

Third, social science research has broadly speaking two methodological branches: qualitative and quantitative approaches to the collection and analysis of data. Most of the times, social scientists commit themselves to one or other of these approaches. However, a number of the founding fathers combined both methods in their work. In particular, Emile Durkheim, W. E. B. Du Bois and Morris Janowitz used – and were good at – both research practices. This is something we should continue. Instead of devoting a lifetime of research to one approach, it makes sense to regard the whole set of methodologies as a toolbox, from which one can pick the instruments that are best to study the problem in hand. Sometimes one needs to work as an anthropologist, some-times as a statistician, and sometimes as both. This may require extra effort. To do anthropological fieldwork one needs to study indigenous languages; to analyse a large data set one needs to master the newest software. Occasionally one needs to analyse visual displays, such as photographs. Sometimes it is best to team up with other specialists, which is something Fotini Christia does. She has already combined various approaches using games as a research instrument during fieldwork in Bosnia (Alexander and Christia, 2011). She also applied experimental designs *in vivo* in the operational environment of Afghanistan (Beath et al. 2013). Now together with colleagues from data sciences she is studying social behaviour in Yemen – for instance religious practices and reac-tions to violence – based on the analysis of millions of items of cell phone data (Christia et al., 2015). Clearly, these are the ways to make real progress in understanding the impact of military operations and foreign (developmental) interventions on conflict and violence.

Towards a military sociology with more 'soul'

Finally, the founding scholars teach us not to limit ourselves to something that military professionals tend to do themselves, which is asking questions about close means–ends relations. As we saw in the introductory chapter, in sociology this is referred to as functional rationality. Studying the ways a bridge can best be destroyed – with a minimum of fuel, ammunition and aircraft damage and a maximum of safety – belongs to this type of rationality. But asking how the destruction of this bridge, with its possible collateral damage, may or may not contribute to resolving the conflict and ending the hostilities belongs to the realm of substantive rationality. Here the means–ends relations are much more complicated and extended. Founding sociologists such as Karl Marx, W. E. B. Du Bois, Morris Janowitz, Arlie Russell Hochschild and Cynthia Enloe have ceaselessly stressed the importance of paying attention to the broader, wider questions, even if this is not always understood or appreciated by others.

Despite a possible lack of support and appreciation, this may be a more fruitful option than will be clear at first sight. Concerns about sustainable production and the natural environment show that what was seen as con-troversial yesterday may well be an accepted truth tomorrow (e.g. Levy et al., 2016). What seemed to be a matter of substantial rationality in days gone by has nowadays developed into a matter of functional rationality. Things can change rapidly.

Management scholars Paul Adler and John Jermier (2005) have argued that management research needs to be more concerned about exploited groups such as lower-level employees and disadvantaged communities as well as the abused natural environment. They argue in favour of advancing their field with more 'soul'. Similarly, one could plead for the development of a military sociology with more 'soul', paying dedicated attention to host nationals who undergo the military's presence and actions, but also to soldiers and veterans who carry the burden of their actions. This should ensure that emphasizing military role performance in terms of 'clean work' (no damage to one's own units, smooth operations, no delays) does not limit a consideration of the basic legitimacy of this role and the military presence per se (Ben-Ari, 1989: 383). It should also prevent one losing sight of the possible damaging impact of military presence and action (Masuch, 1991). In general, it will be conducive to improving the military's effectiveness.

Sociological imagination, again

In order to achieve this, we might do well to resort to the old idea of 'sociological imagination' (Wright Mills, 1959), which implies a basic questioning of the situation and imagining how things could be done differently. It implies that one does not accept the statement that 'there is no alternative', it entails arguments against the tendency to eliminate all alternatives in face of the one solution that is being proposed. It implies scrutinizing the 'military definition of the world reality', as Charles Wright Mills (2000 [1956]: 202) once put it. In fact, it implies critically examining any definition of the world reality.

Bibliography

Adler, P.S. and J. Jermier (2005) 'Developing a field with more soul: standpoint theory and public policy research for management scholars'. *Academy of Management Journal* 48(6): 941–944.

Alexander, M. and F. Christia (2011) 'Context modularity of human altruism'. *Science* 334: 1392–1394.

Autessere, S. (2014) 'Going micro: emerging and future peacekeeping research'. *International Peacekeeping* 21(4): 492–500.

Beath, A., F. Christia and R. Enikolopov (2013) 'Empowering women through development: evidence from a field experiment in Afghanistan'. *American Political Science Review* 107(3): 540–557.

Ben-Ari, E. (1989) 'Masks and soldiering: the Israeli army and the Palestinian uprising'. *Current Anthropology* 4(4): 372–389.

Berger, P. and Th. Luckman (1984) *The Social Construction of Reality: A Treatise in the Sociology of Knowledge*. Harmondsworth: Penguin.

Christia, F. (2012) *Alliance Formation in Civil Wars*. Cambridge: Cambridge University Press.

Christia, F., L. Yao, S. Wittels and J. Leskovec (2015) 'Yemen calling: seven things cell data reveal about life in the Republic'. *Foreign Affairs*, 6 July.

Collins, R. (2011) 'C-escalation and D-escalation: a theory of the time-dynamics of conflict'. *American Sociological Review* 77(1): 1–20.

Ender, M.G. (2009) *American Soldiers in Iraq: McSoldiers or Innovative Professionals?* London and New York: Routledge.

Giddens, A. and Ph.W. Sutton (2013) *Sociology*. 7th edn. Cambridge: Polity Press.

Grutzpalk, J. (2002) 'Blood feud and modernity: Max Weber's and Emile Durkheim's theories'. *Journal of Classical Sociology* 2(2): 115–134.

Levy, D., J. Reinecke and S. Manning (2016) 'The political dynamics of sustainable coffee: contested value regimes and the transformation of sustainability'. *Journal of Management Studies* 53(3): 364–401.

Masuch, M. (1991) 'The determinants of organizational harm'. *Research in the Sociology of Organizations* 9: 79–102.

Olonisakin, F. (2000) *Reinventing Peacekeeping in Africa: Conceptual and Legal Issues in ECOMOG Operations*. The Hague and Boston: Kluwer Law International.

Pouligny, B. (2006) *Peace Operations Seen from Below: UN Missions and Local People*. Bloomfield, CT: Kumarian Press.

Resteigne, D. (2012) *Le militaire en opérations multinationales: regards croisés en Afghanistan, en Bosnie, au Liban*. Brussels: Bruylant.

Ruffa, Ch. (2014) 'What peacekeepers think and do: an exploratory study of French, Ghanaian, Italian and South Korean armies in the United Nations Interim Force in Lebanon'. *Armed Forces and Society* 40(2): 199–225.

Shields, P. and D.S. Travis (2017) 'Achieving organizational flexibility through ambidexterity'. *Parameters* 47(2): 65–76.

Turner, J.H. (1991) *The Structure of Sociological Theory*. Belmont, CA: Wadsworth.

Wright Mills, C. (2000 [1956]) *The Power Elite*. New edn. Oxford and New York: Oxford University Press.

Wright Mills, C. (1959) *The Sociological Imagination*. New York: Oxford University Press.

Zerubavel, E. (1997) *Social Mindscapes. An Invitation to Cognitive Sociology*. Cambridge, MA. and London: Harvard University Press.

Index

Abolitionist movement 80, 132, 138
aboriginal communities 23
absolutism 120–1
abstract thinking 4, 6, 22, 57, 73, 79, 98, 105
Abu Ghraib 176
abuse 101, 145, 173, 176, 203
accountability 11
accountancy standards 108–9
activism 11, 65–77, 127, 136, 170, 177, 185
Addams, J. 5, 65–77, 79, 114, 121, 127; and city improvements 66–8; and Enloe 169–70, 177–8; and future studies 197, 200; and peace activism 66–8; and peacekeeping 68–75; and pragmatism 72–5; and UN 68–72
Adler, P. 4, 203
administrative studies 4, 73, 143
administrative styles 29, 146–51, 153, 164
admirals 40
affiliations 9, 12, 15, 51–2, 56, 126
Afghanistan 2, 11, 27–8, 30, 40, 46; and Addams 71, 75; and Du Bois 86; and Elias 132, 138–9; and Enloe 173, 175; and Foucault 109, 111; and future studies 199, 202; and Goffman 97–8; and Hochschild 158, 165; and Janowitz 125; and Lammers 149–51; and Latour 189; National Security Forces 145; and Simmel 52–4, 56, 61
Africa 10–11, 13, 15, 41, 45, 47–8, 84, 96, 112–13, 124, 139, 147, 181, 199
African Americans 66, 78–9, 81–5, 107, 172–4
African Union (AU) 27, 68
airports 114–15, 201
Algeria 33, 43, 83, 132
Ali, M. 82

alienation 37, 45–8, 62, 93, 99, 101, 114, 157, 159
all-volunteer forces 1, 46, 82, 124–7, 131, 135–6, 138, 161, 174
Allende, S. 41
altruistic suicide 29–31
ambidexterity 13–14
American Journal of Sociology 51, 57, 65, 75, 118
American Sociological Society 66
American Soldier 119
Anglo-Saxon model 45, 125, 175, 199
Angola 43
animator role 97
anomic suicide 30
anomie 30, 61, 159
anthropology 6, 24–5, 162, 175, 181–2, 199, 202
anti-Semitism 22
Aoi, C. 70
apartheid 79, 84–5
Arab Spring 12
Arab states 12
Arabian Sea 125
Arabic language 95
architecture 184, 191–2
Argentina 123, 132, 173
armed forces 1–2, 11–14, 16–17, 26–8, 30, 32; and Addams 73; and Du Bois 82; and Elias 131, 133, 135–7; and Enloe 173, 175; and future studies 196, 199–200; and Goffman 92, 101–2; and Hochschild 158; and Janowitz 122–4, 127; and Lammers 144–5, 150–3; and Latour 185; and Marx 38, 44; and minority relations 83–5; rich and poor 43–5, 47; and Simmel 61
Asia 1, 41, 84, 95, 113, 124, 172
Asian Americans 83

assessment 26, 143
assimilation 27, 80, 87, 91, 175
asylum seekers 112–13, 139–40
Atlanta Sociological Laboratory 78
Atlanta University 78
Australia 6, 32, 59, 124, 174
Autessere, S. 70, 198
author role 97
authoritarianism 13, 98, 133
authority 13, 15–17, 55, 94, 121,
　147, 152
autonomy 39, 48, 58, 87, 100, 110, 122,
　131, 144, 148, 189
AVFs 118–29, 161
Axelrod, R. 56

Bali 31
Balkan states 19
Baltic states 28, 85, 126, 139
baptising ceremonies 92–3
Bar, N. 161
barter system 51
Bauman, Z. 10, 190
Beck, U. 68
Belgium 27–8, 33, 45, 54, 67, 81, 83–4,
　94, 124, 147, 152, 175
Ben-Ari, E. 5, 101, 161–3, 165
Benedict, R. 118
Bentham, J. 106
Berlin University 51
Beyoncé 83
bias 6, 60, 74, 79, 82, 88, 101, 134, 150
bikers 26
Bin Laden, O. 16
biology 81, 157, 177
black communities 78–85
Black Lives Matter 83
Black Power 83
Bloody Sunday 84
blueprint policies 98
body counts 109
Boëne, B. 2
Bolivia 13, 84, 87, 92
bomb disposal 24
border controls 68, 99, 101, 105, 112–15,
　152, 170
Bosnia 45, 56, 69, 82, 86, 149, 191, 202
Bourdieu, P. 4, 135, 169, 181
Braender, M. 138
brain-drains 70
Brazil 33, 44
Breaking the Silence movement 177
Bremer, P. 149
Brendel, D. 73

Britain 12, 14, 23, 27–8, 32–3, 37–8; and
　Addams 65; and Du Bois 78, 81, 83–4;
　and Elias 131–3, 136; and Enloe 172,
　174–6; and Foucault 106, 108; and
　Hochschild 165; and Janowitz 124; and
　Lammers 146–8, 150–2; and Latour
　187; and Marx 40, 44, 46; and Simmel
　59–61
broadcasting 42, 125, 147, 200
brothels 172
Brussels Airport 114
Bryan, C.J. 30
Buddha 191
budgets 39–40, 58–9, 73, 113, 122, 133,
　152, 183
Bulgaria 125, 132, 199
Bulge, battle of 81
bullying 101
Bundeswehr 61–2
bureaucracy 5–6, 8–21, 38, 48, 54, 58–9;
　and Addams 74; and Du Bois 86; and
　Elias 134; and Foucault 108; and future
　studies 197; and Goffman 94, 99; and
　Hochschild 159; and Janowitz 122; and
　Lammers 145, 147; and Latour 185,
　189–90; street-level bureaucracy
　91–104
Burk, J. 2, 5, 82, 118, 120
Burt, R. 52, 59
business practices 108

cadets 108, 143
Caforio, G. 2
Callon, M. 187
camaraderie 23
Cambodia 68, 133
Camelot project 187
Canada 6, 24, 28, 46, 59, 91, 124, 150,
　165, 174, 181
capitalism 8, 45, 124
Caplow, T. 56
career patterns/prospects 9, 12, 153
Carlton-Ford, S. 2
case studies 32–3, 132, 148–50, 201
casualties 3, 42, 69, 131–2, 164
Casualty Assistance Officers (CAOs) 164
categorization 196–8
Catholics 55
Caucasus 85
CCTV 115
ceasefires 56
Central and Eastern Europe 48, 112,
　125, 199
certification 27

chains of command 47
Chaka Zulu 10
Challenger 188–9
Chambers, P. 124
charismatic authority 15–17
Chayes, S. 53
Chechnya 40
Chicago School 66
Chicago University 118
children 47, 70, 166, 172, 177
Chile 41, 121
China 32, 37, 44, 48, 172, 174, 199
Chomsky, N. 169
Christia, F. 55–6, 198, 202
Christians 56
city improvements 66–8
civil inattention 100
civil rights 84, 111, 125, 132
civil servants 9, 12–13, 70, 86, 122, 149
civil service issue 12–13, 86
civil society 48, 61, 72, 112, 136, 196
civil wars 1, 12, 38, 56, 66, 80–1, 134,
    145, 192
civil-military relations 1, 4, 47, 68, 71, 73,
    95, 118, 121–4, 149, 197–8
civilization process 94, 130–5
class/class struggle 37, 43–4, 79–80, 183
classical sociologists 2, 4, 37–8, 130, 135,
    140, 159, 196–204
classified material 28
Clausewitz, C. von 55
climate change 68
Clinton, H. 149
cliques 93, 96
closed organizations 91–2
Coalition Provisional Authority 149
coercion 11, 13, 15, 46, 83, 108, 124,
    147, 152
cold side 3
Cold War 39, 46, 57, 122–3, 125, 184,
    186
collateral damage 3, 131, 190, 202
collectivism 95
collectivization 98
Collège de France 105
Collins, R. 5, 8, 31, 55, 101, 161, 200
colonels 38, 42
colonialism 1, 37–8, 43, 59, 67, 73; and
    Du Bois 79, 83–4; and Elias 132; and
    Enloe 170; and Foucault 111; and
    Hochschild 164; and Lammers 146–8;
    and Latour 181, 185
comfort women 172
command and control 146

commodification 45–8, 157, 197
Common Security and Defence Policy
    (CSDP) 111
Commonwealth 59
communism 32, 37, 48, 112
comparative analysis 29, 31–4, 124,
    143–4, 146, 150–1, 153, 165, 197,
    201–2
concomitant variations 32
concordance theory 41, 123
conflict 51–68, 100, 112, 121, 139–40,
    144–5; conflict mediation 5; conflict
    prevention 40, 120; frozen conflict 72;
    and future studies 197, 200, 202; and
    Hochschild 158, 160; and Lammers
    153; and Latour 184
Congo 33, 47, 70–1, 73–4, 124, 134,
    145–6, 153, 166
Coning, C. de 70
conscience collective 25, 92
conscientious objectors 82, 145
conscription 1, 43, 46, 84–6, 94, 124–7,
    131, 135, 145–6, 151, 161, 174–5
conservatives 157
constabulary forces 73, 121
contractors 39, 46–7
control organizations 147
Cooley, C. 23
cooperation 18, 27–8, 56–7, 66, 72, 80–2,
    87, 114, 143–56, 200
coordination game 41
corporations 38–9, 47, 122
Coser, L. 79, 160
cosmopolitanism 52, 138
coups 12, 27, 41–2, 121–3, 143
courts 26
crime 22, 31, 47, 57, 66–7, 95, 106, 113,
    132, 140, 172
Crimea 133, 139
critical analysis 8, 37–40
Cuba 48, 81
culture 22–36, 52, 60, 66, 68, 84; culture
    studies 25; and diversity 85–7; and
    Enloe 174, 177; and Foucault 107; and
    future studies 199; and Goffman 92–3,
    95; and Hochschild 161–3, 165; and
    Lammers 144, 150–1, 153; and Latour
    185, 191–2
current contexts 2, 5–6, 11, 23, 28, 68;
    and Du Bois 79; and Elias 130, 134;
    and Enloe 169, 175; and Foucault 105,
    112; and future studies 196, 199; and
    Janowitz 124; and Latour 183, 191
cybersecurity 13, 190–1

cyberspace 189–91
Cyprus 71
Czarniawska, B. 187

D-Day 118
Dandeker, C. 2, 5, 105
data sciences 202
De Swaan, A. 133
de-personalization 92, 163
deaths 11, 42–3, 46, 82, 132, 164, 190
dedovschina 94
defence industries 172
deference 95
dehumanization 162–3
demilitarization 170
democracy 14, 38, 70–1, 74, 81, 112,
    121, 123, 134, 137, 173, 175, 184, 197
Democratic Republic of Congo *see*
    Congo
denial 57
Denmark 27, 138, 150
deserters 42, 145–6
deterrence 57
developing states 14–15, 37, 40, 44–5,
    121–4, 131, 145, 172
deviance 106–7, 137
Dewey, J. 4–5, 72, 121, 127, 200
diasporas 66
dictatorships 71, 132
differentiation 87, 102, 108
diffusion of beliefs 199–200
digital technology 186, 190–1
Dimaggio, P. 152
diplomacy 39–40, 111, 151, 158, 184
disaster relief 39, 170–1
discipline 10, 18, 26, 92, 105–17, 136,
    143, 157, 185
discrimination 75, 81–3, 88, 100
diversity 5, 52, 78–90, 197
division of labour 9, 11, 22, 24, 48, 120,
    122, 187
divorce 25, 30–1, 164, 173
double bind process 138–9
double consciousness 80, 107
Douglas, M. 25
draft system 40, 43, 46, 118, 124, 126–7,
    131, 135, 143, 161
dramaturgy 101–2
dressage 107
Dreyfus Affair 22
drones 11, 13, 110–11, 189–90, 198
Du Bois, W.E.B. 4–5, 18, 37, 51, 66,
    78–90; and cultural diversity 85–7; and
    Enloe 169; and Foucault 107; and

future studies 197, 202; and
    Hochschild 157; and military 80–3; and
    minority relations 83–5
Durkheim, E. 4–5, 19, 22–36, 44, 51, 62;
    and comparative analysis 31–4; and Du
    Bois 87; and Elias 130; and Foucault
    105, 107; and future studies 197,
    201–2; and Goffman 92; and
    Hochschild 157, 162; and Janowitz
    118, 124; and Lammers 144, 150; and
    Latour 183; and military culture 25–8;
    and primary groups 23–5; and suicide
    29–31
Dutch 10–11, 26, 28, 33, 45, 84, 86–7,
    125, 132, 143, 147–50, 152, 164, 186
Dutch East Indies 33, 43
Dutch language 6
duties 94
dyads 52, 97
dys-civilization 133–4

East 6, 200
East Germany 61
East Timor 68
Eastern Slavonia 68
ecology 191
Ecuador 84
egoistic suicide 30
Egyptians 9
El Salvador 68
elections 38, 70, 122, 157, 173, 197
Elias, N. 4–5, 94–5, 105, 107, 125,
    130–42; and civilization process 130–5;
    and decline of violence 130–5; and
    Enloe 178; and future studies 197, 201;
    and habitus in combat 135–8; and
    Hochschild 157, 162, 164; and
    international relations 130, 138–40;
    and Latour 190
elites 5, 9, 12, 14, 38–40, 56, 58, 120,
    147–9
emotional labour 158–64
emotions 5, 91, 99, 102, 137, 139–40,
    157–68, 197
Ender, M. 2, 5, 10, 164, 175, 198
Engels, F.W. 37, 44
engineering 11, 24, 29, 39, 108, 119, 184,
    186, 188
England, L. 176
English language 6–7, 28, 52, 59, 95–6,
    130, 149
enlightenment model 119
enlisted personnel 10, 24, 31, 43, 45–6,
    81–2, 86, 173–5

Enloe, C. 5, 26, 136, 169–80, 183, 197;
and future studies 202; and
militarization of women 171–3; and
women in military 173–6
entertainment industry 172
entrepreneurs 14
environmental issues 138, 184, 186,
202–3
Erdogan, R. 42
Eritrea 174
Espinoza, E. 82
Estonia 27, 85, 126, 151
ethics 3, 8, 48, 122, 190
ethnicity 11, 19, 43, 60, 78, 83, 85, 100,
136, 169
ethnography 32
Europe 1–2, 4–6, 13, 28–9, 37–8, 44; and
Addams 71; and Du Bois 80, 83–4; and
Elias 130, 132–3, 139; and Foucault
105–6, 111–14; and future studies
199–200; and Janowitz 118–19, 124–5;
and Lammers 143, 146, 149, 151–2;
and Latour 187; and Marx 46, 48; and
Simmel 58
European Union (EU) 68, 111, 113,
152, 200
Europol 105
evaluation 99–100, 108, 110, 175
evidence-based practice 16
exclusion 38, 54–5, 57, 59, 67
experts 3, 8, 24, 39–40, 74, 177
exploitation 14, 37, 43, 172, 203

face theory 95
Facebook 30
faits divers 87–8, 176–8
fake news 41
families 9, 14, 23–4, 30–1, 92, 96,
111, 137, 159–60, 164–5, 172–3,
190, 198
Fanon, F. 44
Far East 124
Farrell, T. 61
Farsi language 56, 95
fatalistic suicide 31
fatwa 56
Feaver, P. 122–3
feigning 159
femininity 170, 174
feminism 65–6, 125, 169–80
feminization 170
fieldwork 33, 56, 101, 162–3, 182,
198, 202
Finland 126

First World War *see* World War I
Five Eyes 59
flags 23
Follett, M.P. 4
Foucault, M. 4–5, 68, 105–17, 160, 170,
190; and border management 112–15;
and future studies 197, 199; and
governmentality 111–12; and
international relations 111–12; and
panopticon 106–11
founding fathers 2, 19, 51, 118, 127, 143,
157, 196–7, 202
fractionalization 56
fragging 24, 145
fragmentation 24, 55, 59
France 14, 22, 26, 33–4, 40, 44; and
Addams 67; and Du Bois 83–4;
and Elias 132, 135; and Enloe 172,
174; and Foucault 105–6; and
Goffman 93; and Janowitz 125; and
Lammers 146–8, 150–2; and Latour
181, 187, 192
Franco, F. 192
fraternization 93–4
French language 2, 6, 96
French Revolution 45
Frontex 105, 114
frustration 31, 41, 100–2, 149, 157,
164, 166
functional rationality 3, 17, 70, 98,
121, 202
future studies 153, 196–204

Gabon 172
game theory 41, 56–7
Gaza 136
gaze of power 107–8, 113, 115
Gazit, N. 101
gender 2, 5–6, 65, 70, 74–5, 80, 82–3,
98, 125, 136, 169–80, 197
generals 38, 40, 42, 56
genocide 11, 134
Georgia 85
German language 6, 51
Germany 8, 11, 22–3, 28, 51–2, 59–62;
and Addams 66, 68; and Du Bois 81,
83; and Elias 130, 136; and Enloe 174;
and Hochschild 165; and Janowitz
118–19, 125; and Lammers 146–8,
150–2; and Latour 187, 192
Gerth, H. 38
Gestapo 59
Ghana 33, 41
GI resistance 43, 46, 82, 145

Giddens, A. 4
globalization 157, 166, 170
Goffman, E. 4–5, 51, 91–105, 107, 111,
  157–8; and admission to military 91–4;
  and future studies 197, 201; and
  Hochschild 162–3; and interaction
  rituals 91, 94–9; and language
  mediation 91, 94–9; and street-level
  bureaucrats 91, 99–102
Goldstein, J. 132, 134, 176
good practice 72
gossip 57
governance 68, 73, 75, 108, 147
governmentality 105, 111–12
Graner, C. 176
Granovetter, M. 52, 54, 59
Gray, J. 133
Greece 113, 126, 132, 151
greedy institutions 160, 173
Greeks 10, 59, 98
Grenada 123
grief 157, 164, 173
Griffith, J. 30
group formation 23–5, 28, 51–2, 55–6,
  66, 83, 87–8, 119, 182, 197
Guam 172
La Guerra del Gaz 84
guilt 119, 157, 162, 166
Gurkhas 84

habitus 130–42
Haddad, S. 12
haircuts 92–3
Haiti 33
Hajjar, R.M. 97
Harig, C. 33
Harvard University 57, 78, 132
hegemony 176
Heinecken, L. 48
Hellum, N. 175
Helmand Province 28, 61
Hendrix, W. 143
heroic suicide 29
hierarchies 9, 13, 24, 26, 43, 58,
  82, 94, 108–10, 137, 144, 147,
  153, 170
high/low capacity regimes 134
Hindi language 95
Hispanic Americans 83
historians 3, 80, 130, 164, 198
Hitler, A. 15–16
HIV/AIDS 70
Hochschild, A.R. 4–5, 91, 102, 157–68,
  197, 202; and emotional labour 160–4;

and emotional work/management
  158–60; and Post-Deployment
  Disorientation 165–6; and PTSD
  165–6
Hoedemaekers, I. 97
Holocaust 10–11, 133
homelessness 66
homogenization 108
hooliganism 130, 138
Hoskin, K. 108
host states 18, 46–7, 52–3, 56, 60–1,
  69–74; and Du Bois 85–7; and Elias
  132, 137; and Enloe 171, 178; and
  Foucault 111, 113; and future studies
  197–201, 203; and Goffman 94–9;
  and Lammers 149–50, 153; and
  Latour 190
hot side 3
Howard, L. 71, 74
Hull House Museum 66, 72
human rights 73, 136, 184
human-system relations 107, 181–6,
  189, 192
humanitarian missions 33, 67, 114, 132
humour 159, 163
Hungary 112, 125, 199
Huntington, S. 118, 122–3
Hurricane Katrina 39, 170–1
Hussein, S. 12
Hutus 133
hypocrisy 69, 71

Ideal Types 8–9, 122
identity 25, 56, 86–7, 175
ideology 23, 31, 37, 45–6, 83, 97,
  187, 199
imagination 203
impression management 100–1
inclusion 78–90, 136
India 13, 40–1, 44, 102, 123, 147–8
Indian Wars 81
indigenous communities 13, 84, 120, 123,
  200, 202
Indochina 147
Indonesia 132, 143, 149, 164, 172
industry 39–40, 108, 124, 143–5,
  172, 186
inequality 5, 37–8, 42–3, 67, 70, 82, 84,
  107, 172, 183, 197
infantry 10, 23–4, 27, 95, 175
informalization 137–8
information sharing 54, 58–60, 189
infrastructure 47, 73, 98, 191–2
Ingesson, T. 33

inner direction 26
innovation 3, 10, 14, 60–1, 97, 119–20,
153, 182–9, 197
inscription devices 182
institutions 68, 105, 114, 124, 144–5,
147; and Enloe 171; greedy institutions
160, 173; and Latour 185; and
separation approach 123; total
institutions 91–104, 107, 111,
160, 197
integration 22, 28, 30, 55, 61, 71, 78,
81–5, 87–8, 145–6, 175
intelligence 11, 24, 45, 57–60, 95, 98,
105, 111, 170, 188
interaction style 1, 15, 22–3, 51, 57,
60; and Addams 73–4; and Elias 139;
and Enloe 172; and future studies
197, 200–1; and Goffman 91, 94–100,
102; and Hochschild 158; and Latour
190, 192
intermediaries 147
internalization 92, 106–7, 131–2, 136,
151–2
International Campaign to Ban
Landmines (ICBL) 170
international community 69, 112
International Governmental Organizations
(IGOs) 111
international relations (IR) 3–4, 39,
111–12, 120, 130, 138–40, 186
internationalization 143
Internet 16, 37, 99, 110, 190
interpreters 60, 87, 96–9
intifadas 162
involved outsiders 96
Iran 12, 191
Iraq 2, 10, 12–13, 17, 30, 33; and Addams
71; and Du Bois 82, 86; and Elias
132–3, 139; and Enloe 171, 175–6;
and Foucault 111; and Janowitz 123,
125; and Lammers 149–50; and Latour
184, 191; and Marx 40, 46; and
Simmel 52, 61
ISAF 28, 53
Islam 8, 86, 184
Islamic State 16, 31, 134
isomorphism 14, 151–3, 199
Israel 6, 24, 33, 43, 101, 123, 126, 146,
161, 174–7
Israeli Defence Force (IDF) 87, 136, 161,
163, 174, 176
Italy 27, 33, 66, 113, 125, 151–2, 187
Ivory Coast 181
Iwo Jima, battle of 86

Janowitz, M. 5, 13, 23, 25, 73, 118–29;
and all-volunteer forces 124–7; and
civil-military relations 121–4; and Du
Bois 81; and future studies 197, 200,
202; and professional soldiers 120–1
Janus face 26
Japan 27, 31, 86, 135, 146, 172, 174
Japanese Americans 173
Jensen, E. 182
Jermier, J. 203
Jews 8, 11, 22, 66, 119, 133
jihadism 16
Joas, H. 2, 75
Johnson, J. 181
joy 102, 157–8
judges 106

Kaddafi, M. 71
kamikaze squads 31
Kanter, R.M. 87
Karpinsky, J. 176
Kelly, B. 159
Kelty, R. 47
Kenya 33, 43
KGB 59
Khmer Rouge 133
King, A. 10, 23, 135–6, 175
Kleinreesink, E. 165
Knöbel, W. 2, 75
Korea 33, 139, 172
Korean War 82, 123
Kosovo 163, 165
Kümmel, G. 2

labour markets 30, 48, 86, 160
laissez-faire 148
Lammers, C. 5, 27, 82, 143–56, 197, 199;
and administrative style 146–51, 153;
and cooperation 143, 151–3; and
isomorphism 151–3; and mutinies
143–6; and occupational style 146–51,
153; and strikes 143–6
language mediators 46–7, 53, 60, 74,
96, 200
large-scale firms 38
Lasswell, H.D. 39
Latin America 15, 41, 83–4, 96, 124, 132
Latour, B. 4–5, 110, 181–95, 197;
and cyberspace 189–90; and
infrastructure 191–2; and innovation
184–9; and nature 191–2; and new
stuff 189–91; and unmanned devices
189–91
Latvia 85

law 9–10, 15–16, 26, 59, 99–100, 114, 134, 196
law enforcement 26, 59, 99
Law, J. 187
Lazarsfeld, P. 119
leadership 8–21, 31, 40, 44, 53, 55, 67, 79–80, 110, 123, 145, 149, 159, 198
league tables 108
Lebanon 33, 61, 71, 123, 151
legal authority 10, 15, 131, 135–6, 144, 190
Leonhard, N. 61
Levy, Y. 5, 43, 87
liberations 149
Liberia 163, 165
Libya 1, 40, 71–2, 133–4
life chances/living standards 31, 37, 70, 84, 165
limitations 16–17
Lingalese language 74
linguists *see* interpreters; language mediators
Linklater, A. 138
Lipsky, M. 5, 99–101
Lithuania 85, 126
lobbying 122
logistics 8, 11, 27, 39, 53
loneliness 30
Long-Term Missions 112
looting 47, 146, 171
Low Countries 185
loyalty 12, 23–4, 26, 86, 147–8, 160
Luhman, N. 4
lumpenproletariat 44
lying 57
lynchings 81

McChristal, S. 16
McDonaldization 10
macro-level 2, 4, 8, 34, 131, 133, 196–7
Macve, R. 108
Mafia 16, 66
Malaya 32, 43, 132
Malesević, S. 2, 11, 133
Mali 86
managed hearts 157, 159
management studies 73
managerialism 109, 159
Mannheim, K. 3, 121
Marcuse, H. 118
marginalization 84
market armies 46–7
market sector 108, 184, 196
marriage 25, 30, 57, 65, 97, 172–3

Martineau, H. 65
Marx, K. 4–6, 15, 37–50, 54, 66, 79; and alienation 45–8; and commodification 45–8; and Enloe 169; and Foucault 105, 107; and future studies 197, 202; and Goffman 99; and Hochschild 157; and inequality 42–3; and Janowitz 120–1; and Lammers 143–4; and military coups 41–2; and military power elites 38–40; and poverty 43–5
masculinity 26, 101, 177
masculinization 170
Mastroianni, G.R. 29–31
Maurice of Orange 10
Mead, G.H. 66
means-to-ends relations 3, 72, 121, 202
mechanical solidarity 24
media 1, 16, 42, 171, 176, 198
Mediterranean 119
memoirs 165
mental health/illness 29–31, 91, 105, 130
mercenaries 45
merchants 1
merit 9–10, 12, 15, 85
Merkel, A. 151
Merlingen, M. 111
Merton, R.K. 13, 70, 119
meso-level 2, 133, 196–7
metaphors 66, 98, 107, 171
meteorologists 11
metis 98
metrics 109, 113–14
Mexico 113
micro-level 2, 23, 51, 101, 111, 131, 134, 196–7
Middle Ages 1, 130–1, 138
Middle East 1, 15, 60, 95, 124, 134, 191
migration/immigration 43, 60, 66–8, 71, 79, 96, 112–14, 139
militarism 66–7, 131, 170–1
militarization 170–3
military 1–6, 8, 10–14, 16–19, 22, 68; admission to 91–4; and critical analysis 37–40; and culture 22–36; and diversity 78–90; and emotional labour 160–4; and emotions 157–68; and feminism 169–80; and inclusion 78–90; and innovation 184–9; and intelligence 57–60; military groups 22–36; military mothers 173; military wives 172–3; and minority relations 83–5; and power elites 38–40; and race 78–90; and science 181–95; and technology 181–95

military sociology 1–2, 28, 41, 45, 54, 94, 117–18, 120, 123–4, 143, 198, 200–3
military studies 4–5, 8–15, 28, 33, 42–3, 48, 196–204
military-industrial complex 39, 124, 143
militias 47, 73, 124, 146
mimesis 152
minorities 2, 52, 60, 80–5
modernity 98, 184, 190
Moelker, R. 26
Mohammed, Prophet 15
Moore, B. 83
morality 29, 46, 57, 66, 68, 109, 161, 166, 178, 183, 190
Mort, M. 187
Moskos, C. 5, 28, 46, 71, 78, 82, 118, 126
Mouzelis, N.P. 93
Mozambique 68
mujahedin 56
multinational missions 27–8, 69, 87, 150, 189
music 6, 8–21, 79–80, 138, 157
Muslims 13, 56, 86–7
mutinies 42, 82, 143–56

Nagl, J. 32
naked power 9, 15–16, 147, 150
Namibia 68
naming 84, 92, 137
Napoleon, Emperor 1, 124
NASA 188
National Solidarity Programme (NSP) 75
Nationale Volksarmee (NVA) 61–2
nationalism 18–19, 43, 69, 125
Native Americans 38, 81, 83, 86
native elites 147–9
NATO 27–8, 41, 45, 59, 69, 71, 112, 139, 149, 151–3, 175, 199
nature 191–2
Navajo code talkers 86
Nazis 11, 83, 118–19, 130, 147–8, 174, 192
NCOs 94, 173
Nepal 44, 84
nepotism 11, 14
Netherlands 26, 48, 67, 83, 124, 133, 143, 146–7, 149, 165, 187
networks 51–4, 67, 147, 182, 185–8, 192, 197
neuroendocrinology 181
New Zealand 59, 174
NGOs 114
Nigeria 44

Nightingale, F. 173
Nobel Prize 65, 67, 170
non-combat situations 61, 101
normal damage 111
normalization 108, 110, 112
norms 15, 25, 58, 97, 108, 112, 131, 140, 152–3, 159, 178
North 6
North America 32
North Vietnam 12
Northern Africa 147
Northern Ireland 12, 84
Norway 27, 126, 147, 150, 175
novels 13
Nowak, M. 57
Nuciara, M. 2
number distributions 51–4, 87

Obama, B. 149, 164
obedience 10, 26, 93, 107
object orientation 184
objective civilian control 122
occupational style 143, 146–51, 153
Office of Strategic Services (OSS) 118
officers 10–11, 13–14, 16–17, 24, 28, 39; and Du Bois 80, 82–5; and Elias 132, 136; and Enloe 173; and Foucault 108, 113; and Goffman 93–4; and Hochschild 158, 164–5; and Janowitz 120, 122–3, 126; and Lammers 143, 146, 152–3; and Marx 43; and Simmel 61–2
Olonisakin, F. 198
Olympic Games 83
operas 18
Operation Enduring Freedom 28
operational styles 32–3, 150, 170, 199, 201
organic solidarity 24
Organization of Security and Cooperation in Europe (OSCE) 111–12
organization studies 4, 8, 10, 13–14, 37, 73; and emotions 157–68; and Foucault 107–9; and future studies 197, 199; and Goffman 91, 101–2; and Janowitz 122; and Lammers 143–7, 150, 152; and Latour 181, 185, 188, 192; organizational learning 71, 74
Orwell, G. 107
other/s 95, 105, 111, 120, 131, 139–40, 157–8, 163, 177, 200–1
outsourcing 46, 48, 127, 151, 197
overviews 2, 185, 196, 201

Pacific 31, 119, 172
pacifism 2, 133
Pakistan 44, 123
Palestinians 136, 177
panopticon 106–11, 115, 160, 190
para-military forces 102, 105, 124
Parsons, T. 4
partnerships 52–4, 59, 112
Pashtun language 95
Pasteur, L. 182
paternalism 153
patriarchalism 15
patrimonialism 9, 11–12, 14–15, 134
patriotism 173
peace 1–2, 26, 55, 65–77, 81, 134; and
    Elias 139; and Enloe 169–70, 174,
    177–8; and Hochschild 163–4; and
    Latour 191–2; peace activism 66–8;
    peace weaving 67–8, 72
peacekeeping 6, 13, 45, 65–77, 101, 112;
    and Enloe 177–8; and future studies
    199; and Janowitz 121, 126; and
    Lammers 153; and participatory
    missions 74–5, 200; and practical
    missions 73; and provisional missions
    74; unintended consequences of 70
peasants 1, 79, 130
penal systems 106
People's Republic of China *see* China
performance indicators 108–10
Perrow, C. 12, 188
personnel turnover 126–7, 198
Petraeus, D. 17
Philippines 172
philosophy 22, 72, 105–6, 121, 181
Pilster, U. 101
Pinker, S. 132–4, 178, 190
piracy 125
Plato 17
platoons 3, 23–4, 28, 136
pluralism 66, 73–4
Poland 11, 66, 79, 112, 125, 139,
    151–2, 199
police/policing 11, 13, 68, 78, 88,
    99–102; and Elias 131–2, 134–5; and
    Enloe 160–70; and Foucault 105, 110,
    113–14; and Hochschild 158, 162, 164;
    and Janowitz 124; and Lammers 149
policy formation 39, 57, 75, 82, 98, 100,
    112, 114, 119, 145, 170
politeness 95
political armies 41
political science 3–4, 6, 33, 37, 56, 118,
    177, 183, 198

politicians 17, 38, 56, 58, 109–11, 122–3;
    and Elias 138–9; and Enloe 171–2; and
    future studies 199; and Hochschild
    161, 166; and Janowitz 126–7; and
    Lammers 149, 151–2; and Latour 182,
    190, 192
pollution 138
polymetes soldiers 98–9, 200
Portugal 28, 132, 150
positions in networks 51–4
post-colonialism 41
Post-Deployment Disorientation 165–6
post-military society 131
Pouligny, B. 198
poverty 31, 41, 43–5, 66–72, 131,
    139–40, 165–6
Powell, C. 184
Powell, W. 152
power games 94, 140
power relations 38–40, 56, 107, 139, 144
power-knowledge mechanisms 112
pragmatism 5, 65–77, 120–1, 127, 200
primary groups 23–5, 28, 119
principal agent relations 122–3
principal role 97
prisoners of war 23, 118
privacy 92, 111
private sector 39, 46–7, 114, 170, 197
process dynamics 72
productivity 109, 113
professionalization 45, 71, 73, 85–6, 112,
    118–29; and Elias 136; and Enloe 175;
    and future studies 197, 202; and
    Hochschild 158, 160, 162, 164; and
    Lammers 146, 153
profit 46, 70, 97, 146, 158, 172
progress 68, 82, 99, 109, 184–5,
    192, 202
proletariat 44
propaganda 56, 118
prostitution 70, 172
protest movements 42, 46, 67, 83, 144,
    146, 163, 177
Protestants 8, 55
Prüfert, A. 2
Prussia 146
psyche 25
psychiatry 73
psychogenesis 131
psychology 18, 22, 31, 52, 99, 119, 132,
    157, 177, 190
PTSD 165–6
public opinion 1, 125
public relations 39

qualifications 9–10, 12, 85
quantification 109, 183, 201

race 6, 9, 24, 37, 65–6, 78–90, 100, 119,
    125, 172, 174–5, 197
racial profiling 100
railways 11
rational-legal authority 15–16
rationalization 9–10, 14–18, 143, 147
rebellions 145–6
reconnaissance 187, 189
reconstruction 13, 126–7, 149
recruitment 12, 14, 30, 84, 86, 91;
    and Elias 133; and Enloe 173–4;
    and future studies 198; and
    Goffman 96; and Janowitz 120, 123,
    126; and Lammers 143; and Latour
    182, 185
Red Army 85, 174
Red Teams 17
refugees 105, 114, 139–40
regulations 9, 11, 13, 15, 27, 47, 59,
    106, 137
religion 8–9, 11, 15, 22–3, 25, 43, 45, 57,
    65–6, 79, 85–7, 98, 176, 202
representation 1–2, 147
research and development (R&D) 39,
    183, 187
reservists 27, 61, 160, 162–3, 176
Resteigne, D. 54, 198
restraint 136–8, 197, 201
retirees 9, 158, 165
reversibility 99
revolts 42
revolutions 1, 4, 15, 37–8, 41, 81, 107,
    121, 187, 192
rhythm 18
Rietjens, S. 109
risk society 68
rites de passage 92–3
rituals 13, 23, 58, 91–104, 136, 196
Ritzer, G. 5, 10
Roberts, K.H. 23
robots 11, 189
role performance 159–60, 162–3, 170,
    173, 175–8, 203
Romania 132
Romans 9–10, 18
Ron, J. 136, 163
Roosevelt, T. 66
routinization 16
Ruffa, C. 33, 150, 198
rules of game 92, 107
Run for the Wall 26

Russia 27, 39–40, 60, 69, 85, 94, 125–6,
    133, 139, 158, 173–4, 188, 199
Russian language 126
Rwanda 45, 69, 134
Ryan, K. 133

sabotage 146, 185
safety 98, 109, 111, 114–15, 137, 139,
    159–61, 202
sanctions 57, 147
Santin, M. 159
Sasson-Levy, O. 177
Schaub, G. 47
Schiff, R. 123
Schmoller, G. 78
Schuetz, A. 61
Schumpeter, J. 4
science 6, 17, 110, 119, 132, 177,
    181–95, 197
Scotson, J. 139
Scott, J.C. 98–9
Scott, W.J. 29–31
scripted behaviour 159, 161
secession 144
Second World War *see* World War II
secrecy 52, 54, 57–60, 91–3, 188–9, 197
secret societies 57–60, 91–3, 188–9
security forces 12–14, 133
security sector 46–7, 100, 114, 188
security studies 3, 58, 67, 71, 105, 111,
    121, 159–60
Segal, D. 2, 5, 118
Segal, M. 118, 160
segregation 66, 81–2, 177
self-fulfilling prophecies 41
Senegal 44, 83, 172
separation 27–8, 87
September 11 2001 31, 58–9, 114, 149,
    159, 184, 191
Serbo-Croat language 56
Serbs 13, 19
sexual harassment 70
sexuality 85, 105, 131, 136
SHAPE 28
Shaw, M. 131
Shields, P. 5, 65, 67, 73
Shiite Muslims 56
Shils, E. 23, 118
Shirzai, G.A. 53
short-termism 72
Simmel, G. 4–5, 51–64, 80, 87, 91, 95–7;
    and conflict 54–7; and future studies
    197, 200; and Goffman 99; and
    Hochschild 157; and intelligence

57–60; and Latour 185, 188; and networks 51–4; and secrecy 57–60; and stranger role 60–2

simulation studies 57, 186

Singh, N. 41

situational withdrawal 93

slavery 66, 80–1, 131–2, 138

small groups 22–5, 28, 52

snipers 161–2

social construction 79, 82, 199

social facts 22, 31, 198

social media 16, 42, 100, 110, 160

social sciences 5, 29, 32–3, 37, 56, 66, 78, 115, 118, 177, 181–3, 187, 198–9, 201–2

social theory 2, 4–6, 66

socialism 112

socialization 91, 107, 111, 143

socio-materiality discourse 181

sociogenesis 131

sociologists 4–5, 8, 18–19, 23, 26, 28; and Addams 66–8; and Du Bois 78–9; and Elias 130–1, 133, 140; and Enloe 175; and Foucault 105; and future studies 198–9, 201–2; and Goffman 91, 94, 98; and Hochschild 157–8, 160, 163; and Janowitz 120, 125–6; and Lammers 143, 152; and Latour 181, 187–8, 192; and Marx 38, 44; and Simmel 51, 54, 58, 60–2

sociology 1–3, 22, 37–8, 51, 55, 57–8; and Addams 65–6, 75; basic/applied sociology 119; connected sociology 6, 169, 200; and controversies 183; and Du Bois 78–9, 81, 88; and Durkheim 22; and Elias 130, 135, 138; and Foucault 106–7, 117; founding fathers of 2, 19, 51, 143, 196, 202; and future studies 195, 199–200; and Goffman 91; Hochschild 157, 159, 166; and imagination 203; and Janowitz 119, 121, 127; and Lammers 144, 146, 150; and Latour 181, 183; and method blending 201–2; of military operations 198–9; military sociology 1–2, 28, 41, 45, 54, 94, 117–18, 120, 123–4, 143, 198, 200–3; and Simmel 62; and soul 202–3; and Weber 8, 16–17

Soeters, J. 67, 73, 97

software 17, 202

solidarity 23–4, 75

Somalia 24, 45, 69, 82, 134

Sorrow Songs 79

South 6, 200

South Africa 27, 44–5, 48, 79, 84, 174

Southeast Asia 124

sovereignty 149

Soviet Union 8, 37, 39–40, 43, 48, 85, 98, 174, 199

space security 13

Spain 28, 83–4, 87, 113, 132, 185, 192

Spanish language 6, 28, 96

special operations forces 14, 27, 54, 68, 93, 136, 175

sports officials 130, 137–8

squads 23, 28

Stalin, J. 16

standardization 9–11, 15, 18, 26

Starr, E.G. 66, 72

state 1, 4, 8, 10, 12, 39; and Elias 131, 136, 138; and Foucault 111; and Janowitz 121–3; and Lammers 151; and Marx 45, 47; and Simmel 59, 63; simplification of 98–9

states of emergency 16

statistics 22, 29, 68–9, 101, 108–10, 112, 119, 124, 132, 144, 174, 202

stereotypes 68, 88

Stewart, R. 33

stigmatization 140

Stinchcombe, A.L. 2

Stouffer, S. 118

strangers/stranger role 51, 60–2, 80, 96, 157, 159, 185, 188–9, 197

strategic cultures 151

strategic interaction 95, 98, 100

stratification 38

street-level bureaucracy 91–104

stress 97, 159–60, 165–6, 173, 190, 198

strikes 143–56

strong ties 52, 54

structural holes 52–3

structural inertia 59

Stuxnet 191

Sub-Saharan Africa 41

substantive rationality 3, 17, 121, 169, 190, 202

Sudan 1

suicide 29–31, 166, 197

Sunni Muslims 56

Super Bowl 83

supercooperators 56–7

supra-national institutions 68, 114, 138, 196

surveillance 105–17, 189–90, 197

Swahili language 45, 95

Sweden 125–6, 163

sympathetic understanding 66, 68

Syria 1, 40, 131, 133, 139

Taleb, N.N. 133
Taliban 61
Talmadge, C. 12
Tarde, G. 4
targets/target-setting 3, 11, 67, 72, 74, 101, 121, 157, 161–2, 190
taxation 131
Tblisi uprising 85
technology 6, 10–11, 27, 44–5, 69, 110, 113, 125, 153, 161, 181–95, 197, 199
Teitler, G. 146
tele-soldiers 189–90
terrorism 1, 13, 31, 58, 68, 92, 101, 105, 111, 113–14, 133, 140, 172, 191
tertius gaudens 97
tertius iungens 97
Thailand 124, 172
Thakur, R. 70
Thomas theorem 81
Thomas, W.I. 66
threat perceptions 126, 138–9
Tierney, K. 170
Tilly, C. 134
tit-for-tat strategy 56
Tocqueville, A. de 4
tokenism 87–8, 190
torture 19, 96–7, 106, 137
torturing ties 96–7
total institutions 91–104, 107, 111, 160, 197
totems 23, 191
traditional authority 15–16
trafficking 16, 70, 114, 172
training 23–8, 31, 39, 45, 60, 73; and Du Bois 82; and Elias 136; and Foucault 107, 110, 112; and future studies 198; and Goffman 92–4; and Hochschild 161–3, 166; and Janowitz 125–6; and Lammers 152; and Latour 181, 186
traitors 96, 147
Traugott, M. 44
trauma 31, 165
triads 52, 55–6, 97
tribes/tribalism 9, 11, 15, 23, 32, 53, 123, 126
tributary labour 45
Truman, H. 82
Trump, D. 40, 151
Turkey 27, 41–2, 121–3, 126, 133, 151
Turner, M. 59
Tuskegee Airmen 81
Tutsis 133

Uganda 166
Uiterwijk, D. 187

Ukraine 85, 126, 133, 139
unemployment 44
uniforms 92, 100, 114, 162–3, 185
unintended consequences 70
unions 48, 67, 147, 151
United Kingdom (UK) *see* Britain
United Nations (UN) 17, 27, 33, 40, 44–5, 68–74; and cooperation 153; Department of Peacekeeping Operations 71; and Elias 134; and Enloe 172, 177–8; and Foucault 112; and future studies 199–200; and Goffman 100; MONUSCO 71; peacekeeping 68–72; UNFICYP 71; UNIFIL 33, 71
United States (US) 1–2, 5–6, 10, 12–13, 17, 199–200; and Addams 65, 67, 71–3, 75; Air Force 27; Army Academy at West Point 83; Congress 40; Corps of Engineers 39; and Du Bois 78–9, 82–4, 88; and Durkheim 23–4, 26–32; and Elias 132, 135; and Enloe 172–4, 176; and Foucault 107–9, 112–14; and Goffman 93, 98; and Hochschild 157, 160, 163–5; and Janowitz 118–20, 123–6; and Lammers 145–52; and Latour 184, 186; Marine Corps 86, 158, 162, 175; and Marx 37–40, 42, 44–6; National Guard 170–1; Navy 23; and race relations 81–3; and Republicans 126; and Simmel 51, 53–4, 59, 61; WAC 83
unmanned devices 186, 189–91
Urdu language 95
Uruguay 44

validation 186
value-rationality 17
Van Bladel, J. 94
Van den Bogaert, S. 54
Van Doorn, J. 125, 143
Van Veen, M. 186
Vaughan, D. 188
Veblen, T. 4
veil 79, 88
veterans 25–6, 30, 61, 164, 203
victories 120–1, 185
Vietnam War 18, 24, 32, 42–4, 46, 125; and Elias 132, 135; and Enloe 172; and Lammers 145; and Latour 185, 187; Vietcong 12, 82, 109, 158
violence 1–4, 10–11, 16–19, 31–2, 39–40, 47; and Addams 65–7, 70, 72; decline of 130–42, 164, 178, 190; and

Du Bois 88; and Enloe 171, 177–8;
and Foucault 107, 112; and future
studies 197–8, 200–2; and Goffman 94,
99, 101; and Hochschild 157–8, 160–2,
166; and inequality 43–4; and Janowitz
120, 125; and Lammers 144–6; and
Latour 183, 192; and Simmel 55
volunteers/volunteer forces 1, 46, 78,
81–2, 86, 124–7, 131, 135–6, 138,
161, 174, 197

Waitoolkiat, N. 124
war-cries 18
warlords 56
wars 1–2, 4, 11–12, 16, 18–19, 23–4; and
Addams 67–8, 71; and Du Bois 81–2,
84–5; and Durkheim 26–8, 31–2; and
Elias 130–1, 138–9; and Enloe 171–8;
and Foucault 109, 112; and future
studies 198; and Hochschild 158, 166;
and inequality 42; and infrastructure
191–2; and Janowitz 120, 125; and
Lammers 143, 147, 150; and Latour
184–5, 190–2; and Marx 38–40, 42,
46; and nature 191–2; and poverty
43–5; and Simmel 55–6
weak ties 52–3, 95, 200
weapons 27, 33, 38, 108, 122, 153,
170–1, 184, 189–91
Weber, M. 4–6, 8–21, 38, 48, 58, 62; on
authority 15–17; on bureaucracy 8–15;
and Du Bois 78, 80, 86; and Durkheim
22; and Foucault 105, 107–8; and
future studies 197; and Goffman 99;
and Janowitz 122; and Lammers 143–5,
147; and Latour 185; on leadership
15–17; on music 17–19
Wehrmacht 23, 118
Weibull, L. 163, 165
Weick, K. 23
West 1, 6, 8, 10–14, 16, 37–9; and
Addams 68–9, 72–3; and civil-military

relations 121–4; and Du Bois 86; and
Elias 132, 137, 139; and Enloe 172,
174; and Foucault 112; and future
studies 200; and Goffman 95–6, 98;
and Hochschild 166; and Janowitz 126;
and Lammers 145, 149, 151–2; and
Latour 184; and Marx 43–7; and
Simmel 52, 54, 56, 60
West Africa 181
West Bank 136, 162
West Germany 61
West Point 83, 108
whistle blowing 146
white supremacism 80, 85, 107
wicked problems 145
Winslow, D. 24
women in military 173–6
Women's International League for Peace
and Freedom (WILPF) 67, 170
women's rights 65, 67, 70, 132, 140, 169
Woolf, V. 170
Woolgar, S. 182
world risk society 68
World War I 1, 19, 22, 62, 67, 75, 80–1,
84, 130, 185–6
World War II 1, 11, 23, 31, 39, 42–3;
and Addams 68; and Du Bois 81, 83,
85–6; and Elias 135; and Enloe 172–3;
and Janowitz 118–20, 124; and
Lammers 146, 148, 150; and Latour
186; and Simmel 61
World War III 39–40
Wouters, C. 137
Wright Mills, C. 4–5, 38–40, 120,
169, 203

Xhosa language 45

Yemen 1, 134, 202
Yugoslavia 13, 112, 125

Zulu language 45

Made in United States
Orlando, FL
16 August 2023